Kernel Projects FOR Linux®

GARY NUTT

University of Colorado

Boston San Francisco New York
London Toronto Sydney Tokyo Singapore Madrid
Mexico City Munich Paris Cape Town Hong Kong Montreal

Sr. Acquisitions Editor: Maite Suarez-Rivas
Assistant Editor: Lisa Hogue
Production Supervisor: Helen Reebenacker
Cover Design: Leslie Haines/Gina Hagen
Text Design: Suzanne Heiser
Composition: Publisher's Design and Production Services, Inc.
Copyeditor: Laura Michaels
Manufacturing Buyer: Caroline Fell

Reprinted with corrections, March 2001

Library of Congress Cataloging-in-Publication Data

Nutt, Gary J.
Kernel projects for Linux/Gary Nutt.
p. cm.
Includes bibliographical references and index.
ISBN 0-201-61243-7
1. Linux. 2. Operating systems (Computers) I. Title.
QA76.76.063 N885 2001
005.4'469—dc21 00-035576

2 3 4 5 6 7 8 9 10-MA-2-01

This book is dedicated to my three siblings

Dolores—along with my Mother, my greatest supporter through my early years

Bill—my academic role model and (along with my wife) my lifelong closest friend

Greg—my gentle brother and role model for all things artistic

Preface

TO THE STUDENT

Experience has shown that the best way to learn the details of how an operating system (OS) works is to experiment with it—to read, modify, and enhance its code. However, OS software, by its nature, must be carefully constructed. This is because it directly controls the hardware used by all of the processes and threads that execute on it. As a result, experimenting with OS code can be difficult, since an experimental version of the OS might disable the test machine. This laboratory manual provides you with a learning path for studying the Linux kernel with as little risk as possible. By learning about the Linux kernel in this way, you will develop a technique by which you can learn and experiment with other kernels as well. Consider this learning path to be a graduated set of exercises. First, you will learn to inspect various aspects of the OS internal state without changing any code. Second, you will extend the OS by writing new code to read (but not write) kernel data structures. Third, you will reimplement existing data structures. Finally, you will design and add your own functions and data structures to the Linux kernel.

The Linux kernel is written in the C programming language. Therefore you need to be relatively proficient in using C before you can study the kernel. If you know C++, then you will not have difficulty understanding the source code, though when you add or change parts of the kernel code you will not be able to use objects.

This manual is designed as a companion to a general OS textbook. It consists of two parts. Part 1 offers an overview of the Linux design. If you are using this manual at the beginning of your first OS course, you might discover that Part 1 discusses several topics that are new to you. However, work your way through it to get a feeling for how Linux is built. It gives the "big picture" but not many details. Then go back to Part 1 as needed as you work the exercises.

Part 2 consists of a dozen laboratory exercises that help you to learn to use Linux. Each exercise is a self-contained unit consisting of the following sections:

- Introduction
- Problem Statement
- Attacking the Problem

The exercises link the general concepts and the Linux details. Each begins with an introduction that explains Linux concepts and details relevant to the exercise. The introduction explains how the generic concepts that you will have learned in lecture and textbooks are realized in Linux. The next part of the exercise presents the problem on which you will be working. It includes detailed Linux-specific information that you need to solve the problem. Sometimes, a quick review of the pertinent parts of Part 1 will help you to frame the work of the exercises before you dive into the details.

Your school's laboratory probably has already been set up as a Linux lab. For you to solve most of the exercises in this manual, the laboratory administrator will provide you with a copy of the Linux source code and superuser permission to create new versions of the OS. Do not abuse your privilege as a superuser! You need this privilege in order to modify the kernel, but you must not use it for other purposes. This manual includes a CD-ROM, containing the Linux source code, that you can use to install Linux on your own computer.

Good luck with your study of operating systems. I hope that this exercise manual is a valuable learning tool for exploring OS concepts in Linux.

TO THE INSTRUCTOR

Today, abstraction is the basis of most software that is written—in the classroom or in practice. Students are taught to think of software solutions in terms of objects, components, threads, messages, and so on. This perspective teaches them to leverage the power of the hardware to solve increasingly complex tasks. In this way, they reduce programming time while reusing lower-level abstractions. At the bottom of all of these abstractions is the operating system—processes and resources (and sometimes threads). Application software and middleware use these OS abstractions to create their own higher-level abstractions. These range from accounting packages, spreadsheets, and missile trackers to windows, databases, objects, components, messages, and continuous media streams.

This trend toward the heavy use of abstraction prompts some to argue that OSs are no longer worthy of serious study, since they are largely transparent to the application programmers working at higher layers of abstraction. However, the OS is still fundamental because its design and implementation are the basis of the design and implementation of all of the other abstractions. Programmers will always be able to write better middleware and application programs if they understand how OSs work. Moreover, the need for people who understand basic OS technology remains, whether they are to write drivers for new devices, to create new microkernel servers, or to provide new systems capable of efficiently handling evolving requirements such as continuous media.

Typically an OS instructor has to decide whether an OS course should focus on issues and theory or provide an environment in which students can experiment with OS code. The 1991 (and draft 2001) IEEE/ACM undergraduate course recommendation describes a course that consists of a substantial amount of time spent on issues, but also includes a significant laboratory component. Even though the trend is toward courses based on conceptual materials, students and instructors seem to agree that hands-on experience is invaluable in learning about OSs. Many courses attempt to follow the IEEE/ACM lead by dividing the course into lecture and laboratory components, with the lecture component focusing on issues and theory and the laboratory component providing some form of hands-on exercises.

The IEEE/ACM recommendation supports the idea that the laboratory component should allow students to learn how to use the OS mechanisms, specifically by focusing on the OS application programming interface (API) as the primary mechanism for experimentation. The philosophy behind this approach is that students must learn how to *use* an OS before they can really understand how to *design* one. This philosophy drives a companion book on programming Windows NT via the Win32 API [Nutt, 1999] and one on laboratory exercises [Nutt, 2000].

However, in a late 1998 survey of 78 universities conducted by Addison-Wesley, 43 indicated that they teach OS *internals* in the introductory OS course. Of these 43, 26 use a variant of UNIX as the target OS, 13 use Linux, 10 use an unspecified version of UNIX, and 3 use MINIX. Eight said that they use some other OS as the subject system (such as Nachos), and the remaining 9 did not specify the OS that they use. The survey clearly showed that a significant fraction of the community teaches OS internals as a component of an introductory OS class, despite the IEEE/ACM recommendation and despite the heavy use of conceptual OS textbooks. It also showed that most of these courses use two books: a traditional OS theory book (such as [Silberschatz and Galvin, 1998] or [Nutt, 2000]) and a reference book (such as [Stevens, 1993], [McKusick, et al., 1996], or [Beck, et al., 1998]). Of course, no single-term undergraduate course can possibly cover all of the material in both a theory book and a book that describes an entire OS. The lack of a good laboratory manual forces the instructor to have students buy a supplementary book that contains *much* more information than they will have time to learn in a single academic term. Further, the instructor will have to learn all of the material in both books, as well as learn the subject OS, derive a suitable set of exercises, and provide some form of guidance through the OS reference materials so that the students can solve the exercises.

This textbook is a laboratory manual of Linux internal exercises. It complements an OS theory book by providing a dozen specific exercises on Linux internals that illustrate how theoretical concepts are implemented in Linux. The instructor does not need to become a "complete" Linux kernel expert or derive a set of exercises (either with full documentation for the exercise or with pointers to appropriate sections in a supplementary reference book). Instead, the instructor, lab assistant, and students can use this manual as a self-contained source of background data and exercises to study how concepts are implemented. Thus the less expensive laboratory manual replaces a general reference book, while providing focused information for a set of kernel internals exercises. For the student who wants to understand related information that is not required in order to solve the exercise, the background material for exercises provides pointers to reference books (and the literature).

A single-semester OS course consists of 15 weeks of course material. In my experience, many undergraduate students have difficulty doing a substantial programming exercise in less than one and a half to two weeks. This means that my students have been able to complete perhaps six to eight programming assignments in a semester. This manual provides enough exercises to allow you to choose a subset that best suits your students' backgrounds and your preferences. Most of the exercises include options that allow you to vary the assignments from term to term (thereby reducing the probability of public solutions from previous terms). As mentioned previously, my intention is to release frequent editions of this manual. I expect that the new editions will have new exercises that require new solutions.

Also provided is a solution to each exercise. Thus more difficult exercises can be chosen, and as necessary you can distribute parts of the solution that are not published in the manual.

None of these exercises are as difficult as building a new kernel from scratch. Rather, they emphasize having students study the existing Linux kernel by modifying or extending its components. The first ones are easy, and the background material is comprehensive. Later exercises increase in difficulty, with decreasing amounts of "handholding" information. Exercises 1 and 2 will ordinarily require a week or less to complete, but the last third of the exercises are likely to require a couple of weeks each. If your students need extra practice with C programming, you might carefully consider using Exercises 1 and 2 as tutorials. This might require that you provide a little extra assistance, especially with the concurrency elements of Exercise 2.

THE CD-ROM VERSION OF LINUX

Any hands-on study of an OS must commit to a particular version of the OS. With the rapid evolution of Linux, Version 2.2.*x* will be out of date by the time that the book is published. In an attempt to avoid the problem of the book and the OS code being out of sync, I have included the source code for Version 2.2.14. This first edition of the manual was originally written for Version 2.0.36. Then it was updated for Linux Version 2.2.12 just before it went into the publication cycle. As the book was going to the printer, I discovered that only 2.2.14 (and not 2.2.12) was available for distribution with the manual. Small differences exist between 2.2.12 and 2.2.14—generally in coding style rather than content. However, some of these differences show up in a couple of exercises. Specifically, watch for them in the virtual memory and scheduler parts of the kernel code. I will correct them in the next edition. I decided that including a complete 2.2.14 installation was better than the manual's having no CD-ROM. Though newer versions of the source code will be available when you use this book, I encourage you to install this version on your laboratory machines so that your students will have a software environment that is reasonably consistent with the manual. My best wish is that I will be able to release new editions of the manual that roughly track the Linux releases; the next edition might use, for example, Version 2.6*x*.

ACKNOWLEDGEMENTS

This manual represents years of effort—mine as well as other people's—learning about Linux. I benefited considerably from the assistance, insight, and contributions of the teaching assistants for Computer Science 3753: Operating Systems at the University of Colorado, namely: Don Lindsay, Sam Siewert, Ann Root, and Jason Casmira. Phil Levis provided interesting and lively discussions of Linux and the exercises. And when I first installed Linux on a machine, it worked, though not as well as it did after Adam Griff polished the installation.

Many of the exercises derive from projects and exercises in the undergraduate and graduate OS classes at the University of Colorado. In particular, Exercise 3 was created by Sam Siewert in spring 1996 for Computer Science 3753. Exercise 4 takes some material from another exercise created by Sam Siewert. Exercise 9 comes from a course project that Jason Casmira did in Computer Science 5573 (the graduate OS class) in fall 1998. Exercise 10 was first designed by Don Lindsay in fall 1995 and refined by Sam Siewert in spring 1996. Exercise 1 also appears in my companion OS textbook [Nutt, 2000], and Exercise 2 is an extension of another one that also appears in that book. Exercises 11 and 12 resemble exercises for Windows NT that appear in another of my manuals [Nutt, 1999]; Norman Ramsey created the original Windows NT exercises.

Many reviewers helped make the manual much better than its original draft. Richard Guy used the first public draft of the manuscript in a course at UCLA. Paul Stelling (UCLA) did a careful reading of the draft, correcting errors and providing insight into good and bad aspects of it. Simon Gray (Ashland University) provided particularly lucid and insightful comments on the exercises. The following also provided helpful comments that greatly improved the manual: John Barr (Ithaca College), David Binger (Centre College), David E. Boddy (Oakland University), Richard Chapman (Auburn University), Sorin Draghici (Wayne State University), Sandeep Gupta (Colorado State University), Mark Holliday (Western Carolina University), Kevin Jeffay (University of North Carolina at Chapel Hill), Joseph J. Pfeiffer (New Mexico State University), Kenneth A. Reek (Rochester Institute of Technology), and Henning Schulzrinne (Columbia University).

The Addison Wesley staff was very helpful in preparing this work. Molly Taylor and Jason Miranda provided wide ranges of assistance in handling reviews and otherwise supporting the early stages of development. Lisa Hogue finished the process, particularly by saving the day by finding a version of the Linux source code that could be distributed with the book. Laura Michaels did her usual diligent job in copy editing the work, Gina Hagen helped with production and Helen Reebenacker was the production editor. Last, but not least, Maité Suarez-Rivas, the acquisition editor, recognized the need for the book and relentlessly pushed forward to make it happen.

All of these people helped to produce the content, but of course, any errors are my responsibility.

Gary Nutt

Boulder, Colorado

Contents

part 1

Overview of Linux

Linux is a contemporary, open implementation of UNIX, available at no cost on the Internet. Since its introduction in 1991, it has become a highly respected, robust operating system (OS) implementation, enjoying great success as a platform for studying contemporary OSs, especially the internal behavior of a kernel. Just as significant, Linux is now used in many corporate information processing systems. Thus studying Linux internals provides valuable career training as well as being an excellent means of educational experimentation. Today, several new companies provide industrial-strength support for Linux.

1 The Evolution of Linux

Linux has evolved within the UNIX community. The UNIX OS was introduced to the public in a classic research paper in 1973 [Ritchie and Thompson, 1973]. UNIX established two new trends in OS design. First, previous OSs were huge software packages, typically the largest software package that ran on the computer, and they were designed for a specific hardware platform. By contrast, UNIX was intended to be a small, no-frills OS that could be made to run on any small computer. Second, the UNIX philosophy was that the OS *kernel* should provide the minimum essential functionality and that additional functionality should be added (as user programs) on an as-needed basis. For these reasons, UNIX was revolutionary. Within half a dozen years, it had become the preferred OS by programmers in multivendor hardware environments (universities, research laboratories, and system software development organizations).

Even though the UNIX kernel could be ported onto a new hardware platform without the entire OS's having to be redeveloped, the source code was owned by AT&T Bell Laboratories. Other organizations could obtain the right to use the source code (for example, to port it onto their preferred computer hardware) by paying a licensing fee to AT&T. By 1980, however, many universities and research labs had obtained the source code and were busily modifying it to meet their own needs. The most prominent work at that time was at the University of California at Berkeley under a Defense Advanced Research Projects Agency research contract. Commercial computer vendors had also begun to use the UNIX source code to derive their own versions of the UNIX OS.

By 1985, two primary versions of UNIX were running on many different hardware platforms: the main line version from AT&T Bell Labs (called *System V UNIX*) and an alternative version from the University of California at Berkeley (*called BSD UNIX*). The primary hardware platform for *BSD UNIX* was the DEC VAX, so BSD UNIX was more specifically called Version *4 BSD UNIX*, or *4.x BSD UNIX*. Both the AT&T and BSD versions implemented system call interfaces that were recognizable as UNIX, though they differed from each other in several details. In particular, substantial differences existed in the way that the two OS kernels were implemented. The competition between System V and BSD UNIX systems was very active, with programmers swearing by one version or the other. By 1988, AT&T and the leading commercial proponent of 4.x BSD UNIX (Sun Microcomputers) reached a business agreement by which these two leading versions would be merged into a common version of UNIX, called the Sun Solaris OS.

Meanwhile, other computer makers were pushing for an alternative implementation of the UNIX system call interface. As a result by 1989, a committee had been formed to develop a standardized interface. The result was an API, a *system call interface*, called *POSIX.1*.[1] Using POSIX, everyone was free to design and build kernels that provided the functionality that it specified. For example, a group of OS researchers at Carnegie Mellon University led by Richard Rashid developed the *Mach* OS that had a POSIX/UNIX system call interface. Mach was an alternative to the 4*x* BSD and System V UNIX kernel implementations. Eventually, a version of Mach was used as the basis of the Open Systems Foundation OSF-1 kernel. The first technique used to implement the POSIX/UNIX interface in Mach was simply to incorporate substantial amounts of

[1] The system call interface is often simply called "POSIX," though that term can be misleading because the POSIX committee developed several different APIs and only the first of the standards addresses the kernel system call interface. This book considers only POSIX.1, so it often uses the more popular, but less accurate, designation of POSIX to refer to the POSIX.1 system call interface.

BSD UNIX code into the Mach kernel. However, by Version 3, Mach had been redesigned as a *microkernel* with servers. Although this version of the microkernel contained no licensed source code, the BSD server still implemented the 4.*x* BSD system call interface by using the BSD source code [Tanenbaum, 1995].

On a smaller scale, in 1987 Andrew Tanenbaum designed and implemented a complete version of UNIX named MINIX. "The name MINIX stands for mini-UNIX because it is small enough that even a nonguru can understand how it works" [Tanenbaum, 1987]. MINIX implements a once-popular version of the AT&T UNIX system call interface called *Version 7 UNIX*, the basis of both BSD and System V UNIX. Tanenbaum distributed MINIX as a supplement to his OS textbook, providing also a comprehensive discussion of how the kernel was designed and implemented. He noted that MINIX " . . . was written a decade after UNIX, and has been structured in a more modular way" [Tanenbaum, 1987]. That is, it is based on a microkernel with servers, as opposed to the monolithic design of BSD and System V UNIX. MINIX was initially quite successful as a pedagogical OS, but it eventually lost some of its support because of its main feature—its simplicity. It was small enough to study but not robust enough to use as a practical OS.

In 1991, Linus Torvalds began creating the first version of Linux.[2] Although apparently inspired by the success of MINIX, he intended his OS to be more robust and useful than MINIX. Torvalds released his Linux source code to anyone who wanted to use it (by making it freely available over the Internet under the GNU Public License). It quickly caught on as a significant implementation of POSIX. Linux was the first version of UNIX for which the source code was completely free. Soon, people worldwide began to contribute their own modifications of and enhancements to Torvalds's original code. Today, the Linux distribution includes the OS, as well as a wide range of supplementary tools written by many different contributors. In addition to the original Intel 80386/80486/80586 (also called the x86 or i386) implementation, implementations were created for the Digital Alpha, Sun Sparc, Motorola 68K, MIPS, and PowerPC. By 1996, Linux had become a significant OS. By a year later, it had become an important part of the commercial OS scene, while continuing in its first role, as a free implementation of the UNIX interface.

Following the UNIX philosophy, Linux is actually the nucleus, or *kernel*, of an OS rather than the complete OS. The UNIX kernel was introduced as a minimal OS

[2] The **comp.os.minix** newsgroup had a few postings from Torvalds in early 1991 in which he let the world know that he was working on a public implementation of POSIX.

that implemented the bare necessities and left the software to provide the desired bells and whistles to libraries and other user-mode software. The early UNIX kernel followed the principle of "small is beautiful." In the intervening quarter of a century, new features were continually added to it, thereby creating "creeping featurism" that caused it to grow quite large. Today, UNIX can no longer be considered a minimal set of OS functionality.

Though Linux is usually thought of as "UNIX kernel," in 1991 it was started as a new design without the collection of hacks and patches that existed in the then current kernels. It has attempted to follow the "small is beautiful" philosophy of early UNIX, while still implementing POSIX. However, because it is freely available, anyone can add features to the kernel. Thus it is susceptible to the same "creeping featurism" that grew the UNIX kernel. The Linux kernel is still relatively small but is growing very rapidly. The Version 2.2 Linux kernel is larger and more complex than the Version 2.0, which is larger and more complex than Version 1.

This manual discusses the design and implementation of the Version 2.2 Linux kernel. The exercises and explanations were based on the latest stable release of Linux in early 2000, Version 2.2.12. Part 1 of this manual describes the kernel's overall organization. The exercises in Part 2 focus on different aspects of the kernel, each providing considerably more detail about the part of the kernel that is relevant to the exercise.

2 General Kernel Responsibilities

The UNIX family of OSs divides functionality into two classes. In the first, the kernel executes with the CPU in supervisor mode (see Part 1, Sections 2.2.2 and 3.2), whereas in the second, all other OS components execute with the CPU in user mode. This manual focuses on the Linux kernel. In general, the kernel is responsible for abstracting and managing a machine's hardware resources and for managing the sharing of those resources among executing programs. Because Linux implements a UNIX-style interface, the general definitions of the resource abstractions and sharing models are already determined. The kernel must support processes, files, and other resources so that they can be managed with the traditional UNIX system calls. Linux differs from other systems that implement a UNIX interface in the data structures and algorithms that it uses to meet those responsibilities.

2.1 Resource Abstraction

Resource abstraction is the creation of software (usually) to simplify the operations that must be applied to the hardware to cause it to function properly. For example, a device driver is a software resource abstraction that hides the details of how the physical device is manipulated to perform an input/output (I/O) operation. Once a device driver has been implemented, other software can use it to read or write the device without having to know details such as how to load commands and data into the device's controller registers. Abstraction can also be used to create resources that have no particular underlying hardware; examples of such resources are messages and semaphores. Abstract data types and objects are common software mechanisms that are used to create abstract resources.

Historically (and in Linux), the computer's components are abstracted into processes and resources. In conventional computers, an object program (produced by the compiler and loader) is placed in the machine's executable memory (called *random access memory*, or RAM). A *process* is an abstraction of the CPU operation that executes the object program.

Linux is a *multiprogrammed* OS. That is, it has been designed so that multiple programs can be loaded into RAM at once and the OS will execute one program for a while and then switch to another that is currently loaded in memory. The RAM is *space-multiplexed*—divided into blocks called *memory partitions*, each of which contains a program ready for execution. The CPU can then be *time-multiplexed*, that is, when a process is allocated the CPU, no other process can use the CPU for a specified period of time. Time-multiplexing enables the CPU to execute the programs currently loaded in different memory partitions. The OS must keep track of which program is being executed for which user (by using some previously allocated set of resources). The process abstraction allows the OS to control the execution of each instance of a program. For example, the OS can decide which process should execute and which should be made to wait for the CPU to become available. All of the aspects of the OS that implement the process abstaction are known as *process management*.

Resource management is the procedure for creating resource abstractions and allocating and deallocating the system's resources to and from the processes as they execute. A *system resource* is any logical component that the OS manages and that can be obtained only by having the process request the use of the resource from the OS. For example, RAM is a system resource. A portion of RAM must be allocated to a process when the process begins and must be made available to other processes when the process releases it. The memory resource manager is responsible for controlling the use of the machine's executable memory. Another system resource is the CPU, a specialized OS resource that is controlled by the kernel, though historically it has been treated as a special case compared to other system resources.

Other resources that the kernel manages include all of the system's devices, which are resources with their own abstraction models. Storage devices are normally abstracted so that information stored on them appears as a logical byte stream, commonly called a *file*, a special case of a resource. In UNIX, an attempt is made to have every resource other than the CPU and executable memory look like a file.

2.2 *Sharing Resources*

The Linux notion of a resource implicitly relies on the idea that processes can request resources, use them, and then release them. When a process requests a resource, it ordinarily needs exclusive use of that resource. *Exclusive use* of a resource means that when a unit of the resource is allocated to one process, then no other process has access to that unit of resource. Two critical aspects apply to this resource management: the competition to acquire units of a resource and the assurance of exclusive use.

2.2.1 Managing Competition for Resources

Competition for a resource is controlled by that resource's manager. The OS must contain a component that will be responsible for accepting requests to use each resource, for allocating the resource to a process, and for retrieving a resource when a process releases it. Following is the simplest model for using a resource (see Figure 1.1).

1. Process P requests K units of resource X from the manager for resource X.
   a. If K units of resource X are available, then the manager allocates them to process P (marking its internal *assigned* and *available* data structures to indicate that they are allocated and unavailable to other processes).
   b. If K units are not available, then the manager for resource X blocks process P while it waits for K units of X to become available. P will be prevented from further execution until the resource manager for X allocates the K units to P.
2. When at least K units of resource X become available through a deallocation by some other process P_i, the manager for X chooses one

Figure 1.1 Resource Manager Schematic

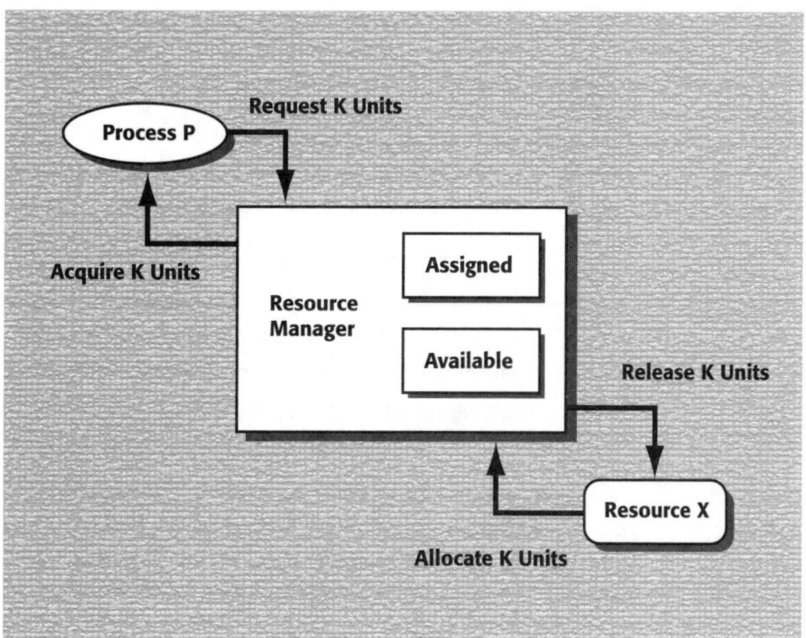

of the waiting processes whose request can be satisfied, say P, and then allocates the K units of resources to the process.

3. Process P is once again ready to execute by using the K units of resource X.

Notice that the CPU resource also conforms to this model of behavior. That is, when processes P_i and P_j are ready to execute, but the CPU resource is being used by some other process, P_k, then P_i and P_j are blocked, waiting for the CPU to become available. When P_k gives up the CPU, the scheduler will choose a waiting process, say P_i, and allocate the CPU to it. Thus the scheduler is simply a resource manager for the CPU resource.

2.2.2 Exclusive Use of a Resource

The OS uses many different mechanisms to assure that a process has exclusive use of an allocated resource, depending on the nature of the resource. The way that the CPU is given exclusively to a process differs from the way that memory or a device might be dedicated to the process. This is because, as mentioned earlier, the CPU is time-multiplexed. Choosing efficient and effective mechanisms to assure exclusive use of each resource is one of the challenges of designing an OS.

A process is given exclusive use of the CPU by assuring that other processes cannot interrupt the process's execution (unless those other processes are "more important" than the running process). Exclusive use of memory is assured through hardware memory protection mechanisms. These mechanisms prevent the CPU from accessing memory that is not allocated to the process that is currently using the CPU. Exclusive use of devices is assured by preventing the CPU from executing an I/O instruction for the device unless it is performed on behalf of the process that has been allocated the device.

Creating mechanisms to guarantee exclusive use of a resource can be very difficult. Over the years, OS and hardware designers have evolved to use a model of operation whereby the mechanism to assure exclusive use is implemented partly in the OS and partly in hardware. A key aspect of this approach is that the hardware "knows" when the OS is executing on the CPU. This allows the hardware mechanisms to react to instructions issued by *trusted software*—software that has been carefully designed and analyzed so that it performs exactly as intended. At the same time, the hardware mechanisms ignore attempts to perform instructions that might violate exclusive use (executed by software that is *untrusted* by the OS).

Contemporary CPUs such as the Intel 80286 microprocessor and above are built with a *mode bit* that can be set to *supervisor mode* or *user mode*. When the CPU is in supervisor mode, also called *kernel mode*, it is presumed to be executing trusted software and the hardware will execute any instruction in its repertoire and reference any memory address. When the CPU is in user mode, it is presumed to be executing untrusted software and the hardware will not execute *privileged instructions* (such as I/O instructions) and will reference only the memory allocated to the process that is currently using the CPU.

The mode bit is a very powerful mechanism. Linux and other contemporary OSs use it to ensure the exclusive use of the system's resources. The entire Linux kernel executes in supervisor mode (thus in all UNIX-like systems, this is also often called *kernel mode*), and all other software executes with the CPU in user mode. The Linux kernel is trusted software, whereas all other programs are untrusted software that has not been analyzed to determine its correctness. This means, for example, that only kernel code can actually execute device I/O instructions. All user-mode software must ask the kernel, via a system call to the kernel, to perform an I/O operation.

An obvious challenge in designing the hardware and the OS is to determine a safe means by which user-mode software can cause the CPU to change the mode to supervisor mode so as to execute the kernel and then to change it back to user mode after it has finished its work. Part 1, Section 3 discusses CPU modes in greater detail. Complete details for the way that the Intel 80386 and higher hardware, called the i386 architecture in the Linux source code, and Linux accomplish this is deferred until Exercise 5.

2.2.3 Managed Sharing

In some cases, two or more processes need to share a resource. For example, one process reads a file that contains the number of hours that each employee worked and a second writes payroll checks. While the second process is writing the check for record *i*, the first process could be reading the hours for record *i* + 1. How can the first process teil the second process the amount of the check that it should write? If the two processes share a block of memory, then the first process can write the amount for record *i* into the shared memory and then immediately start reading record *i* + 1. When the second process is ready to write the check for record *i*, it can read the amount from the shared memory.

The barriers that the system uses to enforce the exclusive use of a resource (for example, to prevent one process from reading or writing the memory that had been allocated to another) generally prevent sharing strategies. To accommodate sharing when it is needed, the OS must make some provision for violating the exclusive use mechanism when both processes want to share a resource. Just as the mechanism that is used to enforce exclusive use varies among resources, so does the mechanism for allowing resource sharing. This adds a new level of complexity to the design of the resource manager.

2.3 *A Partition of OS Functions*

OS designers partition the functions that must be performed by the OS into the following four categories.

- **Process and resource management**. Process and resource management is the heart of a multitasking OS. It creates the software environment that is the illusion of multiple virtual machines, with their own logical resources being used by multiple processes.
- **Memory management**. Memory management is responsible for allocating memory to processes, for protecting allocated memory from unauthorized access, and sometimes for automatically moving information back and forth between the memory and storage devices. The Linux memory manager employs *virtual memory* based on paging. Systems with virtual memory provide the most general functionality, accomplishing all the goals of allocation, protection, and automatic movement. However, virtual memory carries costs—in time, space, and hardware.
- **Device management**. A computer can be configured with a wide array of different device types. Some are low-speed character devices, for ex-

ample a keyboard, touch-sensitive screen, or remote control. Others are high-speed block devices, for example a packet network interface. The device management function provides controlling functions for this array of devices.

- **File management**. File management implements a specialized resource abstraction for storing information on the computer's storage devices (such as disk drives). The file manager also provides directories for organizing collections of files. Like most contemporary OSs, Linux uses a hierarchical file directory. The file manager uses the functionality of the device manager to implement these abstractions.

The UNIX philosophy, to which Linux adheres, is to implement the minimum amount of mechanism for kernel functions, with the remainder being implemented in user space software (libraries, runtime software, middleware, and application programs). A simple example that reflects this philosophy is the way in which files are handled. Applications programs nearly always manipulate records of data instead of linear streams of bytes. In the UNIX philosophy, only byte stream files are implemented in the kernel. If an application intends to organize the stored information as records, then it is responsible for

- defining the data's structure (for example as a C `struct`),
- translating the structure into a byte stream before it is written into a file, and
- translating the byte stream back into a structure after it has been read from the file.

The kernel file mechanism has no knowledge of any application's data structures; it only handles byte streams. User-space code (libraries such as the `stdio` library or the application software) defines the data structures used with each byte stream file.

3 Kernel Organization

The Linux kernel, like most predecessor UNIX kernels, is designed and implemented as a *monolithic* kernel.[3] In the traditional UNIX kernel, process and resource management, memory management, and file management are carefully implemented within a single executable software module. Data structures for each aspect of the kernel are generally accessible to all other aspects of the kernel. Device management, however, is implemented as a separate collection of

[3] There is a trend in many modern OSs, such as Mach and other research OSs, to use a microkernel organization where the normal kernel functions are distributed between a minimal microkernel that executes in supervisory space and a collection of servers that execute in user space. Your textbook provides more information about microkernel organizations.

device drivers and interrupt handlers (that also execute in kernel mode). Each device driver is intended to control a particular type of hardware device, for example, a 1.44 megabyte (MB) floppy disk. The philosophy behind this design is that the main part of the kernel should never be changed; the only new, kernel-space software that should be added to the system is for device management. Device drivers are relatively easy to write and add to the kernel (compared to, say, adding a feature to process management).

As technology evolved, this design assumption became a serious barrier to enhancing the kernel. The first UNIX systems did not support the wide range of hardware components that are common in today's machines, especially not bitmap displays and networks. Rather, the interface between the kernel and the device drivers was designed to support disks, keyboards, and character displays. As hardware evolved to include newer devices, providing appropriate kernel support wholly within a device driver became increasingly difficult. Linux addressed this problem by providing a new "container"—called a *module*—in which to implement extensions to the main part of the kernel (see Figure 1.2). A module is an independent software unit that can be designed and implemented long after the OS has been compiled and installed and that can be dynamically installed as the system runs. The interface between a module and the kernel is more general than the one used with UNIX device drivers. It provides the systems programmer with a more flexible tool with which to extend the kernel functionality than do device drivers. In fact, modules have proved to be so flexible that they are sometimes used to implement device drivers. You will learn to write a module to extend the kernel in Exercise 4 and to implement a device driver in Exercise 9

Figure 1.2
Kernel, Device Drivers, and Modules

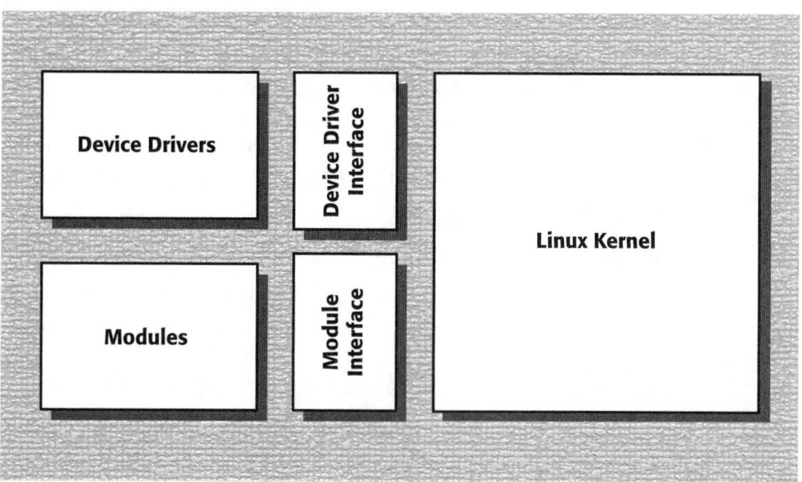

3.1 Interrupts

The kernel reacts to service requests from any active, external entity. In some cases, the external entity is a process that performs a system call (described in Part 1, Section 3.2). In other cases, a hardware component can request service from the kernel by issuing an interrupt. An *interrupt* is an electronic signal produced by an external component (such as a device) that is fielded by the CPU hardware, thereby causing the CPU to begin executing a program sequence that is independent of the one that it was executing at the time that the interrupt occurred. Usually, the interrupt signals that a device has finished an I/O operation that was started earlier by a device driver. However, sometimes it signals an event, such as the physical clock device's having just "ticked."

In the i386 architecture, the hardware behavior of an interrupt can be represented by the algorithm shown in Figure 1.3. The basic part of the fetch-execute hardware algorithm has the program counter (PC) holding the address of the next instruction to be executed. When it is time to execute the instruction, the instruction is copied from memory into the instruction register (IR). The control unit part of the CPU then decodes and executes the instruction from the IR.

When an external component wants to obtain service, it makes an *interrupt request* (IRQ) that sets a conceptual interrupt request flag, **InterruptRequest**, in the CPU. As shown in Figure 1.3, the control unit hardware checks **InterruptRequest** at the end of each fetch-execute cycle. If an IRQ occurred, then the hardware algorithm causes the CPU to cease executing the sequence of instructions addressed by the hardware PC. It then causes the CPU to branch to an *interrupt service routine* (ISR) (also generically referred to as an *interrupt handler in other OSs*) for this IRQ, by writing the address of the ISR into the PC with the **restore_PC(IRQ)** function in the algorithm description. The ISR address is stored in a kernel table that was set up when the kernel was initialized. When the branch occurs, the hardware saves the original PC value (the address of the next instruction to be executed) of the interrupted process.

When the ISR begins executing, the CPU registers will contain values that are being used by the interrupted process (excluding the PC). The ISR immediately saves all of the general and status registers of the interrupted process and copies its own values into every CPU register so that it can run the main part of the ISR routine to handle the interrupt occurrence.

A problem can result if an interrupt occurs while one ISR is in the middle of execution when the second IRQ occurs. That is, before the CPU can finish handling the first interrupt, it could restart due to the occurrence of a second

Figure 1.3

The Hardware Process's Algorithm

```
InterruptRequest = FALSE;
...
while (haltFlag not set during execution) {
   IR = memory[PC];          /* Fetch into the IR */
   PC++;                     /* Point the PC at the next instruction */
   execute(IR);              /* Execute the current instruction */
   if (InterruptRequest)  {
                             /* Interrupt the current process */
     save_PC();              /* Save the PC */
     restore_PC(IRQ);        /* Branch to the ISR for this IRQ */
}
```

interrupt. Depending on exactly which part of the ISR is currently being executed for the first interrupt, the CPU state could be lost or the interrupt processing for the first device operation might never be completed.

Of course, some parts of the ISR can be interrupted and then resumed later without harm. A problem occurs, however, if one ISR begins to execute and to save the state of the process that it interrupted. If it is in the middle of saving CPU register contents when another IRQ occurs, then the second ISR will start saving registers, saving some values from the original process and some from the interrupted ISR execution. When the first ISR is eventually allowed to complete, it will continue saving the register contents of some process other than the one that it originally interrupted.

The second ISR will not behave correctly and might even cause the first I/O operation to fail, thereby resulting in a race condition. A *race condition* is a situation in which two or more entities, A and B (such as ISR executions) might occur in either order. If A occurs before B, the system changes to one state, but if B occurs before A the system changes to a different state. This race condition between the execution of the ISR and the occurrence of another IRQ must be avoided if the machine is to perform I/O operations reliably. You can handle this race condition by incorporating another mechanism to explicitly prevent interrupts from interrupting the handler. Machines such as the i386 that incorporate interrupts also include an interrupt-enabled flag. Linux provides a kernel function (cli()) to set the interrupt-enabled flag to FALSE and another kernel function (sti()) to set the flag to TRUE. These two functions are used throughout the kernel when it is important to avoid a race condition caused by interrupts. How do you know when to use cli() and sti()? By carefully analyzing the context in which any piece of the code executes. Clearly this will be more difficult in a monolithic kernel than in a more modular kernel.

Interrupts do not alter the control flow of the process that is executing on the CPU. Rather, they simply delay the process's execution by running extra programs "behind the process's back." Once **sti()** has been executed, the **InterruptEnabled** flag is set to **TRUE**.

3.2 Using Kernel Services

As suggested by Figure 1.4, user programs view the kernel as a large *abstract data type* (ADT) (similar to an object) that maintains state and that has a number of functions on its public interface, the *system call interface*. This ADT provides OS service to a user program whenever the program calls a function on its public interface. The exact nature of the service depends on the particular function that is called, its parameters, and the state of the OS when the function is called. Hence, the public interface specification for the kernel is the main description of the OS's functionality. In the case of Linux, the system call interface is nominally defined by the POSIX.1 specification. It is only nominal because any version of Linux might not implement some of the fine details of the specification and because the specification does not completely specify the semantics of the interface. However, the POSIX.1 specification is sufficiently com-

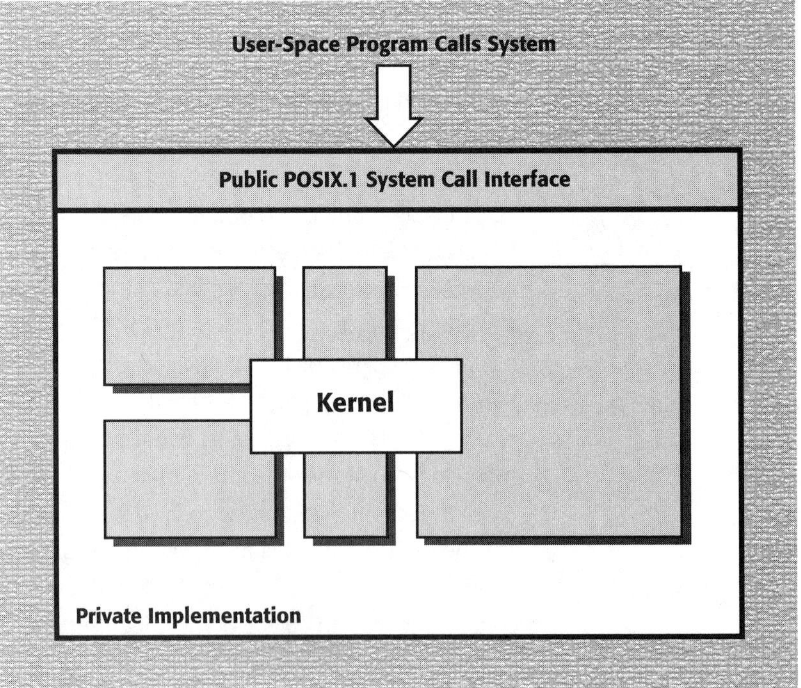

Figure 1.4
The Kernel as an ADT

plete that programmers are generally willing to accept it as a basic OS interface specification.

In a continuation of the ADT analogy, the POSIX implementation is private, so implementations might differ by system, and even by Linux implementation version. In theory—and generally in practice—the boundaries between device drivers or modules and the kernel are not discernible to the user program. These differences are characteristics of the internal design and not of the public interface. Thus POSIX defines functions that normally are implemented in the kernel, device drivers, or modules. If the function is implemented in a device driver or module, then when a user program invokes the function, the kernel will field the call and pass it through an internal interface to the appropriate device driver or module. In a Linux POSIX implementation, some functions might even be implemented as user-space programs. For example, most versions of Linux rely on library code to implement the thread package [Beck et al., 1998].

If the kernel ADT were actually implemented as a C++ object, it would be a *passive object*. That is, the kernel software does not have any internal thread of execution or process; it is simply a collection of functions and data structures that maintain state. Any process that uses kernel services—the process is an *active entity*—makes a kernel request by (logically) making a procedure call on POSIX. That is, a process that is executing outside of the kernel begins to execute the kernel code when it makes the system call. This contrasts with the idea that the process that is executing user code might obtain service from a distinct kernel process. In Linux, the process executing the user program also executes the kernel programs when a system call is made.

Conceptually, then, whenever a process executing an application program desires service from the OS, it calls the appropriate OS function through POSIX. Before the call the process is executing the application program, and after the call (but before the return) it is executing the kernel software. However, recall that the kernel is executed with the CPU in supervisor mode but the application program is executed in user mode. When the process performs the system call, the CPU must change from user to supervisor mode, and when the system call returns the CPU must change from supervisor to user mode. The return case is simple to handle, since one of the privileged instructions that can be executed when the CPU is in supervisor mode is to switch the CPU mode from supervisor to user mode. Here is the dilemma: How can a user mode program switch the CPU to supervisor mode with the assurance that once the switch is done the CPU will be executing trusted kernel code and not untrusted user code? If the program is executing in user mode, it must be able to direct the hardware to switch to supervisor mode; the instruction must not be a privileged instruction. If there were an ordinary (not privileged) instruction to switch the mode, then there would be nothing to prevent a program from executing the instruction then executing privileged instructions.

Normally, the compiler translates any function call into machine language statements that prepare actual parameters for passing then a procedure call instruction on the entry point of the target function. In the case of kernel calls, this would have two significant implications:

1. Every kernel routine (and hence the entire kernel) will be linked into every application program.
2. Every kernel routine will immediately have to execute a machine instruction to switch the CPU to supervisory mode before performing the work.

Notice that because the kernel code would be linked into the user program, the kernel code would be readable by the process while it was executing in user mode. So it would be possible for the user program to copy the machine instruction for switching to supervisory mode and then to use that instruction to switch the mode to run untrusted software.

CPUs that incorporate the mode bit also usually incorporate a hardware trap instruction. A *trap instruction* is an instruction that causes the CPU to branch to a prespecified address (sometimes as a function of an instruction operand) and also to switch itself to supervisory mode. Of course, the details of each machine's trap instruction are unique to that machine. A trap instruction is not a privileged instruction, so any program can execute a trap. However, the destination of the branch instruction is predetermined by a set of addresses that are kept in supervisory space and that are configured to point to kernel code.

Suppose that the assembly language representation for a trap is

```
trap  argument
```

Figure 1.5 depicts the following behavior of a trap instruction.

1. Switch the CPU to supervisor mode.
2. Look up a branch address in a kernel space table.
3. Branch to a trusted OS function.

The trap instruction provides a safe way for a user-mode process to execute only predefined software when it switches the mode bit to supervisor mode.

Here is a summary of the actions performed to accomplish a system call.

1. For a system call, F, a stub procedure is used to invoke F (the stub is also named F).

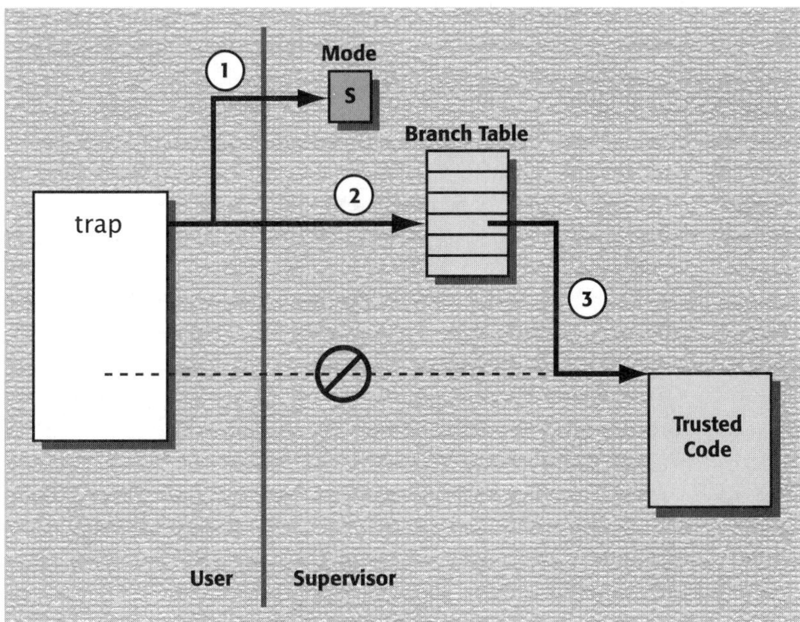

Figure 1.5
The Trap Instruction Operation

2. The stub is linked into the (user-space) calling program.
3. When a process executes the call to F at runtime, control is transferred to the stub procedure rather than directly to the kernel.
4. The stub procedure validates the parameter values being passed to the kernel procedure. In addition, it can, in principle, authenticate the process that calls the stub procedure.
5. The stub procedure executes a trap instruction that switches the CPU to supervisory mode. It then branches (indirectly through a kernel table that contains kernel function entry points) to the entry point for the target kernel function.

Because the trap instruction is compiled into the stub procedure, a user-space program cannot easily determine the trap's destination address. Even if it could, it would be unable to branch indirectly through the kernel-space function table. As a result, it cannot directly invoke a kernel function and instead must use the system-provided stub. In Exercise 5, you will add a system call to Linux by adding an entry to the system table for your kernel function.

3.3 Serial Execution

Linux is a multiprogramming kernel. Kernel functions, however, are normally executed as if they are in a *critical section*. That is, once a process calls a system function, the function normally runs to completion and returns before the CPU is allocated to a different process. However, IRQs can interrupt the execution of a system call to perform an ISR. This type of kernel is *single-threaded*, since (ignoring the ISRs) only one thread of execution is allowed to execute in the kernel at any point in time. One thread of execution cannot start a function call and become interrupted by the scheduler to let another process run (and possibly make a kernel call). This approach has at least two important implications.

1. A kernel function can update various kernel data structures without being concerned that another process will interrupt its execution and change related parts of the same data structures. Race conditions among processes do not occur. (However, race conditions between the process and the interrupt-induced execution might occur.)
2. When writing a new kernel function, always keep in mind that you cannot write code that will block, waiting for a message or other resource that only some other process can release. This type of code might produce deadlock in the kernel.

3.4 Daemons

This section earlier explained how normal processes execute kernel code. That is, there is no special "kernel process" that executes kernel code. While this is accurate, several user-transparent processes called *daemons* are started when a Linux machine is started and must exist in order for the OS to operate correctly. For example, if the machine is connected to a network, a daemon process must exist to respond to incoming network packets, another daemon process will log system messages and errors, and so on. The particular daemons that are running on any Linux installation vary according to the way that the system administrator has set up the machine (this is explained further in the following subsection on booting a Linux machine).

By convention, daemon processes execute programs whose names end with the character "d." For example, the network daemon is usually called **inetd** and the system logging daemon is **syslogd**. You can make a good guess as to what daemons are running on your Linux machine by typing the following line to your shell:

```
ps aux | more
```

The **ps** command reports the process status, and the **aux** parameters indicate that you want a report in user format (the **u** parameter) for all processes (the **a** parameter), including those without a controlling terminal (the **x** parameter). As you scan the resulting list, look for commands that end with the character "d" and that have a TTY field of "?" (indicating no controlling terminal). Typically, you will see **syslogd**, **klogd**, **crond**, and **lpd** running on your system. You can find out what each of these daemons is doing by looking at the **man** page for the program that the daemon is running (for example, use **man syslogd** to read the **man** page for **syslogd**).

3.5 *The Booting Procedure*

Every computer has a sequence of instructions that are executed whenever the computer is powered up or restarted. Similarly, every OS has a sequence of instructions that it executes prior to beginning normal operation. Computer hardware designers determine the hardware bootup procedure when they construct the machine.

Contemporary i386 machines, for example, typically are designed to support Microsoft OSs, so they incorporate the Basic Input/Output System (BIOS) at a prespecified location in the system's read-only memory (ROM). When the computer is started, it begins executing from BIOS code. The BIOS first runs the manufacturer's hardware booting sequence by executing the Power-On Self Test (POST). The POST performs various diagnostic tests to check the memory and devices for their presence and for correct operation. The POST usually takes several seconds, possibly even a couple of minutes. When the POST has completed, the machine is ready to load and start the OS.

3.5.1 The Boot Sector

The OS is loaded from the system's *boot disk*. An i386 system treats the A: floppy disk drive as the default boot disk if it contains a diskette; otherwise, one of the system's hard disk drives is treated as the default boot disk.

A boot disk must be configured to contain a *boot record* at the disk's first logical sector. The boot record fits onto a single 512-byte disk sector (often called the *boot sector*). The boot sector is organized as shown in Figure 1.6 [Beck, 1998; Messmer, 1995].

After the POST finishes executing, the BIOS copies the boot record from the disk into memory. The boot record also includes various parameters that de-

Figure 1.6
Boot Sector

0x000	0x002	**<A jump instruction to** 0x*0XX*>
0x003	. . .	**Disk parameters (used by BIOS)**
0x*0XX*	0x1fd	**Bootstrap program**
0x1fe	0x1ff	0xaa55 **(the magic number for BIOS)**

scribe the disk's physical layout. These parameters are stored in well-known locations in the boot record and include the number of tracks and the number of sectors per track. When the boot record is loaded, the BIOS program can read these parameters from the well-known addresses. Further, once the boot record has been loaded, BIOS branches to the first location in the program and then immediately branches to location `0x0`*XX* (the value *XX* is `3e` for the Linux boot record and `1e` for the MS-DOS boot record). The small program stored in the boot record then can load a more sophisticated loader from other sectors on the disk; it is the more sophisticated loader that loads the OS.

Hard disks can have an additional level of abstraction, called *disk partitioning*. In a partitioned hard disk, each partition is treated like a physical disk above the abstract machine that accesses the physical disk (BIOS, in MS-DOS). A hard disk can be partitioned to have up to four logical disks, each with its own set of logical sectors. If a disk partition is a *bootable disk partition*, then its logical sector number 0 will be a boot sector. In a partitioned disk, the physical head 0, track 0, sector 1 (the first logical disk sector) contains a partition sector rather than a boot sector. The *partition sector* provides information that describes how the hard disk is partitioned into logical disks. When the hardware is powered up, it goes to head 0, track 0, sector 1 and begins executing code. A partitioned disk has a 446-byte bootstrap program at the first byte in the sector. An unpartitioned disk has a jump instruction to start the execution on the boot program stored at location `0x0`*XX* in the sector. After the bootstrap program is a 64-byte partition table for the disk. This table contains space for the four partition entries, each of which describes the portion of the physical disk that is used for its partition (the starting sector of the partition, ending sector, number of sectors in the partition, and so on). The last 2 bytes of the partition sector contain a magic number, `0xaa55`, to identify the partition sector.

An i386 computer can be booted with Linux by using a Linux boot disk whose boot record contains a Linux boot program rather than a Windows OS boot program. For a partitioned hard disk, loading different OSs in different partitions is possible. Windows OSs can handle multipartitioned disks by designating one of the partitions as the *active partition*; the system will always boot from the active partition.

Linux provides a special *Linux Loader* (LILO) that can be placed in the system boot record to allow the user to choose at boot time which partition is to be the active partition. In this case, LILO will be loaded in the boot record so that the BIOS will run it after the POST.

3.5.2 Starting the Kernel

When the machine is powered up, the hardware fetch-execute cycle begins, thereby causing the control unit to repeatedly fetch and decode instructions and the arithmetic-logic unit to execute them. The hardware is now executing some "process" that can be called the *hardware process*. The hardware process is not a Linux process because it starts when the hardware starts, long before the kernel has even been loaded. After the POST has completed, the boot record has been read, and the loader has placed the OS into primary memory, the booting procedure begins to run kernel code to initialize the computer's hardware. The computer is then ready to start the kernel, by setting the CPU in supervisor mode and branching to the main entry point in the kernel. This main entry point is started in the boot sequence (rather than being started as a conventional main program), so it is not an ordinary C program with the conventional main header line.

Once the main entry point has been entered, the kernel initializes the trap table, the interrupt handler, the scheduler, the clock, the modules, and so on. Near the end of this sequence, it initializes the process manager, thereby signifying that it is prepared to support the normal process abstraction. The hardware process then creates the *initial process*. The initial process is allocated the first entry in the kernel's process descriptor table, so it also is referred to internally as *process 0*, or `task[0]`, or INIT_TASK. The initial process then creates the first useful Linux process to run the `init` program and begins to execute an idle loop. The initial process's only duties after the kernel is initialized is to use idle CPU time. That is, it uses the CPU when no other process wants to use the CPU (the initial process also is sometimes called the *idle process*).

The first real process continues to initialize the system, now using higher-level abstractions than were available to the hardware process. It starts various daemons, starts the file manager, creates the system console, runs other `init` programs from `/etc`, `/bin`, and/or `/sbin`, and runs `/etc/rc` (if necessary).

Starting the kernel is a complex procedure, and opportunities for something to go wrong abound. In several places in the procedure, various alternatives are checked in case the default boot algorithm fails. By the time that the kernel initialization has completed, the initial process is enabled and several other daemons will have been started. Chapter 3 of Beck, et al. [1998] provides a more detailed discussion of the steps involved in starting the kernel.

3.6 Logging In to the Machine

During initialization, the kernel creates one process on each communication port that can be used to support user logins. Each of these processes will run a copy of the **getty** program (see Figure 1.7). The **getty** process initializes itself and then waits for a user to begin using the port. When the user begins to use the port, **getty** runs the **login** program, expecting a user identification on the first line and a password on the second line. Once the port's **login** program obtains the identification and the password, it verifies the user's identity by looking up both in the system's **/etc/passwd** file. Each entry is a line in this file and has the form

```
jblow:eNcrYPt123:3448:35:Joe Blow:/home/kiowa/jblow:/bin/bash
```

An entry is a *record* for a different user, with fields in the record separated by the semicolon (":") character. In the example record,

- **jblow** is the user login,
- **eNcrYPt123** is an encrypted copy of the password,
- the next two numbers, **3448** and **35**, are the user ID and group ID, respectively,
- **Joe Blow** is the user's real name,
- **/home/kiowa/jblow** is the user's home directory, and
- **/bin/bash** is the path to the shell command line interpreter preferred by the user.

If this authentication is successful, then the **login** process changes the current directory to the user's home directory and executes the specified shell program so that the user can interact directly with the **login** process by using the shell.

A user who logs into a UNIX machine simply begins using a process that was created when the machine was started. (Starting a shell involves many more details, but conceptually, this description is accurate.) Thus the user's process is executing a shell program (for example, the Bourne shell, the C shell, or the Korn shell) with a unique copy of the data and stack segments for the shell execution. The unique data includes the user's environment variables, such as the PATH variable. When the user logs off the machine, the **login** process returns from its shell call and waits for the next user to log in.

3.7 Control Flow in the Machine

Ultimately, the behavior of the computer is controlled by the action of the hardware process—remember, there is only one hardware process. This process executes the algorithm shown in Figure 1.3 until the computer is halted. Even though the kernel might switch from running one program—for example, an ISR or a user program—the hardware process operates at a level of abstraction *below* the kernel. Therefore the hardware process has no notion of software

Figure 1.7
The getty Program

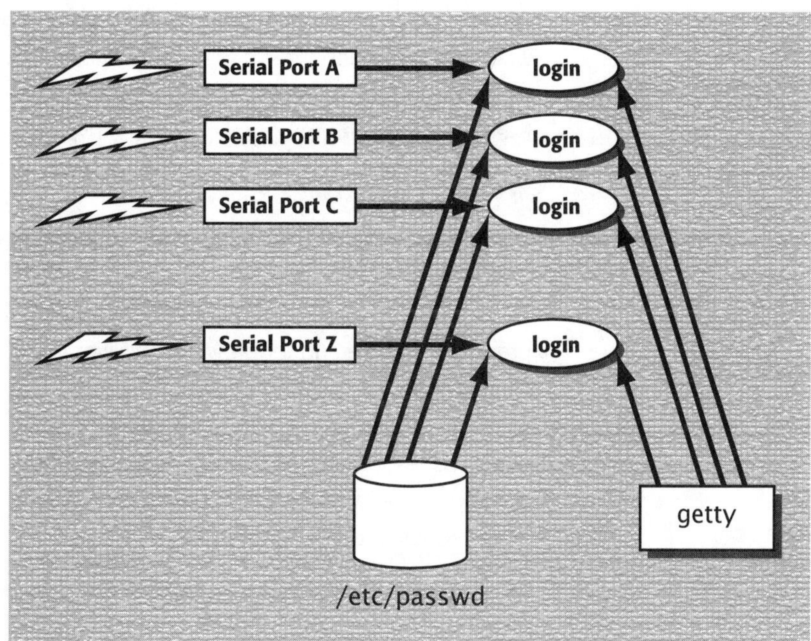

processes, ISRs, or other kernel abstraction; instead, it just fetches and executes instructions. At this low-level view of the behavior of the computer, even interrupts are nothing more than branch instructions.

Figure 1.8
The Hardware Process

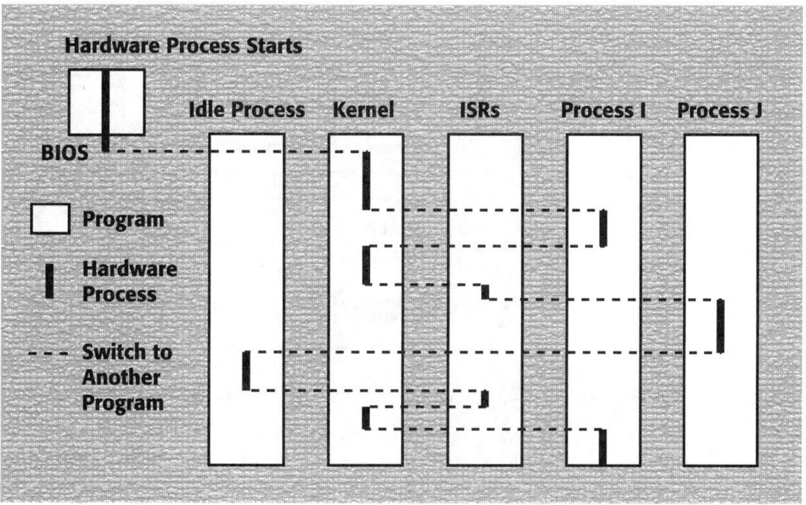

Figure 1.8 provides an intuitive visual description of the behavior of the hardware process. When the machine is powered up, the hardware process starts executing the fetch-execute cycle on the BIOS program (including the POST). Eventually, it runs kernel code and (in this hypothetical example) executes code on behalf of Linux process i returns to the kernel, returns to an ISR, and so on.

4 Process and Resource Management

The process manager is responsible for creating the process abstraction that programmers use and for providing facilities so that a process can create, destroy, synchronize, and protect other processes. Similarly, resource management involves creating appropriate abstractions to represent entities that a process might request (and to block their execution if the resources are unavailable). In addition to abstraction, resource managers must provide an interface by which a process can request, acquire, and release resources.

To illustrate the job of the process manager, following is a summary of a program's execution at various levels of abstraction (see Figure 1.9).

- **Hardware level**. The hardware fetches an instruction from the memory location addressed by the PC, executes it, fetches the next one, executes that one, and so on. It does not distinguish one program from another; all programs are simply sets of instructions in the primary memory. As a result, only the notion of the hardware process executing stored instructions applies, with no further abstraction such as a Linux process occurring.

Figure 1.9
Process Abstraction

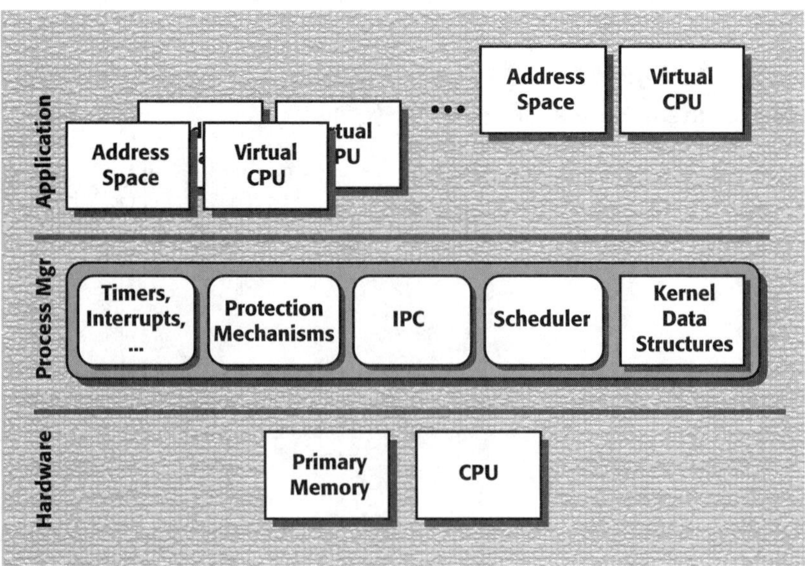

- **Process manager level**. The process manager creates a collection of idealized *virtual machines*, each of which has the characteristics of the host CPU when it is running in user mode. The process manager uses the hardware level to create a Linux process by using timers, interrupts, various protection mechanisms, interprocess communication (IPC) and synchronization mechanisms, scheduling, and a collection of data structures. Applications interact with the process manager (by using the system call interface), for example,
  - to create instances of the virtual machine (with **fork()**),
  - to load the address space with a particular program (by using **exec()**), and
  - to synchronize a parent and a child virtual machine (with **wait()**).
- **Application level**. The application level uses conventional Linux processes. The process's address space is the memory of its virtual machine (containing the text, stack, and data segments). The virtual CPU instructions are the user-mode hardware instructions augmented by the system call interface functions, and the virtual resources (including devices) are manipulated via the system call interface.

The process manager must manipulate the hardware process and physical resources to implement a set of virtual machines. It also must multiplex the execution of the virtual machines on top of the single physical machine. (Linux supports multiprocessor CPUs, but in this manual the focus is only on the single CPU implementation.) It further must provide facilities to accommodate sharing: protection and synchronization.

In discussions of the kernel code, the terms *task* and *process* are used almost interchangeably. This manual generally uses *task* when the execution occurs in supervisor mode and *process* when execution occurs in user mode. A process, when created, is usually created with a new *address space*—a set of virtual addresses that the process can read or write as it executes. From the kernel perspective, this means that when the hardware process is executing on behalf of another process, it can read and write only the addressable machine components that correspond to the virtual address in its address space.

4.1 Running the Process Manager

The portion of the kernel that handles process scheduling (like all other parts of the kernel) is executed only when a process begins executing in supervisor mode, either due to a system call or an interrupt (see Figure 1.10).

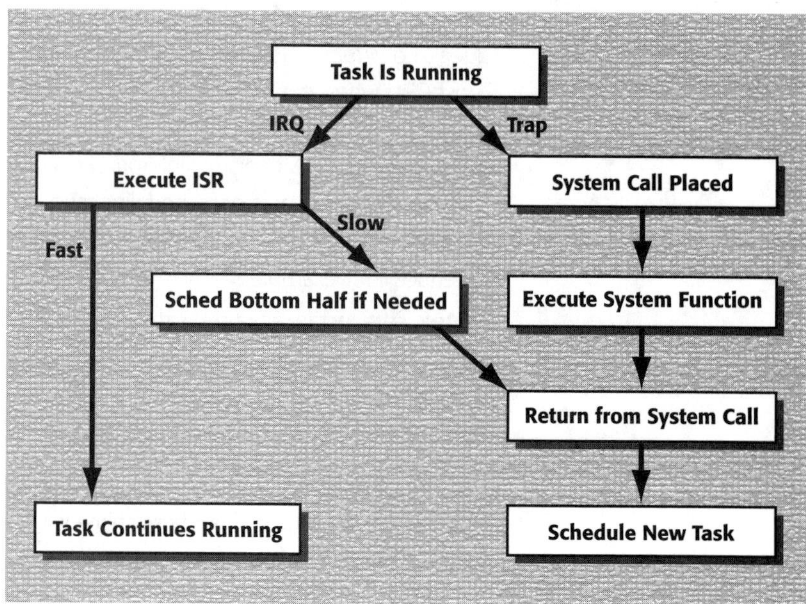

Figure 1.10
Part of Task Control Flow in the Kernel

4.1.1 System Call

Suppose that a process is executing user-mode software and it makes a system call. The process traps into the kernel code to the entry point for the target function. The function is executed by the kernel task that corresponds to the user process that made the system call. When the function completes its work, it returns to the kernel so that it can perform a standard set of tasks in the ret_from_sys_call code (a block of assembly language code in the kernel). This code block dispatches any accumulated system work. For example, it handles signals, completes certain forms of pending interrupt processes (called "executing the bottom halves of pending interrupt handlers"), and schedules other tasks.

The system call is completed with the calling process in the TASK_RUNNING state (ready to use the CPU when it is available) or in the TASK_INTERRUPTIBLE or TASK_UNINTERRUPTIBLE state if the kernel cannot complete the requested work immediately. If the task is blocked (or it has used its entire time slice), then the scheduler is called to dispatch a new task.

4.1.2 Interrupts

When an IRQ occurs, the currently running process completes the execution of its current instruction and then the task starts executing the ISR for the corresponding IRQ. Linux differentiates between fast and slow interrupts. A *fast inter-*

rupt is an interrupt that takes very little time to complete. While a fast interrupt is being processed, other interrupts are disabled. Once that interrupt is handled, the other interrupts are reenabled and the user process is continued.

A *slow interrupt* involves more work. After the interrupts are disabled, the task executes the ISR. The ISR can have a bottom half, which contains work that needs to be performed before the interrupt handling is completed but that does not have to be done in the ISR itself. The pending bottom half work is scheduled in a kernel queue for the next time that bottom halves are to be processed (see the **ret_from_sys_call** processing in the system call description).

Slow interrupts can, themselves, be interrupted. Therefore the queue of bottom half work can build up when nested interrupts occur. If the same ISR is invoked two or more times before the bottom halves are run, then the corresponding bottom half will be run only once even though the ISR executed multiple times. When the slow interrupt finishes the ISR, it executes the **ret_from_sys_call** block of code.

4.2 Creating a New Task

A new task/process is created when its parent process invokes the **fork()** system call. When the kernel creates a new task, it must allocate a new instance of the *process descriptor* so that it will have a data structure to hold all of the information that it needs to manage the new task. In the Linux kernel, the process descriptor is an instance of the **struct task_struct** data type.

The *process table* keeps the collection of process descriptors for each task/process. Older versions of the Linux kernel incorporated a static array of pointers to **task_struct** instances. The current version replaced the static table with an array of pointers. In either case, the idle task occupies the first slot in the list or table (hence the designation of **task[0]** for the idle process).

Each process descriptor may be linked into one or more lists (in addition to the process table), depending on the current state of the process. For example, a process in the **TASK_RUNNING** state is in a list pointed to by a static kernel variable (named **current**) that indicates which processes are currently ready to use a CPU. If the process is blocked, waiting for an I/O operation to complete, then it appears in a list of processes that are waiting for an interrupt from the device. You will begin a detailed study of the **struct task_struct** in Exercise 1 that will culminate in Exercise 9.

The **fork()** system call creates a new process by performing the following steps.

1. Allocate a new instance of a **struct task_struct**, and link it into the **task** list.
2. Create a new kernel space stack for the task to use when it is executing in the kernel.
3. Copy each field from the parent's task descriptor into the child's task descriptor.
4. Modify the fields in the child's descriptor that are specific to the child.
   - Save the new process identifier (PID).
   - Create links to this task's parent and siblings.
   - Initialize process-specific timers (creation time, time left in the current time slice, and so on).
5. Copy other data structures that are referenced in the parent descriptor and that should be replicated for the child process.
- Create a file table and a new file descriptor for each open file in the parent's file table.
- Create a new user data segment for the child task, and then copy the contents of the parent's user data segment into this new segment. (This could be very time consuming, since the data segment could contain megabytes of information.)
- Copy information regarding the signals and signal handlers.
- Copy virtual memory tables.

6. Change the child's state to **TASK_RUNNING**, and return from the system call.

Of course, an **execve()** system call will also greatly influence the contents of the process descriptor, since it causes the process to load and execute a different program than it was executing when it called **execve()**. Briefly, **execve()** causes the kernel

- to find the new executable file in the file system,
- to check access permissions,
- to adjust the memory requirements as necessary, and
- then to load the file for subsequent execution.

This requires updating the details of the memory references in the process descriptor.

The Linux kernel also includes a system call, **clone()**, for supporting threads. The **clone()**and **fork()** calls both invoke the internal kernel function **do_fork()**, so they behave almost the same. They differ in the way that the parent and child data segment is handled. That is, whereas **fork()** copies the data segment, **clone()** divides it (and most of the rest of the parent's address space) between the parent and child tasks. Beck, et al., [1998] points out that even though POSIX specifies calls to invoke threads and that **clone()** is intended to support threads, the 2.0*x* versions of the kernel use the Pthread library to implement them.

4.3 The Scheduler

The *scheduler* is the kernel component responsible for multiplexing the CPU among the programs in memory, that is, among the processes that are in the **TASK_RUNNING** state. It incorporates the policy used to select the next process to be allocated the CPU. The **schedule()** kernel function can be called via a trap. It is also called as part of the **ret_from_sys_call** code block, so it always runs as a task that is associated with a user process or with an interrupt. The scheduler is responsible for determining which runnable task has the highest priority and then for dispatching that task (allocating the CPU to it). In Exercise 9, you will study the Linux scheduler in detail.

4.4 IPC and Synchronization

Two distinct synchronization mechanisms are used in Linux, one within the kernel code itself and the other to provide synchronization mechanisms for user processes. The kernel always executes either as a single task invoked via the system call interface or as activity caused by an interrupt. Kernel activity can never be interrupted by a system call. This is because when either an interrupt is being handled or a system call is being processed, no user process can issue a system call. Therefore the primary need for synchronization within the kernel is to ensure that interrupts do not occur while the current kernel code is in a critical section. This is satisfied by disabling interrupts at the beginning of the critical section (by using the **cli()**— CLear Interrupt—kernel function) and then reenabling them when the critical section is complete (by using the **sti()**—SeT Interrupt—function).

The external synchronization mechanism is based on an event model. The kernel implements an abstract data type called a **wait_queue** to manage events. Each event has a corresponding **wait_queue**; you can add a task to a designated **wait_queue** by using the **add_wait_queue()** kernel function. The **remove_wait_queue()** kernel function removes a single task from the designated wait queue. This abstract data type is the basis of any system call to perform synchronization, such as the System V semaphore system calls. You will learn more about **wait_queue** in Exercise 8.

A user process can perform IPC by using the kernel in any of four different mechanisms.

1. **Pipes (and named pipes)**. Pipes and named pipes export the same interface as files, so much of the implementation is like a file. A pipe uses a 4KB circular buffer to move data from one address space to another via the file `read()` and `write()` system calls. From a process management perspective, this procedure is straightforward. Pipes are discussed further in Exercise 2.
2. **System V IPC**. The System V IPC interface allows user processes to create IPC objects (such as semaphores) in the kernel. The kernel allocates the data structure instance and then associates it with a user-space identifier that is shared among user processes. In the case of semaphores, one process creates the semaphore and then others manipulate it by using the external reference and operations. The semaphore semantics are implemented by using a `wait_queue` instance. System V messages generalize this approach so that structured messages can be saved/retrieved from kernel data structures.
3. **System V shared memory**. The shared memory facility is the generalization of the System V IPC mechanism. A block of memory is allocated in the kernel, and then different processes use an external reference to access the memory. You will study the shared memory implementation in Exercise 6.
4. **Sockets**. The socket is a special case of network socket functionality. A socket implementation requires the kernel to allocate and manage buffer space and socket descriptors. These kernel entities are normally used by the network code, though they can also be used in the UNIX name domain as a specialized form of pipe. A socket differs from a pipe in that it is full-duplexed and is designed to use a protocol for reading and writing information.

4.5 Protection Mechanism

Protection mechanisms come in two flavors:

- Address space isolation
- File protection

Address space isolation is the primary form of protection mechanism. Its use depends on a process's being able to define a set of virtual addresses that cannot be read or written by any other process (except by using the IPC and memory-sharing mechanisms mentioned in the previous section). In Linux, the address space protection scheme is built into the virtual memory mechanism, which is discussed in the next section.

With *file protection*, processes and files are associated with users, with each file having an owner user identified by a user ID (**uid**). A user can be associated with one or more groups, each having a group ID (**gid**). Each file can have read, write, and execute permission for the file owner, for a process that is in the same group as the owner, or for any other process (called world permissions). The kernel checks the **uid** and the file permissions whenever it manipulates a file to see if a process is authorized to access a file.

5 Memory Management

The memory manager is responsible for the following activities.

- Allocate blocks of the system's primary (or executable) memory on request.
- Ensure exclusive control of a block once it has been allocated.
- Provide a means by which cooperating processes can share blocks of memory with each other.
- Automatically move information between the primary and secondary memories.

Linux uses a *demand paged virtual memory model* as the basis of its memory management design. In this model, each process is allocated its own virtual address space. Processes reference virtual addresses, and the system maps each such reference into a primary (also called *physical*) memory address prior to accessing the memory location. The kernel and the hardware together ensure that the contents of the virtual memory location are placed into the physical memory and that the corresponding virtual address is bound to the correct physical memory location when it is referenced by the process.

As with all demand paged virtual memory managers, the basic unit of memory allocation and transfer is a *page*. In the i386 implementation, each page contains 2^{12} (4,096) bytes. Because Linux uses a paged virtual memory approach, the general characteristics of the manager's responsibilities are as follows.

- Blocks are allocated and deallocated as physical memory page frames.
- The protection mechanism is on a page-by-page basis.
- Memory sharing is based on pages.
- Moving pages back and forth between the secondary and primary memories controls automatic movement through the memory hierarchy.

5.1 *Managing the Virtual Address Space*

Each process is created with its own virtual address space. In the i386 architecture, a virtual address is 32 bits wide, meaning that the space contains addresses for 4GB. Because a page is 2^{12} bytes, an address space contains 2^{20} pages.

Each virtual address space is divided into segments: a 3GB *user segment* and a 1GB *kernel segment*. A programmer can use any address in the user segment to reference all of its code and data by having the OS *map* information into specific virtual addresses. Unmapped virtual addresses simply are not used. The virtual addresses in the kernel segment are permanently mapped and are associated with fixed physical memory addresses used by the kernel. This means that every process's virtual address space shares the same kernel segment, since the kernel virtual addresses all map to the physical addresses used by the kernel.

Each of the kernel and user segments is further partitioned into *code sectors* and *data sectors*. Each virtual address contains within the sector a sector identification and an offset. When the CPU is in the instruction fetch phase, it always references a code sector (in either the user or kernel segment). Therefore the compiler does not bother to generate the sector identification as part of the address used by an instruction (special object code formats for Linux are not needed).

Whenever a process is executing, its state includes a *segment selector*. If the process is executing in user space, then the segment selector is set to **user**; if it is executing in the kernel segment, the selector is set to **kernel**. The memory manager forms the virtual address by using the value of the segment selector with the offset address that the process provides. Linux provides macros for setting the segment selector for each of the four segments in the virtual address space.

A process, when initialized, defines its virtual address space by specifying the set of virtual addresses that it will be using. The kernel provides a function, **do_mmap()**, that reserves a set of virtual addresses in the virtual address space. Thus the procedure to determine the virtual addresses to be used includes reading the executable file to determine the load map (and virtual addresses) for the executable file. The **do_mmap()** function is called by **execve()** when it loads a file. Other parts of the OS can also call **do_mmap()**; for example, the **brk()** system call invokes **do_mmap()** when it needs to add more space to the heap used to support **malloc()**. Once virtual addresses have been mapped, the corresponding file contents are associated with a block of virtual addresses. However, the contents of the virtual addresses are stored in secondary memory (on the disk), where they will remain until they are referenced as the process executes in the virtual address space.

5.2 The Secondary Memory

A paging system is designed to have (the mapped part of) each process's virtual address space defined in secondary memory. The Linux system may be configured so that an entire disk partition is dedicated to holding these virtual address spaces, or the virtual address spaces may be saved in individual files kept in an ordinary partition. For historical reasons, this disk partition is called a *swap device*; if files are used, then each file is called a *swap file*. (In some OSs, for example Windows NT, these entities are more accurately called *paging disks* and *paging files*.) A compile-time constant (MAX_SWAPFILES) number of swap devices or files are possible; the default value is 8.

When a virtual address is mapped, corresponding physical space is reserved in the swap device/file. However, no primary memory is allocated or loaded as a result of the mapping operation. When the process is ready to run, the pages that contain the entry point of the program that it is using are loaded into the primary memory. As the process executes, the memory manager translates each virtual address referenced by the process into the physical address that contains the information that was copied from the swap device/file when the page was loaded.

5.3 Handling Missing Pages

The *system address translation mechanism* (see the next section) can determine that the process is referencing a *missing page*, a page that is not currently loaded in the primary memory but that is defined in the swap device/file. When the process references a missing page, the memory manager copies that page from the secondary memory into the primary memory. Page loading requires that the memory manager find the target page in the swap device/file, copy it into a physical memory page frame, adjust the appropriate page translation table(s), and then complete the memory reference.

Each page frame in primary memory has a kernel data structure of type mem_map_t to provide details about the state of that page frame. A node of type mem_map_t may appear in various lists, depending on whether the page is unallocated, locked, shared, or other. If the page is loaded, then the mem_map_t instance references the inode and offset of the file where the page is stored in the swap device/file. All other information required to manage the page frame (such as locking and sharing) is kept in the **mem_map_t** data structure.

Suppose that the memory manager has determined that it needs to load a page into a page frame. It first will attempt to acquire a *block* of new page frames for the process by calling an internal kernel function, **__get_free_pages()**. This function uses a parameter to select a strategy to be used in seeking a page frame. For example, an interrupt routine searching for space is treated differently than a user process requesting space. The size of the block is a kernel compile-time parameter, normally set to allow blocks to be up to 32 pages. Page frames are managed as a free list of blocks of size 2^k page frames. Page frame blocks are allocated by finding the right size of block or by splitting a larger block. If no block is available, then the page manager attempts to free space. Blocks might have been allocated to the file system to buffer pages being read or written by block devices (see Exercise 12), so the page manager first looks to see if a block exists that can be deallocated from the buffer pool. If it finds no block there, it next attempts to reclaim page frames that were reserved for System V shared memory (see Exercise 6). If the block request still cannot be satisfied, the page manager begins looking at all page frames allocated to hold user-space portions of virtual address spaces by using an approximation of a global least-recently-used (LRU) replacement algorithm.

If a page must be removed from physical memory, then the page manager checks to see if it is *dirty*, that is, it has been written to, so that it differs from the copy that exists in the swap device/file. A page that is not dirty does not need to be written back to the swap device/file.

5.4 Address Translation

The Linux memory manager uses a *demand paged virtual memory strategy*. Processes issue virtual addresses (that have already been mapped), and the memory manager is responsible for determining whether the corresponding page is loaded in some physical memory page frame. If it is not loaded, then the page is found in the secondary memory (the disk) and then loaded into a page frame in the physical memory, as described in the previous section. If the page is currently loaded in some page frame in the physical memory, then the virtual address is translated into the appropriate physical memory address. The physical memory location can then be read or written as desired.

Linux defines an architecture-independent memory model that transcends current-day CPUs and memory management units (MMUs), so it includes components that are not used in the i386 implementation. In the general model, a virtual address is translated into a physical address by using a three-level map. A virtual address, *j*, is partitioned into four parts:

- A *page directory* offset, j.pgd
- A *page middle directory* offset, j.pmd
- A *page table* offset, j.pte
- The offset within the page, j.offset

If a page is loaded into physical memory, the physical address, *i*, for a virtual address *j* is determined by the equation

$$i = \text{PTE}(\text{PMD}(\text{PGD}(\text{j.pgd}) + \text{j.pmd}) + \text{j.pte}) + \text{j.offset},$$

where PTE represents the page table, PMD represents the page middle directory table, and PGD represents the page directory table. Here's what happens (see Figure 1.11).

1. The virtual address is divided into the four parts.
2. The j.pgd part is used to locate an entry in the page directory. This page directory entry references the base of a page middle directory.
3. The j.pmd part of the address is used as offset into the designated page middle directory. This references an entry in the page middle directory that points at the base of the page table to be used.

Figure 1.11
Virtual Address Translation

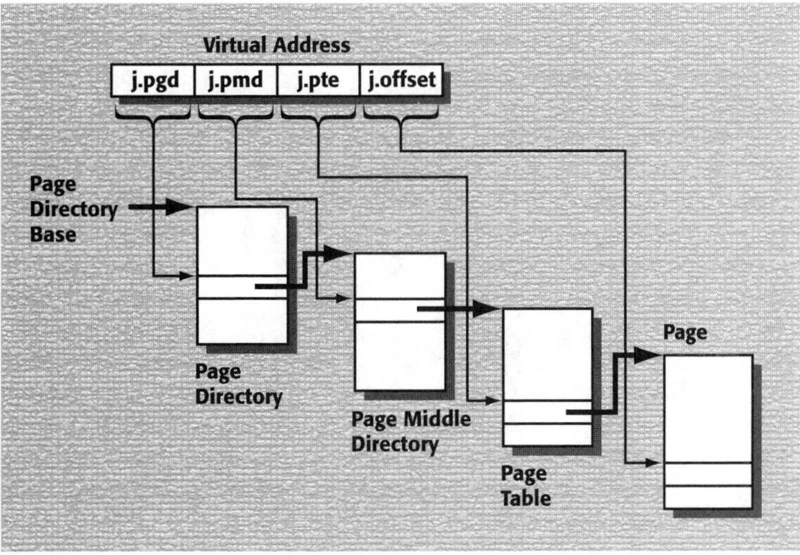

4. The j.pte portion of the virtual address is an offset in the page table. This offset references a page descriptor that contains the physical address of the first location in the page frame that contains the target page.
5. The page offset, j.offset, is added to the page frame address to determine the physical memory address, *i*, for the virtual address, *j*.

Of course, if any map is undefined, a missing page interrupt will be generated during address translation, thereby causing the page manager to load the page and then to map the virtual address.

The i386 microprocessor and compatible MMUs do not have sufficient hardware to support the full three-level translation process, so in this architecture only two levels are implemented. This is accomplished by reducing each page middle directory to only a single entry. Thus the j.pmd part of the address is not used, since the page directory entry points directly at the single entry in the page middle table.

6 Device Management

Two basic approaches to device management in Linux are available:

- Use polling to determine when a device has completed an operation.
- Use interrupts.

In the polling case (see Figure 1.12), the user process performs an I/O request (for example, a **read()** system call on a device) at the system call interface. This

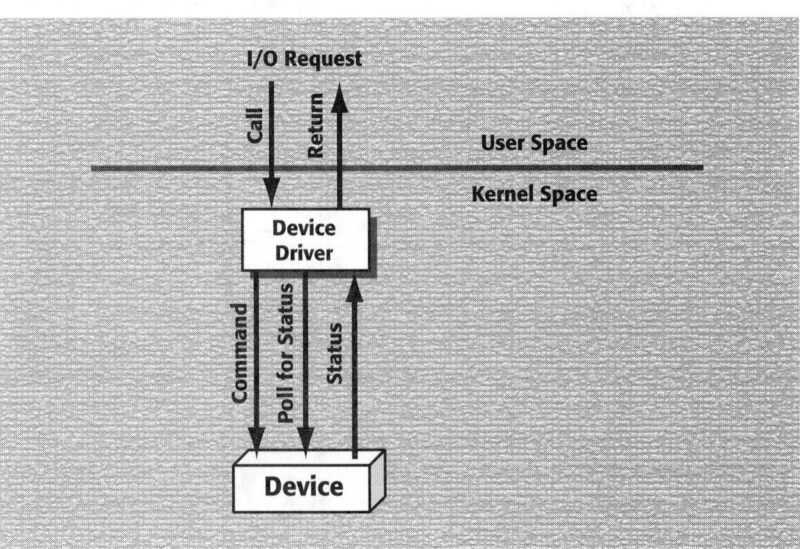

Figure 1.12
Polling Mode I/O

causes the device driver to start the device. The corresponding task then periodically polls the device to inspect its status to determine when the device has completed the operation.

In the case of interrupt mode I/O, a device driver, IRQ, interrupt handler (also called interrupt service routine or ISR), and a device bottom half might be involved in carrying out the operation. As described in Section 4.1 and summarized in Figure 1.13, when a process issues an I/O request to the kernel the device driver checks the status of the device and, if the device is available, starts it on the I/O operation. The task blocks in state TASK_INTERRUPTIBLE while the device is performing the I/O that the task requested. Meanwhile, the device operates autonomously until it completes the operation, at which time it issues an IRQ to the CPU. The IRQ causes the ISR that is associated with the IRQ to be executed. The ISR performs a minimum of the processing tasks associated with the completion of the operation and marks its bottom half for later processing if needed. Once the ISR, and all other ISRs that might have interrupted the original ISR, have completed, the **ret_from_sys_call** code block is executed. This block of code, so-named because it is also run when any system call is completed, runs all marked bottom halves, marks the completed processes as ready (TASK_RUNNING), and then calls the scheduler. Ultimately, the scheduler will dispatch the subject task and will resume operation following its I/O request.

Interrupt mode is generally the preferred I/O technique because it allows the CPU to be allocated to other processes whenever one process is waiting for an I/O operation to complete. However, polling may be used in any of the following situations.

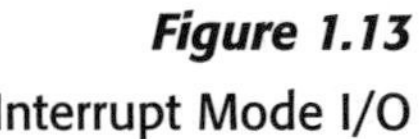
Figure 1.13
Interrupt Mode I/O

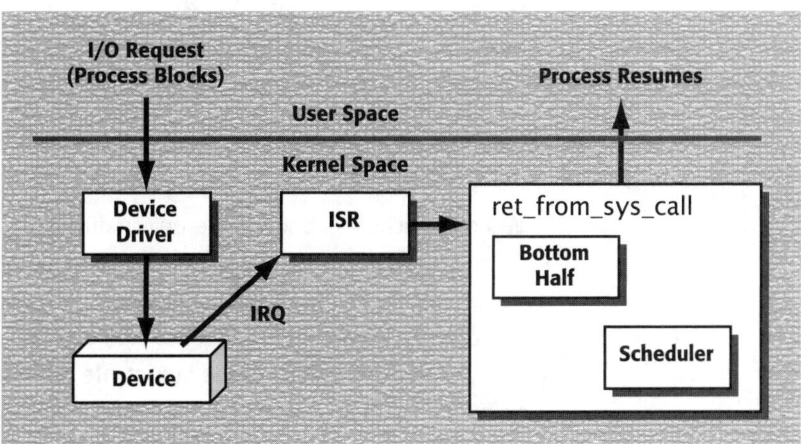

- The I/O operation is so critical to the complete operation of the system that it is deemed worthwhile to have the CPU poll the device for completion without the possibility of other processes running in the meantime.
- The I/O operation is very fast, and the overhead of interrupt management is not considered to be worthwhile.
- The hardware device does not have an interrupt capability.

The remainder of this discussion focuses on interrupt I/O mode.

6.1 The Device Driver

Device drivers and devices are referenced by using major and minor numbers. A *major number* is associated with each device driver that the Linux kernel will use. (Reserving device driver major numbers is a manual procedure whereby a designated person decides which device drivers are "standard" and should have a permanent major number assigned to them.) For example, major number 6 is associated with parallel interfaces, 21 with an SCSI interface, and so on. Temporary major numbers can be assigned as a device driver is being debugged. Each device driver can be used with more than one different physical device, for example a single device driver for a hard disk drive can be used with multiple disk drives on a given machine. The *minor number* is used to distinguish among the physical devices that use a particular device driver.

UNIX devices are classically divided into block devices and character devices. A *block device* is a device whose physical characteristics allow blocks of data to be referenced in any order. A *character device* is a device that reads or writes a single character at a time; the data must be read or written in sequential (byte stream) order. Even though some block devices allow blocks to be read in random order, buffering is used with block devices but not with character devices. (The file manager can predict the order in which blocks will be read, so it can direct the I/O buffering; see the next section.) The APIs for the two classes are different—the functions implemented in a block device driver differ from those in a character device driver. Linux maintains the general distinction, but the differences between the APIs for devices of the two classes are much smaller than in UNIX systems.

When a machine is booted, the device drivers are usually *registered* with the OS. (Linux modules can be used to implement device drivers, and they need not be registered until runtime; see Exercises 4 and 10.) A kernel function is called to register a device. It requires the major number, a character string name for the device, and a list of type `struct file_operations` that identify the entry point for each device operation supported by the driver:

check_media_change()
fasync()
fsync()
ioctl()
lseek()
mmap()
open()
read()
readdir()
release()
revalidate()
select()
write()

The API for the device driver is the same as the file operation API for the file manager. This registration process saves the device driver name and file operations in either the **chrdevs[]** or **blkdevs[]** kernel table (depending whether the device is a character or block device), using the major number as the table index. A temporary major number is assigned to the driver if it is registered with a major number of 0.

6.2 *Handling Interrupts*

Section 4.1 provides a general description of how IRQs and ISRs are used to respond to the occurrence of an interrupt. The ISR is associated with a particular IRQ via an explicit kernel function, **request_irq()**. This function has arguments to specify the IRQ—whether the ISR is for a fast or slow interrupt—the entry point of the ISR, and an argument of type **void** * that can be used to pass arbitrary information (specified as an argument to **request_irq()**. If the IRQ already has an ISR associated with it, then the request fails.

A computer contains a limited number of IRQ identifiers, as determined by the hardware. If two different devices must use the same IRQ, a master ISR must demultiplex IRQs to a collection of ISRs. It does this by polling the hardware to determine which device actually caused the IRQ, and then it selects the proper ISR from the collection.

The ISR can be constructed to perform any work that is needed to complete the I/O operation after the devices finishes. For example, it might check the device status to ensure that the operation completed successfully. For a read operation, it might also transfer data from the device buffer to primary memory. When one instance of an ISR might get interrupted by a second instance of the same ISR (such as multiple clock ticks that might occur while some series of ISRs are being executed), parts of the ISR work can be relegated to a bottom half. The ISR can then mark the bottom half for later execution, thereby effectively postponing some of its processing. When **ret_from_sys_call** runs, it will detect the marked bottom half and run it before calling the scheduler.

A maximum of 32 different bottom halves can be marked for execution. If still more postponed processing is required (and there is no bottom half marker slot available), then the work can be enqueued in a task queue for subsequent execution. A *task queue* is a list of functions with the prototype

```
void (*routine)(void *);
```

This list is executed, one after the other, after the bottom halves have all been run. The task queue functionality distinguishes among functions that are scheduled with interrupts disabled, that are from within an ISR or bottom half, or under any other circumstance.

7 File Management

The Linux file manager defines a single internal view of files that application programs use to read and modify files written onto all storage devices. Each type of storage device implements the common view in its file manager. For example, a disk that contains files written by using MS-DOS (or a Windows OS with DOS-compliant format) can be read or rewritten by a Linux application by using the Linux file manager. According to the internal Linux view, a *file* is a named byte stream that can be saved in the secondary storage system. This byte stream is fragmented into a set of blocks, and then the blocks are stored on the secondary storage device according to a strategy chosen by a particular type of file system. The file manager fetches and puts the blocks that contain the portions of the byte stream that an application program writes or reads. That is, it determines which disk blocks should be read or written whenever any part of the byte stream is read or written.

The Linux file manager is designed so that application programs use a fixed set of functions to manipulate files, as specified by POSIX: **open()**, **close()**, **lseek()**, **read()**, **write()**, **ioctl()**, and so on. A file system-independent part of the file manager handles generic aspects of the work, such as checking access rights and determining when disk blocks need to be read or written. Another part of the file manager handles all file system-dependent aspects of the job, such as determining where blocks are located on the disk and directing the device driver to read or write specific blocks. The two parts combined enable Linux to provide a fixed set of operations at the API, while handling files on disks even if the files were written by using a Windows OS, MINIX, or some other OS.

The Linux file manager API is built on an abstract file model that the Virtual File System (VFS) exports. The *VFS* implements the file system-independent operations, and OS designers provide extensions to the VFS to implement all required file system-dependent operations. The Version 2.*x* release can read and write disk files that conform to various formats, including MS-DOS, MINIX, and `/proc`, as well as a Linux-specific format called *Ext2* and others. Of course, specific file system-dependent components are included in Version 2.2.12 to translate VFS operations and formats to/from each of the external formats that are supported. This discussion focuses on the VFS model.

The heart of VFS is the switch. The *switch* provides the canonical file management API to user-space programs and establishes an internal interface used by the different file system translators that support files for MS-DOS, MINIX, Ext2, and so on (see Figure 1.14). A new file system can be supported by implementing a new file system-dependent (translator) component. Each such translator provides functions that the VFS switch can call (when it gets called by a user program) and that can translate the external file representation into the internal one. Thus the translator is responsible for

- determining the strategy used to organize disk blocks on the disk device,
- reading and writing disk properties,
- reading and writing external file descriptor information, and
- reading and writing the disk blocks that contain file data.

Figure 1.14
The Virtual File System Switch

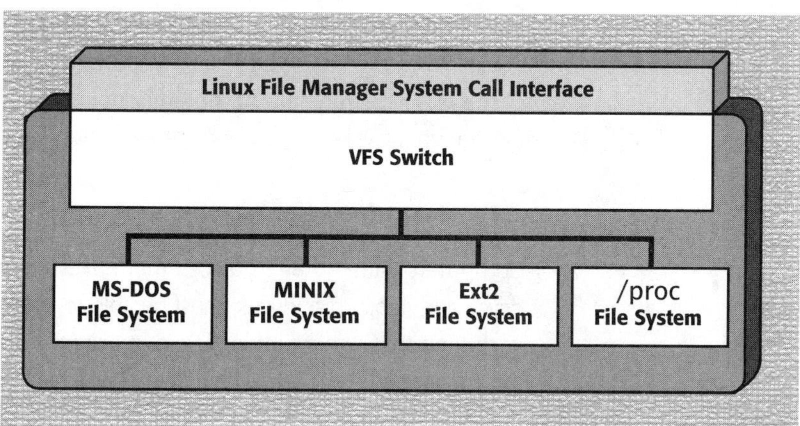

The VFS file system model is patterned after conventional UNIX file systems. A VFS file descriptor is called an *inode* (though it has its own unique format to support the multiple file system approach). Whereas VFS will contain its own format for a file descriptor, each file system-dependent translator converts the contents of the external descriptor into the VFS inode format when the file is opened. It then operates on its own inode data structure. Conversely, when the file is closed, the contents of the internal inode are used to update the external file descriptor.

The VFS inode includes the file access rights, owner, group, size, creation time, last access time, and last time that the file was written. It also reserves space for the pointer mechanism that the specific file system uses to organize the disk blocks, even though VFS does not know how these pointers will be organized (that information is encapsulated in the file system-specific translator component). VFS also supports directories, so it presumes that the external file directories contain at least the name of each file stored in the directory, as well as the address of its file descriptor (almost all file systems contain this minimum amount of information).

VFS assumes the following minimum structure regarding disk organizations.

- The first sector on the disk is a *boot block* used to store a bootstrap program (recall the discussion of the bootstrap process in Section 3.5). The file system does not use the boot block, but it does presume that it is present on every file system.
- A *superblock* contains disk-specific information, such as the number of bytes in a disk block.
- External file descriptors on the disk describe the characteristics of each file.
- Data blocks linked into each file contain the data.

Before VFS can manage a particular file system type, a translator for that type must be written and then registered with VFS. The VFS **register_filesystem()** function informs VFS of basic information that it will need, including the name of the file system type and the entry point of a file system's **read_super()** function that will be used when the file system is mounted.

7.1 Mounting the File System

Computers with storage devices that have removable media, such as tape drives and floppy disk drives, must be able to change the system's file structure each time that a medium is placed in or removed from the device. VFS uses the conventional UNIX mechanism to allow such file systems to be combined into the system's directory hierarchy. (However, Linux, of course, allows heterogeneous file systems to be combined, whereas conventional UNIX combines only homogeneous file systems.) The **mount** command appends a new file system into an existing directory hierarchy. It does this by replacing a directory in the previously mounted file system by the root of the new file system when the corresponding replaceable medium is placed on the system.

For example, suppose that a system contains an optical disk reader. When a particular optical disk is placed in the reader, the **mount()** operation requests that the file manager graft the directory subtree of the optical disk onto an existing file system tree. The device root is treated as a directory in the existing file system hierarchy (see Figure 1.15). In the example, the file **c** has an absolute pathname of **/a/c** because directories **a** and **b** are combined to be the mount point. Once mounted, the file system can be accessed through all normal directory operations, including relative and absolute pathnames and directory traversal operations. To unmount the file system, an **unmount()** command is sent to the file manager. This command prevents access attempts to a part of the file hierarchy that no longer exists.

When a file system is mounted, VFS creates an instance of the **struct super_block** data structure to hold information that it needs to administer the new file system. VFS then calls the new file system's **read_super()** function to retrieve the information contained in the file system's analog of the superblock (from the storage device) and to translate this information and save it in the **struct super_block** data structure.

This superblock includes various fields that VFS needs to administer the file system, particularly the field

```
struct super_operations *s_op;
```

Figure 1.15
The UNIX mount() Command

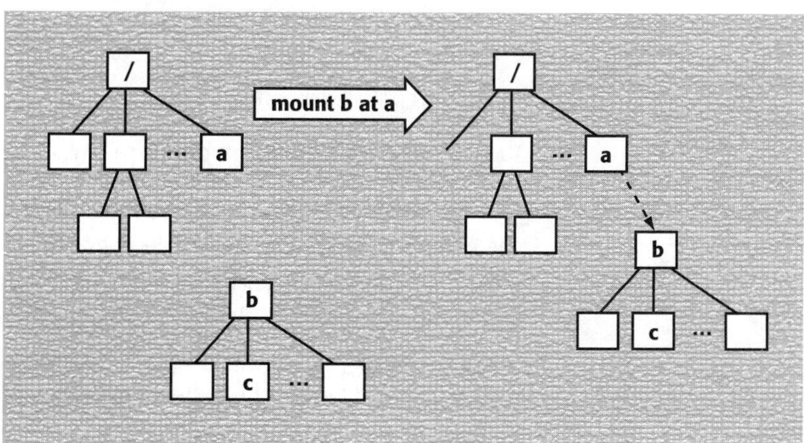

This **s_op** field specifies a collection of functions to write the superblock back to the disk, to read and write inodes on the disk, to check the superblock status, and so on. Thus **read_super()** is the bootstrap function that is bound to VFS when the file system type is registered. After VFS reads the superblock at mount time, it can use the **super_operations** function to manipulate the on-disk superblock as needed. Put another way, **super_operations** defines a public interface for a private, on-disk, superblock abstract data type, thus enabling the translator to implement superblocks and inodes as it chooses.

7.2 Opening a File

To open a file, the file manager searches the storage system for the specified pathname. Searching can be an extended procedure. This is because it requires, for example, opening each directory in the pathname (starting at the highest-named directory in the path), searching the path for the next file or directory in the pathname, and opening that directory or file. If the search encounters a mount point, then it moves from one file system to the other and continues the search. Thus the search might begin in, say, an Ext2 file system but ultimately find the file in an MS-DOS file system.

Once the file manager has located the file in a directory, VFS checks the file and user permissions to ensure that the user's process has permission to open the file. If the process has the correct permissions, then VFS will set up various table entries to manage the I/O. First, an entry is created in the process's *file descriptor table* (see Figure 1.16). Each process has one file descriptor table, and each open file has an entry in that table. An entry is identified by a small integer value that is returned by the call and used for all subsequent references to the file. Note that when the process is created, the file descriptor table is created with the following three entries:

- **stdin** with an entry identifier of 0
- **stdout** with a value of 1
- **stderr** with a value of 2

The next successful **open()** or **pipe()** call will create an entry in the file descriptor table at location 3.

The entry in the file descriptor table points to an entry in the open file table called a *file structure* (it has type **struct file**). The file structure entry holds status information specific to the process that opened the file for the process, for example the value of the file position for this process's use. If two different processes have the file open, then each will have its own file structure entry

Figure 1.16
Kernel File Tables

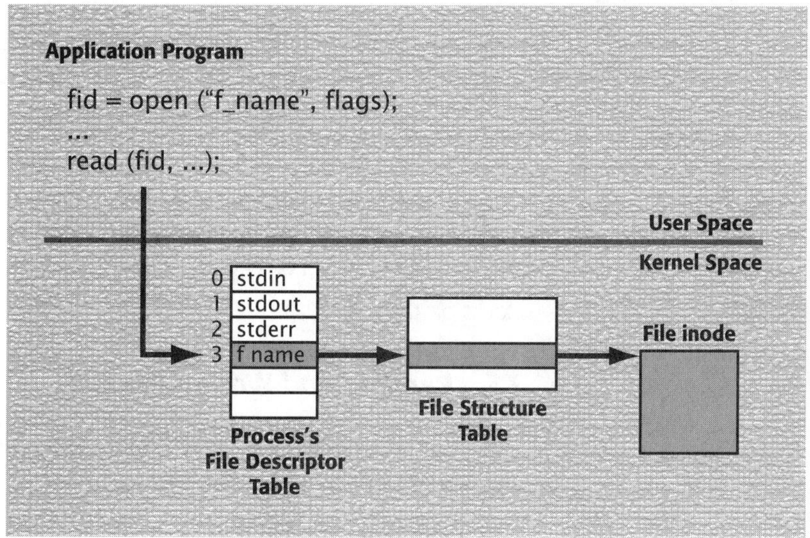

and hence its own copy of the file position. The file structure entry references the VFS inode after it has been constructed in primary memory.

The VFS creates the in-memory inode by reading the external file descriptor (by using the **read_inode()** function specified in the superblock **s_op** list) and translating it into the VFS inode format. Just as the superblock provides a field for a list of **super_operations**, the inode provides the following field to define a list of inode operations:

```
struct inode_operations *i_op;
```

struct inode_operations is a list of operations that VFS will need in order to manipulate the file's blocks, for example **create()**, **lookup()**, **link()**, and **mkdir()**. Also available is a list of default operations that are used if the **i_op** list does not provide an operation.

Inodes allocated in the VFS are allocated to a single, large, linked list. This is useful whenever the VFS intends to scan all inodes. However, access is slow when the VFS wants to reference a particular inode. Therefore inode references are also entered into an open hash table, where they can be accessed with a few (possibly a single) table probe.

Changes to the in-memory version of the inode are not propagated to the external file descriptor on the storage device the moment that the file manager changes them. Instead, the in-memory version of the inode is used to update the external file descriptor in the secondary memory periodically, when the file is closed, or when the application issues a **sync** command. If the machine halts while a file is open and recent changes have been made to the inode, changes to the in-memory inode are likely to differ from the contents of the external file descriptor on the disk. The result can be an inconsistent file system, since the most recent information about the file is lost when the in-memory inode is destroyed. For example, if block pointers in the in-memory inode have changed (with corresponding changes to disk blocks), then the disk might have an external file descriptor that is inconsistent with pointers in various storage blocks on the disk.

7.3 Reading and Writing the File

When the file is opened, an instance of **struct file** (entry in the file structure table) is created. In that file, the field

```
struct file_operations *f_ops;
```

specifies the entry points for **read()**, **write()**, **lseek()**, **select()**, and so on, that are used to perform the file system-specific I/O operations. Also included is a set of default **file_operations** specified in the inode so that if any particular file operation (such as **lseek()**) is not specified in the **f_ops** list, then the function from the default list will be used.

The essential purpose of these routines is to move information back and forth between user-space addresses and the secondary storage blocks. **read()** invokes the file system-specific operations to transfer data from the disk to a system buffer and then to copy the requested number of bytes from the system buffer to the user-space address. **write()** moves data from a user-space address into a system buffer, where it is written to the disk. These routines also must marshal and unmarshal the byte stream.

A file is organized as a sequential byte stream. One implication of this is that applications typically read or write the file as a sequence of bytes rather than randomly access characters in the file. As a consequence, buffering can be used to substantially increase the system's performance. In read buffering, the file system reads ahead on the byte stream, fetching disk blocks that hold parts of the byte stream that appear after the byte currently addressed by the file pointer. In write buffering, a disk block that becomes full is staged for writing whenever the disk device becomes available. As a result, the application does not need to wait for incoming buffers, since they will have been read when they were referenced. In addition, it does not need to wait for write operations, since they will take place as a background activity after the application has logically written the bytes to the stream.

Linux attempts to use as much of the primary memory as it can to provide I/O buffers. It creates a dynamic *buffer cache* whose size depends on the number of page frames that are currently required to support virtual memory. Pages that the virtual memory system does not need can be used in the buffer cache. When a page fault occurs, the buffer cache is one of the first places in which the virtual memory system will search for page frames.

Block buffering is a relatively complex task. This part of the file manager must satisfy each of the following constraints.

- Each file open for reading should have one or more buffers that contain information that has been read from the disk before the process actually requested the information.
- Each file open for writing has a set of buffers that contain information that is to be written to the device whenever it is available.
- Output full blocks that are the same as blocks on the storage device should not be written.
- When the virtual memory does not need all of the physical memory, the buffer cache should be enlarged. When the virtual memory needs more physical memory, the buffer cache should be reduced (without affecting ongoing I/O).
- Buffers can vary in size.
- Buffers can be shared among processes.

7.4 The Ext2 File System

The Ext2 file system is patterned after the BSD Fast File System [McKusick, et al., 1996]. The disk is formatted to contain a set of *block groups*, each of which contains a superblock, group descriptor information, a table of inodes for the files in the block group, and the data blocks.

The superblock contains the following information:

- Number of inodes
- Number of free inodes
- Block details
- Allocation limits
- Last mount and write times
- Errors and status
- Other housekeeping information

A block descriptor holds the details of the blocks within a particular block group. A block may contain descriptions for up to 8,192 blocks for disk block sizes of

1,024 bytes (each block is of size 1,024 = EXT2_MIN_BLOCK_SIZE < EXT2_BLOCK_SIZE < EXT2_MAX_BLOCK_SIZE = 4,096 bytes). The block descriptor also includes the set of inodes for the files in the block group.

To organize blocks, the inode uses a variant of an indexed allocation scheme. It contains pointers to 15 different storage blocks (see Figure 1.17). The first 12 blocks of the file are indexed directly from the first 12 of 15 pointers in the inode. The last 3 pointers are used for indirect pointers through *index blocks*. If the file manager is configured with the maximum-size 4KB blocks, the 12 direct pointers in the inode accommodate files of up to 48KB. If a file requires more than 12 blocks, then the file system allocates an index block and links it into the *single indirect* (thirteenth) pointer of the inode. Hence, blocks 13 to *k* are indirectly addressed from the inode via the indirect block identified by the thirteenth pointer in the inode. Similarly, larger files use the fourteenth pointer to point to a *double indirect* block, and the largest files use the fifteenth pointer to point to a *triple indirect* block.

How large can UNIX files be? This depends on the block sizes as well as the sizes of the disk addresses used in the system. In a simplification of the arithmetic, suppose that an indirect block can store 1,000 disk addresses (ordinarily, the number of disk addresses would be a power of 2, such as 1,024). Then a single indirect block will provide pointers to an additional 1,000 disk blocks.

Figure 1.17
Ext2 File Structure

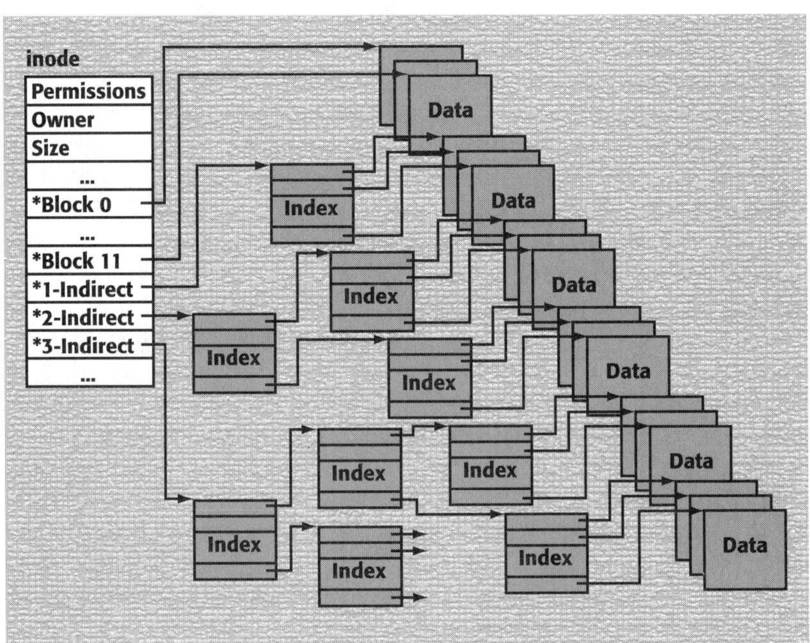

Blocks 0 through 11 are accessed via the direct pointers in the inode, and blocks 12 through 1,011 are accessed indirectly through the single indirect block. The fourteenth block pointer in the inode is the double indirect pointer. It points to a block that contains pointers to blocks of the type referenced from the single indirect field. The double indirect pointer points to a block that points to 1,000 indirect blocks, so blocks 1,012 to 1,001,011 are accessed through the double indirect list. The fifteenth block pointer is the triple indirect pointer. It points to a block that contains double indirect pointers. Again, if each block can store 1,000 block addresses, then the triple indirect pointer indirectly addresses blocks 1,001,012 to the maximum-sized file (under these assumptions) of 1,001,001,011 blocks.

When this block allocation strategy is used, very large files are possible, even though as files grow larger, the access times also increase, due to the indirection. Also, other considerations (designed into the inode structure) prevent a file from reaching this maximum size. For example, with the block sizes given previously, a file using the triple indirect index would require a device capable of storing 4,000GB. Current versions of BSD UNIX do not use the triple indirect pointer. This is partly because of the incompatibility of file sizes with storage device technology and partly because the 32-bit file offsets used in the file system preclude file sizes larger than 4GB.

8 Learning More about Linux

Linux continues to grow in popularity, so many excellent sources of information are available. The exercises in Part 2 of this manual focus on the details of certain aspects of Linux; the areas not covered by the exercises are discussed in the following sources.

- The Linux Documentation Project (**http://metalab.unc.edu/mdw/Linux.html**) is an excellent online collection of articles about all aspects of Linux.
- The second edition of the *Linux Kernel Internals* book by Beck, et al. [1998] is an excellent reference that describes the organization of the version 2.0 kernel and explains many of the details of how individual parts of the kernel are designed.
- Vahalia [2000] on UNIX internals, Bach [1986] on UNIX System V internals, and McKusick, et al. [1996] on BSD 4.4 internals describe how traditional UNIX systems are built and are very good references for Linux.

In the end, people who study Linux internals must read the source code. A complete source code browser site, **http://lxr.linux.no/source/**, helps with this. Also, you should have a copy of the source code on your laboratory machine. It might be loaded anywhere in the file system hierarchy, but usually it is at the path `/usr/src/linux`, that is, `linux` is the root directory of the subtree that contains all of the source code. Exercise 3 discusses the organization of the source code. This manual often refers to source code files by assuming that the current directory is the root directory of the source subtree (for example, `/usr/src/linux`).

part 2

Exercises

This manual's exercises are intended to complement the materials that you learn in your undergraduate OS course. In the lecture part of your course, the focus is on concepts and issues, with side discussions on Linux, UNIX, and/or Windows NT. This manual's goal is to put those theories into practice with a series of hands-on exercises using the Linux kernel.

The exercises use the public distribution of the Linux source code, Version 2.2.12. Version 2.2.14 is included on the CD. By the time that you have completed these exercises, you will have studied and experimented with considerable OS software and will have gained a deep insight into how Linux and other modern OSs are designed.

The exercises address almost all of the aspects of the OS. Following is a summary of what you will do in each.

Exercise 1: Learn about the kernel by having you use the **/proc** file system interface to read the values of various kernel variables. You will gain an intuitive understanding of kernel behavior and learn a valuable tool for inspecting the kernel.

Exercise 2: Gain experience with programming applications that consist of multiple processes. While not focusing on kernel internals, it does provide prerequisite experience with concurrency and file descriptors.

Exercise 3: Your first opportunity to inspect the Linux kernel source code. You will learn how interval timers are implemented in the kernel and then use them to profile a user program.

Exercise 4: Write your first software, which will execute in supervisor mode as part of the kernel. Your solution code will use the loadable kernel module feature first to read the kernel's time variable and then to report it by using the /proc file system interface.

Exercise 5: Add a new system call to the existing Linux kernel. The system function that you implement is simple, but you will learn the details of how the system call mechanism works and then use it to change the system call interface to your copy of Linux.

Exercise 6: Modify the existing implementation of the System V shared memory facility. The modification is not difficult, but it will give you the opportunity to study how this functionality is designed and implemented.

Exercise 7: Learn how Linux implements virtual memory, and then instrument the existing code to provide reports on the virtual memory system's performance.

Exercise 8: Learn about a new synchronization mechanism to the kernel, called the *event*. Events are shared among processes. One process creates an event, and then a community of processes shares the event, much like a barrier.

Exercise 9: Modify the Linux scheduler so that it uses an alternative policy. You will learn the details of how the scheduler works and then how to change it.

Exercise 10: Write your first device driver to implement a FIFO (or pipe) among processes. You will learn about the issues for writing drivers without manipulating hardware.

Exercise 11: Implement a file directory operation on a raw floppy disk driver.

Exercise 12: Complete the MS-DOS-compatible file system started in Exercise 11 by providing the functions for reading and writing the data.

Three factors make kernel programming challenging:

- The lack of good documentation
- The need to be very careful when you change the kernel
- The absence of a robust and safe debugging environment

There is no way around these challenges, except to "bite the bullet" and dive into the project.

As you work through these exercises, notice that to arrive at a solution you generally will not have to write much software. However, you will have to *read* a lot of software in order to come up with a working solution. In addition, you will quickly observe that you need to have a good working knowledge of C or C++. The kernel is written in C and assembly language (though you will rarely encounter the assembly language and can solve all of the exercises without reading it). The discussion includes many code fragments, most taken verbatim from the Linux source code. Also, as part of my pedagogical style, I have included some of my own comments in the code fragments. Each is written with the C++ comment style ("`// Here is a pedagogical comment`") rather than the C comment style ("`/* Here is a verbatim comment */`").

The exercises increase in difficulty from 1 through 12. Considerable assistance is offered in solving the early exercises and much less with the later ones. In this sense, you should solve the last exercise by solving all of those that precede it. Realistically, however, this is too many exercises to do in one term. Figure 2.1 shows that specific dependencies exist among the exercises. The width of the arrow suggests the true strength of the dependency. For example, whereas you'll find it helpful to do Exercise 1 before doing Exercise 4, you really should do Exercise 11 before doing Exercise 12. If you are working on an exercise and are stuck, you might search earlier exercises for help to solve your problem.

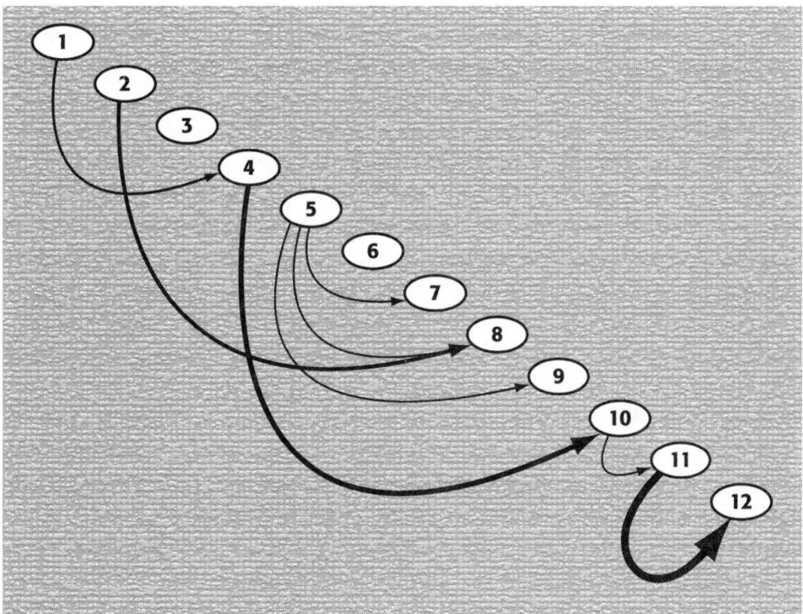

Figure 2.1 Exercise Dependencies

one

Observing Linux Behavior

Exercise Goal: You will learn several important characteristics of the Linux kernel, processes, memory, and other resources. You will write a program to use the `/proc` mechanism to inspect various kernel values that reflect the machine's load average, process resource utilization, and so on. After you have obtained the kernel status, you will prepare a report of the cumulative behavior that you observed.

Introduction

The Linux kernel is a collection of data structure instances (*kernel variables*) and functions. The collective kernel variables define the kernel's perspective of the state of the entire computer system. Each externally invoked function—a system call or an IRQ—provides a prescribed service and causes the system state to be changed by having the kernel code change its kernel variables. If you could inspect the kernel variables, then you could infer the state of the entire computer system.

Many variables make up the entire kernel state, including variables to represent each process, each open file, the memory, and the CPU. Kernel variables are no different than ordinary C program variables, other than they are kept in kernel space. They can be allocated on a stack (in the kernel space) or in static memory so that they do not disappear when a stack frame is destroyed. Because the kernel is implemented as a monolithic module, many of the kernel variables are declared as global static variables. Some of the kernel variables are instances of built-in C data types, but most are instances of an extensible data type, a C **struct**.

In general, the extensible data structures are defined in C header files (also called *include files* or *.h files*) in the Linux source code tree. The Linux source code may be loaded in any subdirectory in your laboratory computer, though the conventional location is in **/usr/src/linux**. Most of the system's **include** files are stored in the **.../linux/include** directory. This directory's exact contents depend on the version of the source. In Version 2.2.12, it includes the directories **asm-generic**, **asm-i386**, **linux**, **net**, **scsi**, and **video**. Also included is a symbolic link named **asm** that points to **asm-i386**. All of the machine-independent **include** files are kept in the **linux** subdirectory, and most of the machine-dependent **include** files are kept in **asm-i386**. The other subdirectories contain miscellaneous other **include** files.

The **include** file **include/linux/sched.h** defines a data structure used for the process descriptor.

```
struct task_struct {
/* These are hardcoded – don't touch */
   volatile long state; /* -1 unrunnable, 0 runnable, >0 stopped */
   ...
   int pid;
   ...
   uid_t uid, ...;
   gid_t gid, ...;
   ...
   };
```

The source code file **kernel/sched.c** contains a declaration of the form

```
struct task_struct * task[NR_TASKS] = {&init_task, };
```

The **task** kernel array variable is the pointer to all of the process descriptors. If you could read the **task** kernel variable and wanted to know the kernel state of a process with a process ID of, say, 1234, you could find the record **task[i]** such that **task[i]->pid == 1234**. Knowing the value **i**, you could then read the value of the **task[i]->state** field to determine the current state of that process. The **task[i]->uid** field is the user ID for the process, and **task[i]->gid** is the group ID for the process. (A process descriptor contains many more fields, as you will discover in subsequent exercises.)

Several other interesting kernel variables are also declared in the **.../linux/kernel/sched.c** file, including

- **long tick**, which defines the amount of time between timer interrupts, and
- **struct timeval xtime**, which is the current system time.

The file **.../linux/kernel/fork.c** contains the declarations **int nr_tasks** and **int nr_running** to define, respectively, the number of tasks in existence and the number that are in the running state. To determine all of the kernel variables that relate to process management, you would need to review all of the source code files in the **.../linux/kernel** directory.

File descriptors—*inodes*—are kept in a hash table, **hash_table**, that is defined in **fs/buffer.c** (in the directory **.../linux**). Each hash table entry includes a **struct inode *inode** field, which is defined in **include/fs.h** (in **.../linux**) as follows.

```
struct inode {
    ...
    uid_t     i_uid;
    gid_t     i_gid;
    ...
    time_t    i_atime;
    time_t    i_mtime;
    time_t    i_ctime;
};
```

The listed fields specify the file owner's user and group IDs (**i_uid** and **i_gid**, respectively), and the three **time_t** fields specify the last time that the file was accessed, the last time that it was modified, and the time at which it was created. The kernel variable, **static struct file * inuse_filps** (declared in **fs/file_table.c**), points to a list of all file descriptors in the system. The **struct file** definition appears in **include/fs.h**.

```
struct file {
    struct file *f_next, *f_prev;
    ...
    mode_t f_mode;
    ...
    struct dentry *f_dentry;
    struct file_operations *f_op;
    ...
};
```

By inspecting the **inuse_filps** kernel list, you can systematically inspect the file descriptor for each file in the system (by following the **f_next** pointer). Each descriptor keeps the protection mode (**f_mode**), a pointer to the inode (via the **f_dentry** pointer; see **include/linux/dcache.h** for the definition of a **struct dentry**), and the list of routines to operate on the file as described in Part 1, Section 7 (**f_op**). Similarly, you can study the files in the **linux/mm** directory to determine the kernel variables that are used to implement the memory manager, the **linux/fs** directory to determine the kernel variables used to implement the file manager, and so on.

A useful first step to understanding the details of Linux implementation is to explore the kernel variables and data structure definitions that are used to write the code. Much of the strategy for solving the problems in the remaining exercises is to focus on a particular aspect of the kernel, to study its data structures and functions, and then to solve the problem. The exercise introduction will help you to determine which parts of the source code tree to focus on for that exercise.

You have not learned enough to be able use a kernel debugger (or to write your own kernel extensions) to read the values stored in kernel variables. However, you can begin to examine some of those values by using existing tools. This exercise takes this latter approach to let you inspect the kernel state and to give you some intuition about how the kernel behaves.

Problem Statement

This exercise is to study some aspects of the organization and behavior of a Linux system by observing values stored in kernel variables.

Part A

Answer the following questions about the Linux machine that you will be using to do these exercises. If your school's lab has several machines, then choose one on which to base your answers.

- What is the CPU type and model?
- What version of the Linux kernel is being used?
- How long (in days, hours, and minutes) has it been since the system was last booted?
- How much of the total CPU time has been spent executing in user mode? System mode? Idle?
- How much memory is configured into it?

- How much memory is currently available on it?
- How many disk read/write requests have been made?
- How many context switches has the kernel performed?
- How many processes have been created since the system was booted?

Part B

Write a default version of program to report the behavior of the Linux kernel by inspecting kernel state. The program should print the following values on `stdout`:

- CPU type and model
- Kernel version
- Amount of time since the system was last booted, in the form dd:hh:mm:ss (for example, 3 days 13 hours 46 minutes 32 seconds would be formatted as `03:13:46:32`)

Part C

Write a second version of the program in Part A that prints the same information as the default version plus the following:

- The amount of time that the CPU has spent in user mode, in system mode, and idle
- The number of disk requests made on the system
- The number of context switches that the kernel has performed
- The time when the system was last booted
- The number of processes that have been created since the system was booted

Part D

Write a third version of the program in Part A that prints the same information as the second version plus the following:

- The amount of memory configured into this computer
- The amount of memory currently available
- A list of load averages (each averaged over the last minute)

This information will allow another program to plot these values against time so that a user can see how the load average varied over some time interval. For this version of the program, you need to provide two additional parameters:

- One to indicate how often the load average should be read from the kernel
- One to indicate the time interval over which the load average should be read

The first version of your program might be called by **ksamp** and the second version by **ksamp -s**. Then the third version could be called by **ksamp -l 2 60**, whereby the load average observation would run for 60 seconds, sampling the kernel table about once every 2 seconds. To observe the load on the system, you need to ensure that the computer is doing some work rather than simply running your program. For example, open and close windows, move windows around, and even run some programs in other windows.

Attacking the Problem

Linux, Solaris, and other versions of UNIX provide a very useful mechanism for inspecting the kernel state, called the **/proc** file system. This is the key mechanism that you can use to do this exercise.

The /proc *File System*

According to McKusick, et al. [1998], the **/proc** file system comes from UNIX Eighth Edition and has been used with 4.4 BSD. "In the **/proc** system, the address space of another process can be accessed with **read** and **write** system calls, which allows a debugger to access a process being debugged with much greater efficiency. The page (or pages) of interest in the child process is mapped into the kernel address space. The requested data can then be copied directly from the kernel to the parent address space." (page 113) In addition, **/proc** can be used to collect information about processes in the system, even though that is not done in 4.4 BSD.

The **/proc** file system is an OS mechanism whose interface appears as a directory in the conventional UNIX file system (in the root directory). You can change to **/proc** just as you change to any other directory. For example,

```
bash$ cd /proc
```

makes **/proc** the current directory. Once you have made **/proc** the current directory, you can list its contents by using the **ls** command. The contents appear to be ordinary files and directories. However, a file in **/proc** or one of its subdirectories is actually a program that reads kernel variables and reports them as ASCII strings. Some of these routines read the kernel tables only when the pseudo file is opened, whereas others read the tables each time that the file is read. (You will learn more details of this behavior in Exercise 4.) Thus the various read functions might behave differently than you expect, since they are not really operating on files at all.

The **/proc** implementation provided with Linux can read many different kernel tables. Several directories as well as files are contained in **/proc**. Each file reads one or more kernel variables, and the subdirectories with numeric names contain more pseudo files to read information about the process whose process ID is the same as the directory name. The directory **self** contains process-specific information for the process that is using **/proc**. The exact contents of the **/proc** directory tree vary among different Linux versions, so you must experiment with the pseudo files to view the information provided.

Files in **/proc** are read just like ordinary ASCII files. For example, when you type to the shell a command such as

```
bash$ cat /proc/version
```

you will get a message printed to **stdout** that resembles the following.

```
Linux version 2.2.12 (gcc version egcs-2.91.66
19990314/Linux (egcs-1.1.2 release)) #1 Mon Sep 27 10:40:35
EDT 1999
```

To read a **/proc** pseudo file's contents, you open the file and then use **stdio** library routines such as **fgets()** or **fscanf()** to read the file. The exact files (and tables) read depend on the specific Linux version that you are using. To find out exactly which file interfaces are available to you through **/proc**, read the **proc** man page on the system.

Using argc *and* argv

If you do Part C or D in addition to Part B, you will need to pass parameters to your program from the shell. For example, suppose that your solution program is named **observer**. To solve Part B, you could call it with

```
bash$ observer
```

whereas to solve Part C or D, you could call with

```
bash$ observer -s
```

If the program is providing the information required for Parts B, C, and D, it might be called by

```
bash$ observer –l 10 600
```

where l means to produce the long report and **10 600** means that the load averages are to be computed once every 10 seconds until 600 seconds have elapsed.

The following code segment is an example for handling the three different ways that **observer** can be called. A C main program may have a header of the form

```
int main(int argc, char *argv[])
```

You may omit the two arguments, **argc** and **argv**, if no parameters are to be passed to the program by the shell. Alternatively, they can be initialized so that **argc** is the number of symbols on the command line and **argv** is an array of pointers to character strings symbols on the command line. For example, if the **observer** program calls with no parameters (the first example previously), then **argc** will be set to 1 and **argv[0]** will point to the string **observer**. In the second example, **argc** will be set to 2, with **argv[0]** pointing to **observer** and **argv[1]** pointing to the string **-s**. In the third example shell command line, you could have **argc** == 4 and **argv[0]** point to **observer**, **argv[1]** to -l, **argv[2]** to **10**, and **argv[3]** to **600**.

The C main program can now reference these arguments as follows.

```
#include  <stdio.h>
  ...
int main(int argc, char *argv[])
    char repTypeName[16];
  ...
// Determine report type
   reportType = STANDARD;
   strcpy(repTypeName, "Standard");
   if(argc > 1) {
   sscanf(argv[1], "%c%c", &c1, &c2);
   if(c1 != '-') {
      fprintf(stderr, "usage: observer [-s][-l int dur]\n");
         exit(1);
   }
   if(c2 ==  's') {
      reportType = SHORT;
      strcpy(repTypeName, "Short");
   }
   if(c2 ==  'l') {
      reportType = LONG;
```

```
strcpy(repTypeName, "Long");
        interval = atoi(argv[2]);
        duration = atoi(argv[3]);
    }
}
    ...
}
```

Organizing a Solution

For Parts C and D, your programs must have different arguments on the command line. Therefore one of your first actions should be to parse the command line with which the program is called so as to determine the shell parameters being passed to it via the **argv** array (see the code on page 62, 63).

You finish initializing by getting the current time of day and printing a greeting that includes the name of the machine that you are inspecting.

```
#include        <sys/time.h>
...
// Finish initializing
    gettimeofday(&now, NULL);  // Get the time of day
    printf("Status report type %s at  %s\n",
                repTypeName, ctime(&(now.tv_sec)));
// Get the host filename and print it
    thisProcFile = fopen("/proc/sys/kernel/hostname", "r");
    fgets(lineBuf, LB_SIZE+1, thisProcFile);
    printf("Machine hostname: %s", lineBuf);
    fclose(thisProcFile);
```

Now you are ready to do the work, that is, to start reading kernel variables by using various **/proc** files. The previous code segment contains an example of how to read the **/proc/sys/kernel/hostname** file. You can use it as a prototype for solving the exercise by reading other pseudo files. This will require some exploration of **/proc** and inspection of the various pseudo files as you investigate different directories.

In Part D, you are to compute a load average. For this, your code needs to sleep for a while, wake up, sample the current load average, and then go back to sleep. Here is a code fragment that will accomplish that work.

```
        while(iteration < duration) {
                sleep(interval);
                sampleLoadAvg();
```

```
            iteration += interval;
}
```

Now you are ready to create the entire solution. Here is all of the code examples that you have seen, put into a single program.

```
#include        <stdio.h>
#include        <sys/time.h>
...

int main(int argc, char *argv[]) {
  ...
  char repTypeName[16];
  ...

/* Determine report type */
   reportType = STANDARD;
   strcpy(repTypeName, "Standard");
   if(argc > 1) {
         sscanf(argv[1], "%c%c", &c1, &c2);
         if(c1 != '-') {
               fprintf(stderr, "usage: ksamp [-s][-l int dur]\n");
               exit(1);
         }
         if(c2 ==  's') {
               reportType = SHORT;
               strcpy(repTypeName, "Short");
         }
         if(c2 ==  'l') {
               reportType = LONG;
               strcpy(repTypeName, "Long");
               interval = atoi(argv[2]);
               duration = atoi(argv[3]);
         }
}

/* Get the current time */
  gettimeofday(&now, NULL);
  printf("Status report type %s at  %s\n",
              repTypeName, ctime(&(now.tv_sec)));

  thisProcFile = fopen("/proc/sys/kernel/hostname", "r");
```

```
    fgets(lineBuf, LB_SIZE+1, thisProcFile);
    printf("Machine hostname: %s", lineBuf);
    fclose(thisProcFile);

/* Code to read the relevant /proc files */
    ...
    while(iteration<duration) {
            sleep(interval);
            sampleLoadAvg();
            iteration += interval;
    }

    exit(0);
}
```

Saving Your Work in a Shared Laboratory

You should keep a copy of all of your source code on a floppy disk so that you have a backup version of your code and can move among different lab machines for different work sessions. To do this, use mtools (see the mcopy shell command). Because the floppy disk is a shared device in a Linux system, you will need superuser permission before you can successfully write to the floppy disk drive.

two

Shell Program

Exercise Goal: You will learn how to write a UNIX shell program. This will give you the opportunity to learn how child processes are created to perform large-grained work and how the parent process can follow up on a child process's work.

Introduction

In Part 1, Section 3.6, you studied how a process is assigned to each login port when the machine is booted up and how a copy of a shell program is executed on behalf of a user that logs in on any port. A *shell*, or *command line interpreter* program, is a mechanism with which each interactive user can send commands to the OS and by which the OS can respond to the user. Whenever a user has successfully logged in to the computer, the OS causes the user process assigned to the login port to execute a specific shell. The OS does not ordinarily have a built-in window interface. Instead, it assumes a simple character-oriented interface in which the user types a string of characters (terminated by pressing the Enter or Return key) and the OS responds by typing lines of characters back to the screen. If the human-computer interface is to be a graphical window interface, then the software that implements the window manager subsumes the shell tasks that are the focus of this exercise. Thus the character-oriented shell assumes a screen display with a fixed number of lines (usually 25) and a fixed number of characters (usually 80) per line.

Once the shell has initialized its data structures and is ready to start work, it clears the 25-line display and prints a prompt in the first few character positions on the first line. Linux systems are usually configured to include the machine name as part of the prompt. For example, my Linux machine is named kiowa.cs.colorado.edu, so the shell prints, as its prompt string,

```
kiowa>
```

or

```
bash>
```

depending on which shell I am using. The shell then waits for the user to type a command line in response to the prompt. The command line could be a string such as

```
kiowa> ls –al
```

terminated with an **enter** or **return** character (in Linux, this character is represented internally by the **NEWLINE** character, '**\n**'). When the user enters a command line, the shell's job is to cause the OS to execute the command embedded in the command line.

Every shell has its own language syntax and semantics. In the standard Linux shell, **bash**, a command line has the form

```
command argument_1 argument_2 ...
```

in which the first word is the command to be executed and the remaining words are arguments expected by that command. The number of arguments depends on which command is being executed. For example, the directory listing command may have no arguments—simply by the user's typing **ls**—or it may have arguments prefaced by the negative "-" character, as in **ls –al**, where **a** and **l** are arguments. The command determines the syntax for the arguments, such as which of the arguments may be grouped (as for the **a** and **l** in the **ls** command), which arguments must be preceded by a "-" character, and whether the position of the argument is important

Other commands use a different argument-passing syntax. For example, a C compiler command might look like

```
kiowa> cc –g –o deviation  –S main.c inout.c –lmath
```

in which the arguments **g**, **o deviation**, S, **main.c**, **inout.c**, and **lmath** are all passed to the C compiler, **cc**.

The shell relies on an important convention to accomplish its task: The command for the command line is usually the name of a file that contains an executable program, for example, **ls** and **cc** (files stored in **/bin** on most UNIX-style machines). In a few cases, the command is not a filename but rather a command that is implemented within the shell. For example, **cd** (change directory) is usually implemented within the shell itself rather than in a file in **/bin**. Because the vast majority of the commands are implemented in files, you can think of the command as actually being a filename in some directory on the machine. This means that the shell's job is to find the file, prepare the list of parameters for the command, and then cause the command to be executed using the parameters.

Many shell programs are used with UNIX variants, including the original Bourne shell (**sh**), the C shell (**csh**) with its additional features over **sh**, the Korn shell, and the standard Linux shell (**bash**). All have followed a similar set of rules for command line syntax, though each has a superset of features.

Basic UNIX-Style Shell Operation

The Bourne shell is described in Ritchie and Thompson's original UNIX paper [Ritchie and Thompson, 1974]. As described in the previous subsection, the shell should accept a command line from the user, parse the command line, and then invoke the OS to run the specified command with the specified arguments. This command line is a request to execute the program in any file that contains a program, including programs that the user wrote. Thus a programmer can write an ordinary C program, compile it, and have the shell execute it just like it was a UNIX command.

For example, suppose that you write a C program in a file named **main.c** and then compile and execute it with shell commands such as

```
kiowa> cc main.c
kiowa> a.out
```

For the first command line, the shell will find the **cc** command (the C compiler) in the **/bin** directory and then, when the **cc** command is executed, pass it the string **main.c**. The C compiler, by default, will translate the C program that is stored in **main.c** and write the resulting executable program into a file named **a.out** in the current directory. The second command line is simply the name of the file to be executed, **a.out**, without any parameters. The shell finds the **a.out** file in the current directory and then executes it.

Consider the following steps that a shell must take to accomplish its job.

1. Print a prompt.

   A default prompt string is available, sometimes hardcoded into the shell, for example the single character string %, #, or >. When the shell is started, it can look up the name of the machine on which it is running and prepend this string to the standard prompt character, for example a prompt string such as **kiowa>**. The shell also can be designed to print the current directory as part of the prompt, meaning that each time that the user types **cd** to change to a different directory, the prompt string is redefined. Once the prompt string is determined, the shell prints it to **stdout** whenever it is ready to accept a command line.
2. Get the command line.

   To get a command line, the shell performs a blocking read operation so that the process that executes the shell will be asleep until the user types a command line in response to the prompt. Once the user types the command line (and terminates it with a NEWLINE ('\n') character), the command line string is returned to the shell.
3. Parse the command.

   The syntax for the command line is trivial. The parser begins at the left side of the command line and scans until it sees a whitespace character (such as space, tab, or NEWLINE). The first word is the command name, and subsequent words are the parameters.
4. Find the file.

   The shell provides a set of *environment variables* for each user. These variables are first defined in the user's **.login** file, though they can be modified at any time by using the **set** command. The PATH environment variable is an ordered list of absolute pathnames specifying where the shell should search for command files. If the **.login** file has a line such as

   ```
   set path=(. /bin /usr/bin)
   ```

   then the shell will first look in the current directory (since the first full pathname is "." for the current directory), then in **/bin**, and finally in **/usr/bin**. If no file with the same name as the command can be found (from the command line) in any of the specified directories, then the shell notifies the user that it is unable to find the command.
5. Prepare the parameters.

   The shell simply passes the parameters to the command as the **argv** array of pointers to strings.
6. Execute the command.

The shell must execute the executable program in the specified file. UNIX shells have always been designed to protect the original process from crashing when it executes a program. That is, since a command can be *any* executable file, then the process that is executing the shell must protect itself in case the executable file contains a fatal error. Somehow, the shell wants to launch the executable so that even if the executable contains a fatal error (which destroys the process executing it), then the shell will remain unharmed. The Bourne shell uses multiple processes to accomplish this by using the UNIX-style system calls **fork()**, **execve()**, and **wait()**.

- **fork()**

  The **fork()** system call *creates* a new process that is a copy of the calling process, except that it has its own copy of the memory, its own process ID (with the correct relationships to other processes), and its own pointers to shared kernel entities such as file descriptors. After **fork()** has been called, *two* processes will execute the next statement after the **fork()** in their own address spaces: the parent and the child. If the call succeeds, then in the parent process **fork()** returns the process ID of the newly created child process and in the child process, **fork()** returns a zero value.

- **execve()**

  The **execve()** system call *changes* the program that a process is currently executing. It has the form

  ```
  execve(char *path, char *argv[], char *envp[])
  ```

  The **path** argument is the pathname of a file that contains the new program to be executed. The **argv** array is a list of parameter strings, and the **envp** array is a list of environment variable strings and values that should be used when the process begins executing the new program. When a process encounters the **execve()** system call, the next instruction it executes will be the one at the entry point of the new executable file. Thus the kernel performs a considerable amount of work in this system call. It must

  - find the new executable file,
  - load the file into the address space currently being used by the calling process (overwriting and discarding the previous program),
  - set the **argv** array and environment variables for the new program execution, and

- start the process executing at the new program's entry point.

  Various versions of **execve()**are available at the system call interface, differing in the way that parameters are specified (for example, some use a full pathname for the executable file and others do not).

- wait()

  The **wait()** system call is used by a process to block itself until the kernel signals the process to execute again, for example because one of its child processes has terminated. When the **wait()** call returns as a result of a child process's terminating, the status of the terminated child is returned as a parameter to the calling process.

When these three system calls are used, here is the code skeleton that a shell might use to execute a command.

```
if(fork() == 0) {
 // This is the child
 // Execute in same environment as parent
   execvp(full_pathname, command->argv, 0);

} else {
 // This is the parent—wait for child to terminate
   wait(status);
}
```

Putting a Process in the Background

In the normal paradigm for executing a command, the parent process creates a child process, starts it executing the command, and then waits until the child process terminates. If the "and" ("&")operator is used to terminate the command line, then the shell is expected to create the child process and start it executing on the designated command but not have the parent wait for the child to terminate. That is, the parent and the child will execute *concurrently*. While the child executes the command, the parent prints another prompt to **stdout** and waits for the user to enter another command line. If the user starts several commands, each terminated by an "&", and each takes a relatively long time to execute, then many processes can be running at the same time.

When a child process is created and started executing on its own program, both the child and the parent expect their **stdin** stream to come from the user via the keyboard and for their **stdout** stream to be written to the character terminal display. Notice that if multiple child processes are running concurrently and all expect the keyboard to define their **stdin** stream, then the user will not know which child process will receive data on its **stdin** if data is typed to the keyboard. Similarly, if any of the concurrent processes write characters to **stdout**, those characters will be written to the terminal display wherever the cursor happens to be positioned. The kernel makes no provision for giving each child process its own keyboard or terminal (unlike a windows system, which controls the multiplexing and demultiplexing through explicit user actions).

I/O Redirection

A process, when created, has three default file identifiers: **stdin**, **stdout**, and **stderr**. If it reads from **stdin**, then the data that it receives will be directed from the keyboard to the **stdin** file descriptor. Similarly, data received from **stdout** and **stderr** are mapped to the terminal display.

The user can redefine **stdin** or **stdout** whenever a command is entered. If the user provides a filename argument to the command and precedes the filename with a left angular brace character ,"<," then the shell will substitute the designated file for **stdin**; this is called redirecting the input from the designated file.

The user can redirect the *output* (for the execution of a single command) by preceding a filename with the right angular brace character, ">," character. For example, a command such as

```
kiowa> wc < main.c > program.stats
```

will create a child process to execute the **wc** command. Before it launches the command, however, it will redirect **stdin** so that it reads the input stream from the file **main.c** and redirect **stdout** so that it writes the output stream to the file **program.stats**.

The shell can redirect I/O by manipulating the child process's file descriptors. A newly created child process inherits the open file descriptors of its parent, specifically the same keyboard for **stdin** and the terminal display for **stdout** and **stderr**. (This expands on why concurrent processes read and write the same keyboard and display.) The shell can change the child's file descriptors so that it reads and writes streams to files rather than to the keyboard and display.

Each process has its own file descriptor table in the kernel (called **fileDescriptor** in this discussion, but labeled differently in the source code); for more on the file descriptor, see Part 1, Section 7.2. When the process is created, the first entry in this table, by convention, refers to the keyboard and the second two refer to the terminal display.

Next, the C runtime environment and the kernel manage the symbols **stdin**, **stdout**, and **stderr** so that **stdin** is always bound to **fileDescriptor[0]** in the kernel table, **stdout** is bound to **fileDescriptor[1]**, and **stderr** to **fileDescriptor[2]**.

You can use the **close()** system call to close any open file, including **stdin**, **stdout**, and **stderr**. By convention, the **dup()** and **open()** commands always use the earliest available entry in the file descriptor table. Therefore a code fragment such as the following:

```
fid = open(foo, O_WRONLY | O_CREAT);
close(1);
dup(fid);
close(fid);
```

is guaranteed to create a file descriptor, **fid**, to duplicate the entry and to place the duplicate in **fileDescriptor[1]** (the usual **stdout** entry in the process's file descriptor table). As a result, characters written by the process to **stdout** will be written to the file **foo**. This is the key to redirecting both **stdin** and **stdout**.

Shell Pipes

The *pipe* is the main IPC mechanism in uniprocessor Linux and other versions of UNIX. By default, a pipe employs asynchronous send and blocking receive operations. Optionally, the blocking receive operation may be changed to be a nonblocking receive (see Section 2.1.5 for details on invoking nonblocking read operations). Pipes are FIFO (first-in/first out) buffers designed with an API that resembles as closely as possible the file I/O interface. A pipe may contain a system-defined maximum number of bytes at any given time, usually 4KB. As indicated in Figure 2.2, a process can send data by writing it into one end of the pipe and another can receive the data by reading the other end of the pipe.

Figure 2.2
Information Flow Through a Pipe

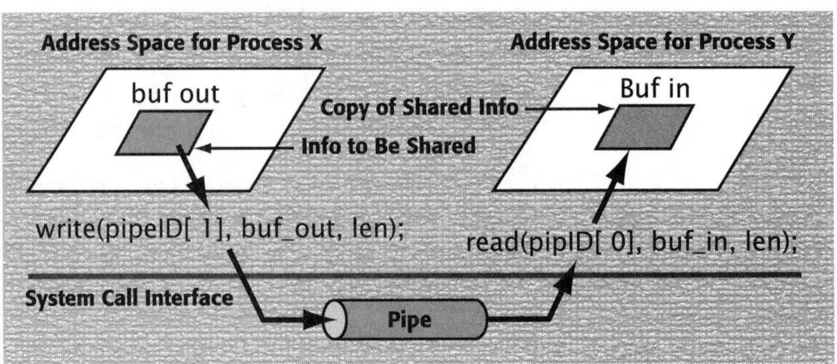

A pipe is represented in the kernel by a file descriptor. A process that wants to create a pipe calls the kernel with a call of the following form.

```
int pipeID[2];
...
pipe(pipeID);
```


The kernel creates the pipe as a kernel FIFO data structure with two file identifiers. In this example code, **pipeID[0]** is a file pointer (an index into the process's open file table) to the read end of the pipe and **pipeID[1]** is file pointer to the write end of the pipe.

For two or more processes to use pipes for IPC (interprocess communication), a common ancestor of the processes must create the pipe prior to creating the processes. Because the **fork** command creates a child that contains a copy of the open file table (that is, the child has access to all of the files that the parent has already opened), the child inherits the pipes that the parent created. To use a pipe, it needs only to read and write the proper file descriptors.

For example, suppose that a parent creates a pipe. It then can create a child and communicate with it by using a code fragment such as the following.

```
...
pipe(pipeID);
if(fork() == 0) { /* The child process */
  ...
  read(pipeID[0], childBuf, len);
  /* Process the message in childBuf */
  ...
} else { /* The parent process */
  ...
  /* Send a message to the child */
  write(pipeID[1], msgToChild, len);
  ...
}
```

A pipe is used in place of a mailbox. In a mailbox, the asynchronous send operation is a normal **write()** system call on the write end of the pipe (pipe descriptor **pipe_id[1]**) and the **read()** operation is a blocking read on the read end of the pipe (pipe descriptor **pipe_id[0]**).

Pipes enable processes to copy information from one address space to another by using the UNIX file model. The pipe read and write ends can be used in most system calls in the same way as a file descriptor. Further, the information written to and read from the pipe is a byte stream. UNIX pipes do not explicitly support messages, though two processes can establish their own protocol to provide structured messages. Also, library routines are available that can be used with a pipe to communicate via messages.

Figure 2.3 illustrates how pipes can be used in Linux to implement concurrent processing between processes A and B (executing **PROC_A** and **PROC_B**, respectively), where A performs some computation ("compute A1"), sends a value **x** to B, performs a second phase of computation, reads a value **y** from B, and then iterates. Meanwhile, B reads the value **x**, performs the first phase of

Figure 2.3
Linux Pipes

```
int A_to_B[2], B_to_A[2];
main(){
   pipe(A_to_B);
   pipe(B_to_A);
   if (fork()==0) { /* This is the first child process */
      close(A_to_B[0]);
      close(B_to_A[1]);
      execve("prog_A.out", ...);
      exit(1); /* Error-terminate the child */
   }
   if (fork()==0) { /* This is the second child process */
      close(A_to_B[1]);
      close(B_to_A[0]);
      execve("prog_B.out", ...);
      exit(1); /* Error-terminate the child */
   }
/* This is the parent process code */
   wait(...);
   wait(...);
}

proc_A(){
   while (TRUE) {
      <compute A1>;
      write(A_to_B[1], x, sizeof(int)); /* Use this pipe to send info */
      <compute A2>;
      read(B_to_A[0], y, sizeof(int)); /* Use this pipe to get info */
   }
}

proc_B(){
   while (TRUE) {
      read(A_to_B[0], x, sizeof(int)); /* Use this pipe to get info */
      <compute B1>;
      write(B_to_A[1], y, sizeof(int)); /* Use this pipe to send info */
      <compute B2>;
   }
}
```

computation, writes a value to A, performs more computation, and then iterates. A process that does not intend to use a pipe end should close so that end-of-file (**EOF**) conditions can be detected.

A *named pipe* can be used to allow unrelated processes to communicate with each other. Typically in pipes, the children inherit the pipe ends as open file descriptors. In named pipes, a process obtains a pipe end by using a string that is analogous to a filename but that is associated with a pipe. This allows any set of processes to exchange information by using a *public pipe* whose end names are filenames. When a process uses a named pipe, the pipe is a system-wide resource, potentially accessible by any process. Just as files must be managed so that they are not inadvertently shared among many processes at one time, named pipes must be managed, by using the file system commands.

Reading Multiple Input Streams

As with any file, the read end of a pipe, a file descriptor, or a socket can be configured, with an **IOCTL()** call, to use nonblocking semantics. After the call has been issued on the descriptor, a read on the stream returns immediately, with the error code set to **EAGAIN**. Also, **read()** will return a value of **0**, thereby indicating that it did not read any information into the buffer. Alternatively, the program can determine whether **read()** succeeded by checking the length value to see if it is nonzero.

Figure 2.4 illustrates the use of the **ioctl()** to switch the read end of a pipe from its default blocking behavior to nonblocking behavior. You can apply this technique to any file descriptor, including **stdin**.

The **select()** command allows a process to poll all of its open input streams to determine which contain data. It then can execute a normal blocking read operation on any stream that contains data. Note that if multiple processes are reading the pipe and each uses a **select()**, then a race condition can result. If you decide to use this approach in your solution, use the **man** page to learn more about **select()**.

Problem Statement

Part A

Write a C program that will act as a shell command line interpreter for the Linux kernel. Your shell program should use the same style as the Bourne shell for running programs. In particular, when the user types a line such as

identifier [identifier [identifier]]

Figure 2.4
Nonblocking read Example

```
#include      <sys/ioctl.h>
int errno;    /* For nonblocking read flag */
...
main() {
  int pipeID[2];
  ...
  pipe(pipeID);
/* Switch the read end of the pipe to the nonblocking mode */
  ioctl(pipeID[0], FIONBIO, &on);
  ...
  while(...) {
  /* Poll the read end of the pipe */
    read(pipeID[0], buffer, BUFLEN);
    if (errno !=EAGAIN){
    /* Incoming info available from the pipe—process it */
      ...
    } else {
    /* Check the pipe for input again later—do other things */
      ...
    }
  }
  ...
}
```

your shell should parse the command line to build **argv**. It should search the directory system (in the order specified by the **PATH** environment variable) for a file with the same name as the first **identifier** (which may be a relative filename or a full pathname). If the file is found, then it should be executed with the optional parameter list, as is done with **sh**. Use an **execv()** system call (rather than any of the **execl()** calls) to execute the file that contains the command. You will need to become familiar with the Linux **fork()**and **wait()** functions and the **execv()** family of system calls (a set of interfaces to the **execve()** system call).

Part B

Add functionality to the shell from Part A so that a user can use the "&" operator as a command terminator. A command terminated with "&" should be executed concurrently with the shell (rather than the shell's waiting for the child to terminate before it prompts the user for another command).

Part C

Modify your shell program from Part A so that the user can redirect the **stdin** or **stdout** file descriptors by using the "<" and ">" characters as filename prefixes. Also, allow your user to use the pipe operator, "|", to execute two processes concurrently, with **stdout** from the first process being redirected as the **stdin** for the second process. Your solution may optionally handle only redirection or only pipes in one command line (rather than both options in the same command line).

Attacking the Problem

Organizing a Solution

The exercise introduction generally describes how a shell behaves. It also implicitly provides a plan of attack, summarized here. This plan describes several debugging versions that you can use for Part A, then apply to the other parts as required.

1. Organize the shell to initialize variables and then to perform an endless loop until **stdin** detects an EOF condition, such as a **Ctrl-D** character or an exit message. Develop a very simple version that prints the prompt character and then waits for the user to type a command. After it reads the command, it should print it to **stdout**.
2. Refine your simple shell so that it *parses* the command line. It should determine the strings on the command line and then put them into a **char *argv[]** array. Also, compute the value for **int argc**. In this debug version, print the contents of **argc** and **argv[]**. You can also detect an **exit** command that will terminate your shell.
3. In the next debug version, use **argv[0]** to find the executable file. In this version, simply print the filename.
   - Construct a simple version that can find only command files that are in the current directory.
   - Enhance your program so that it can find command files that are specified with an absolute pathname.
   - Enable your program to search directories according to the string that is stored in the shell PATH environment variable.
4. Create a child process to execute the command.

Part A

Here is a code skeleton for a shell program.

```
int main () {
  ...
```

```
 struct command_struct {
   char *name;
   char *argv[];
   ...
 } *command;
 ...
// Shell initialization
 ...

// Main loop
 while(stdin is not at EOF) {
   print_to_stdout(prompt_string);
   command_line = read_from_stdin();
  // Determine the command name, and construct the parameter list
   ...
  // Find the full pathname for the file
   ...
  // Launch the executable file with the specified parameters
   ...
 }

// Terminate the shell
 ...
}
```

Determining the Command Name and the Parameter List

You should recognize the **argv** name in the **command_struct** from writing C programs in your introductory programming classes (and from Exercise 1 in this manual). That is, if you write a program and want the shell to pass parameters (from the command line) to your program, then you declare the function prototype for your main program with a line like this:

```
int main(int argc, char *argv[]);
```

The convention is that when your executable program (**a.out**) is executed, the shell builds an array of strings, **argv**, with **argc** entries in it. **argv[0]** points to a string that has the command name **a.out**, **argv [1]** points to a string that specifies the first parameter, **argv [2]** points to a string that specifies the second parameter, and so on. Your program, when executed, reads the **argv** array to get the strings and then applies whatever semantics it wants to interpret the strings.

For example, your program might be run with a command line of the form

a.out foo 100

so that when it begins execution, it will have **argc** set to 3, **argv[0]** will point to the string **a.out**, **argv [1]** will point to **foo**, and **argv [2]** will point to the string **100**. Your program then can interpret the first parameter (**argv [1]**) as, say, a filename, and the second parameter (**argv[2]**) as, say, an integer record count. The shell would simply treat the first word on the command line as a filename and the remaining words as strings.

After your program reads the command line into a string, **command_line**, it parses the line so as to populate the **command_struct** fields (**name** and **argv**). The explanation in the introduction should suffice for you to design and implement code to parse the command line so that you have the name of the file containing the command in **command->name** and (a pointer to) the array of pointers to parameter strings in **command->argv**.

Finding the Full Pathname

The user might have provided a full pathname as the command name word or only a relative pathname that is to be bound according to the value of the PATH environment variable. A name that begins with a "/", "./", or "../" is an absolute pathname that can be used to launch the execution. Otherwise, your program must search each directory in the list specified by the PATH environment variable to find the relative pathname.

Launching the Command

The final step in executing the command is to fork a child process to execute the specified command and then to cause the child to execute that command. The following code skeleton will accomplish this.

```
if(fork() == 0) {
  // This is the child
  // Execute in the same environment as the parent
    execvp(full_pathname, command->argv, 0);

} else {
  // This is the parent; wait for the child to terminate
    wait(status);
}
```

Parts B and C

Getting general code is difficult when more than one special operator is used in one command line, so you should focus on doing the exercise only when "&", "<", ">", or "|" is used and then, not more than one at a time.

three

Kernel Timers

Exercise Goal: You will begin learning about kernel source code by studying the kernel's time management algorithms. First, you will study how the kernel implements interval timers (in part by reading kernel code). Then you will put that knowledge to work by creating a user-space mechanism to measure the execution time of a multithreaded program. As you do the exercise, you also will learn how to use signals.

Introduction

The kernel keeps the current time by reading a clock device and maintaining a kernel variable with the current time. The current time is accessible to user-mode programs via system calls. **gettimeofday()** is the usual interface to the current time maintained by the system. It also is used to determine when the currently running process should be removed from the CPU so that another process can use it, or to keep track of the amount of time that a process executed in user mode or supervisor mode. As background information for doing this exercise, the next sections explain the basic strategy for keeping time and discuss how various time quantities are recorded for each process.

How the Kernel Maintains the Time

Time is stated relative to some important epoch. For example, time in the United States is calculated by using the Gregorian calendar, which is based on a time of zero to be about 2,000 years ago. When you type the **date** command to a shell, the command will read the kernel variable to determine the time, say **Mon Jun 21 09:01:28 MDT 2001**, which can be interpreted to mean that about 2001.5 years have elapsed since the beginning of the epoch.

UNIX systems were not around before about 1970, so they avoid representing time before 1970. This is accomplished by beginning the time epoch at 12 A.M. January 1, 1970 (00:00:00 Greenwich Meridian Time (GMT)). Two **long int** kernel variables keep track of the number of seconds and microseconds, respectively, that have passed since the beginning of the UNIX time epoch. A user-space program can read the system time as follows.

```
#include        <sys/time.h>
...
struct timeval theTime;
...
gettimeofday(&theTime, NULL);
...
```

Here,

```
struct timeval {
   long tv_sec;
   long tv_usec;
};
```

When the code fragment completes, the **timeval** structure will have the variable **theTime.tv_sec** set to the (**long**) integer number of seconds that have passed since 12 A.M. January 1, 1970. **theTime.tv_usec**, also a variable of type **long**, provides the number of microseconds that have elapsed since the last second began. The **date** command translates the kernel time to the local time and to the Gregorian calendar time epoch before it produces a result on **stdout**.

You can see how **gettimeofday()** works by inspecting the kernel function, **sys_gettimeofday**, in the file **kernel/time.c**. (Remember that references to Linux source code assume that the current directory is the root of the subtree that contains all of the source code, usually **/usr/src/linux**.) You might find it interesting to look at the implementation of the i386-specific implementation of the function **do_gettimeofday()** that appears in **arch/i386/kernel/time.c**.

Note that now that you are beginning to inspect Linux source code, you should always use the **grep** shell command when looking for functions and variable names. For example, you can find **do_gettimeofday()** by changing to **arch/i386/kernel** and using **grep** to find the files that contain **do_gettimeofday**.

For the **tv_usec** value to be correct at all times, it must be changed exactly once every microsecond (a millionth of a second). All modern computers use the same basic approach for keeping track of time. The hardware includes a programmable timer device that can be set to issue an interrupt every *K* time units; in the case of Linux machines, *K* is set to be 10 milliseconds. The system can track the passage of time by counting the number of interrupts that have occurred since the system was booted. If the time that the machine was last booted is known, then the current time (more accurately, the time that has elapsed since the machine was booted) can be computed to within 10 milliseconds. In i386 machines, a time-of-day clock runs whether or not the machine is powered up (machines usually have a battery backup that provides power for this clock). The time-of-day clock is not very accurate, but it establishes a base that can be used in conjunction with the 10-millisecond clock.

The clock ISR **timer_interrupt()** in file **arch/i386/kernel/time.c** calls the **do_timer()** function in **kernel/sched.c**. This function increments a counter, in a kernel variable named **jiffies**, each time that it runs. It then marks **TIMER_BH** (the timer bottom half) for execution in the **ret_from_sys_call** sequence (see Part 1, Section 3.1) so that it will run **timer_bh** in **kernel/sched.c**. When the bottom half runs, it updates the system timer as well as a set of timers for each process (*per process timers*; see the next subsection). For the system time, the timer bottom half uses the current value of **jiffies** to compute the current time. It stores the value in **struct timeval xtime**, where the value can be read by other kernel functions (such as **sys_gettimeofday()**).

Per Process Timers

The kernel accumulates time and manages various timers for each process. For example, the scheduling strategy depends on each process's having a record of the amount of CPU time that it has accrued since it last acquired the CPU. Because these time values are associated with each process, they are saved in the process's descriptor. When the kernel creates a task, it allocates a new task descriptor of type **struct task_struct** from the kernel's heap space (i.e., it uses the kernel **kmalloc()** call).

You first saw **struct task_struct** in Exercise 1. This structure contains more than 75 fields, a few of which you have already seen. Next, you will consider the ones related to time values.

```
struct task_struct {
   ...
   long counter;
   ...
   unsigned long policy, rt_priority;
   unsigned long it_real_value, it_prof_value, it_virt_value;
   unsigned long it_real_incr, it_prof_incr, it_virt_incr;
   struct timer_list real_timer;
// Contains tms_utime, tms_stime, tms_cutime, and tms_cstime
   struct tms;
   unsigned long start_time;
   long per_cpu_utime[NR_CPUS], per_cpu_stime[], cutime, cstime;
  ...
};
```

These fields are updated in the **update_process_times()** function located in **kernel/sched.c** (invoked as part of the **ret_from_sys_call** bottom half processing). This function calls **update_one_process()**, which calls other functions to update the values and to decide if a signal should be raised to indicate that a timer has expired. The **counter** field is used to determine whether the process needs scheduling attention.

The interval timers (**it_XXX_value/it_XXX_incr**) use the kernel time to keep track of the following three intervals of time relevant to every process.

- ITIMER_REAL: Reflects the passage of real time and is implemented by using the **it_real_value** and **it_real_incr** fields.
- ITIMER_VIRTUAL: Reflects the passage of virtual time. This time is incremented only when the corresponding process is executing.
- ITIMER_PROF: Reflects the passage of time during which the process is active (virtual time) plus the time that the kernel is doing work on behalf of the corresponding process (for example, reading a timer).

Each of these timers is actually a countdown timer. That is, it is periodically initialized to some prescribed value and then reflects the passage of time by counting down toward zero. When the timer reaches zero, it raises a signal to notify another part of the system (in the OS or a user-space program) that the counter has reached zero. Then it resets the value and begins counting down again.

Each timer is initialized with the **setitimer()** system call.

```
#include        <sys/time.h>
...
setitimer(
    int timerType,
    const struct timerval *value,
    struct itimerval *oldValue
);
```

3

The **struct itimerval** includes the following fields.

```
struct itimerval {
    struct timeval it_interval;
    struct timeval it_value;
);
```

To learn more about the parameters, read the **man** page for **setitimer()**. The general idea is that the **timerType** parameter is set to one of ITIMER_REAL, ITIMER_VIRTUAL, or ITIMER_PROF (which are constants defined in the **sys/time.h** include file). The **value** parameter is used to initialize second and microsecond fields of the given timer. The **it_value** field defines the current value for the timer. The **it_interval** field defines the value that should be used to reset the timer when it reaches zero.

A timer is read with the **getitimer()** system call, as follows.

```
#include        <sys/time.h>
...
getitimer(
    int timerType,
    const struct timerval *value,
);
```

In this case, the **value** parameter is used to return the value of the kernel's clock.

The following code fragment sets ITIMER_REAL and then reads it.

```
#include        <sys/time.h>
...
    struct itimerval v;
    ...
    v.it_interval.tv_sec = 9;
    v.it_interval.tv_usec = 999999;
```

```
v.it_value.tv_sec = 9;
v.it_value.tv_usec = 999999;
setitimer(ITIMER_REAL, &v, NULL);
...
getitimer(ITIMER_REAL, &v);
printf("... %ld seconds, %ld microseconds ...",
   ...,
   v.it_value.tv_sec,
   v.it_value.tv_usec,
   ...);
...
```

When ITIMER_REAL reaches zero, it is reset to (9, 999999) again. However, this code segment does not define any other processing that could be done when the corresponding signal is raised.

Problem Statement

Part A

Use ITIMER_REAL to implement your version of **gettimeofday()**. Set it so that it raises a signal once per second. Use the **signal** facility to determine when ITIMER_REAL has been decremented to zero and to count the number of seconds that have elapsed.

Part B

Design and implement facilities that use the ITIMER_VIRTUAL and ITIMER_PROF interval timers to profile a process. The profile should provide actual time of execution (by using the timer from Part A), CPU time (the time that the process is actually running), user-space time, and kernel-space time. Your program should use ITIMER_VIRTUAL and ITIMER_PROF to report CPU time, time spent in kernel space, and time spent in user space.

Use **gettimeofday()** to compute the program's "wall clock" runtime. All times should have millisecond accuracy, to the extent that your hardware can actually support this. That is, code it for millisecond accuracy, even though you might not get this level of accuracy in reality. Use the **signal** facility to create signal handlers to keep track of the number of seconds of virtual and profile time (raise a signal once per second).

Part C

Write a subject program to spawn two children, with each child recursively computing a Fibonacci sequence for $N = 20$, 30, and 36. The code skeleton for this program is provided in the Attacking the Problem section. Note that Fibonacci(36) might take a couple of minutes to compute. Use the facilities that you implemented in Parts A and B to determine the real time, virtual time, and profile time for each of the three processes.

Attacking the Problem

Organization of the Linux Source Code

All UNIX implementations, including Linux, implement the **ITIMER_REAL**, **ITIMER_VIRTUAL**, and **ITIMER_PROF** functions. However, you might find it helpful (or even necessary) to read the Linux source code to understand how the interval timers work.

The Linux source code is organized in a subtree rooted at the subdirectory **linux** (see Figure 2.5). In my Linux machine, the absolute path to this directory is **/usr/src/linux**; it might be different in yours. The figure does not show all of the directories or any of the files (for example, the kernel image file, **vmlinux**, is stored in the **linux** directory). The **linux** directory contains many files and directories. The directories shown in the figure contain most of the OS source code. The heart of the kernel is kept in two places: **kernel** and **arch/<architecture_type>/kernel**. In this case, you are using the Intel 80x86 architecture, so the **<architecture_type>** is **i386**. The code that implements the memory manager is in **mm** and

Figure 2.5
Linux Source Code Directory Skeleton

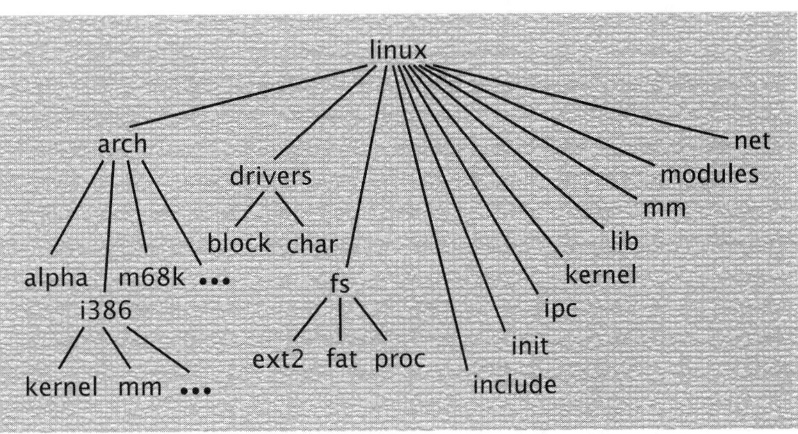

arch/i386/mm. The idea is that architecture-independent code is kept in the subdirectory with the generic function name and the architecture-dependent part of the code (sometimes assembly language) is kept in the **arch** subdirectory. The **itimer** code is all architecture-independent, so **linux/arch/i386/kernel** does not contain an **itimer.c** routine. However **process.c** has its architecture-independent part in **linux/kernel/process.c** and its architecture-specific part in **linux/arch/i386/kernel/process.c**. See Figure 2.6.

You will probably find it worthwhile to browse the **linux** subdirectories to get a feeling for how the overall kernel functionality is distributed across these subdirectories. Located in **linux/kernel/itimer.c** is the implementation for **itimer** (**itimer.c** is part of the general kernel functionality).

Signals

A UNIX system defines a fixed set of signals that can be *raised* by one process, thereby causing another process to be interrupted and to (optionally) *catch* the signal by executing prespecified code for that particular signal. Hence, a *signal implementation* is an OS system mechanism for notifying an application process that some event has occurred. A signal often indicates the occurrence of a hardware event, such as a user's pressing the Delete key or the CPU's detecting an attempt to divide by zero. Signals also may be used to notify a

Figure 2.6
The process.c Implementation

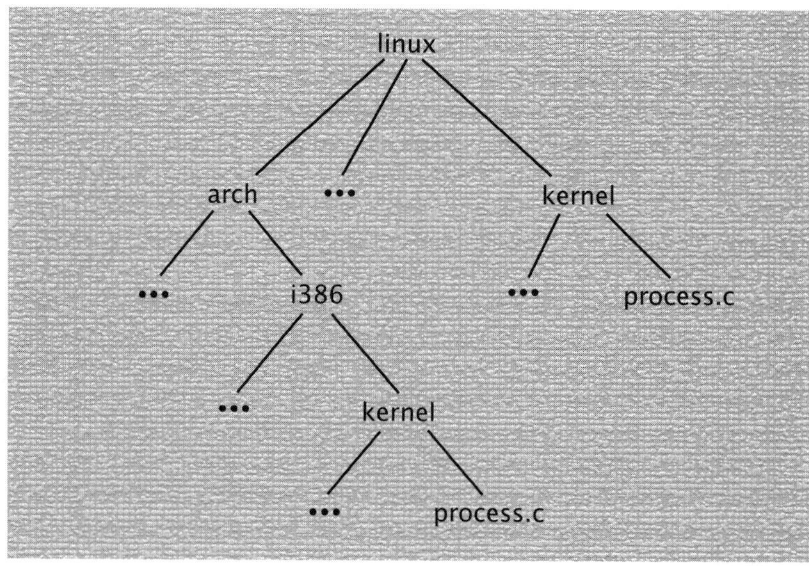

process of the existence of a software condition. You have seen that it can represent the fact that one of the process's three **itimers** has reached zero.

Signals also can be used among application-level processes. Each signal has a type (called a *name*) associated with it. Most contemporary UNIX systems (including Linux) include 31 built-in types. They differ in BSD UNIX (FreeBSD), AT&T System V Release 4 (SVR4), POSIX, and ANSI C. In each version, the system include file, **signal.h** (found in **include/asm/signal.h** in Linux source code trees), defines a number of symbolic names for the signal types. For example, all versions of UNIX define the SIGINT signal type. This signal is raised by the terminal driver when the user presses the terminal interrupt character, usually Delete or **Ctrl-C**. Application programmers are not allowed to create new signals. But most versions of UNIX include **SIGUSR1** and **SIGUSR2**, which can be used for application-to-application signaling.

A signal is raised by calling the **kill()** function and identifying the process to receive the signal and the signal type.[1] Essentially, a receiving application process can cause a signal to be handled in the default way, to be ignored, or to be caught by user-defined code. The **signal()** function is called to identify the signal number and the way that the signal is to be treated. For example, to ignore the **SIGALRM** signal, the process must execute the system call

```
signal(SIGALRM, SIG_IGN);
```

The default handling can be reenabled by calling **signal()** again with the **SIG_DFL** value. The application can process the alarm signal with its own code by supplying a function (that takes an integer argument and returns a **void**) as the second argument to **signal()**.

The following complete program illustrates how a signal handler is registered with the **signal()** function call and how the whole mechanism operates, as well as the form of the signal handler routine itself.

```
#include      <signal.h>
static void sig_handler(int);
int main (void){
  int i, parent_pid, child_pid, status;
/* Prepare the sig_handler routine to catch SIGUSR1 and SIGUSR2 */
   if (signal(SIGUSR1, sig_handler)==SIG_ERR)
```

[1] The name "kill" comes from an early use of signals that meant that one process could send a signal to another to request that the receiver terminate. The name of the function that transmitted the signal was **kill()**. While the types of signals have been extended, the name has not.

```
        printf("Parent: Unable to create handler for SIGUSR1\n");
    if (signal(SIGUSR2, sig_handler)==SIG_ERR)
        printf("Parent: Unable to create handler for SIGUSR2\n");
    parent_pid = getpid();
    if ((child_pid = fork())==0) {
      kill(parent_pid, SIGUSR1);  /* Raise the SIGUSR1 signal */
/* Child process begins busy-wait for a signal */
      for (;;) pause();
} else {
      kill(child_pid, SIGUSR2);  /* Parent raising SIGUSR2 signal */
      printf("Parent: Terminating child ...");
      kill(child_pid, SIGTERM);  /* Parent raising SIGTERM signal */
      wait(&status);  /* Parent waiting for the child termination */
      printf("done\n");
    }
}

static void sig_handler(int signo){
    switch (signo) {
    case SIGUSR1:  /* Incoming SIGUSR1 signal */
        printf("Parent: Received SIGUSR1\n");
        break;
    case SIGUSR2:  /* Incoming SIGUSR2 signal */
        printf("Child: Received SIGUSR2\n");
        break;
    default: break;  /* Should never get this case */
    }
    return;
}
```

This code segment is pedagogic in that it illustrates how signals are raised and caught but does not implement any useful function. It creates a single signal handler, **sig_handler**, that is used by a parent process and a child process with the two calls to **signal()**. Next, it determines its own process identifier by using the **getpid()** system call. It then creates a child so that the parent knows both the parent and child process identifiers but the child knows only the parent's identifier. The child process sends a **SIGUSR1** to the parent and then enters a busy-wait so that it will still exist when the parent sends signals to it. The parent sends a **SIGUSR2** to the child, followed by a termination signal (**SIGTERM**), and then calls **wait()** to obtain the report that the child has been terminated. The child and parent use the same signal handler definition, though the child will never see the SIGUSR1 and the parent will never see a SIGUSR2 signal.

Organizing a Solution

As with all programs, you have many different ways to organize your solution. This section provides a skeleton of a solution. The skeleton uses signals to notify the user processes about time values. Your program must incorporate your own signal handler routines.


```
#include <sys/time.h>
#include <signal.h>
#include <unistd.h>
#include <stdio.h>

long unsigned int fibonacci(unsigned int n);

static long p_realt_secs = 0, c1_realt_secs = 0, c2_realt_secs = 0;
static long p_virtt_secs = 0, c1_virtt_secs = 0, c2_virtt_secs = 0;
static long p_proft_secs = 0, c1_proft_secs = 0, c2_proft_secs = 0;
static struct itimerval p_realt, c1_realt, c2_realt;
static struct itimerval p_virtt, c1_virtt, c2_virtt;
static struct itimerval p_proft, c1_proft, c2_proft;

main(int argc, char **argv) {
  long unsigned fib = 0;
  int pid1, pid2;
  unsigned int fibarg;
  int status;

// Get command line argument, fibarg
  ...
// Initialize parent, child1, and child 2 timer values
  ...
// Enable your signal handlers for the parent
  signal(SIGALRM, ...);
  signal(SIGVTALRM, ...);
  signal(SIGPROF, ...);

// Set the parent's itimers
  ...
  pid1 = fork();
```

```
 if(pid1 == 0) {
 // Enable child 1 signal handlers (disable parent handlers)

 // Set the child 1 itimers

 // Start child 1 on the Fibonacci program
   fib = fibonacci(fibarg);

 // Read the child 1 itimer values, and report them
   getitimer(ITIMER_PROF, ...);
   getitimer(ITIMER_REAL, ...);
   getitimer(ITIMER_VIRTUAL, ...);
   printf("\n");
   printf("Child 1 fib = %ld, real time = %ld sec, %ld msec\n",
       fib, c1_realt_secs,
       elapsed_usecs(c1_realt.it_value.tv_sec,
               c1_realt.it_value.tv_usec) / 1000);
   printf("Child 1 fib = %ld, cpu time = %ld sec, %ld msec\n",
       fib, c1_proft_secs,
       elapsed_usecs(c1_proft.it_value.tv_sec,
               c1_proft.it_value.tv_usec) / 1000);
   printf("Child 1 fib = %ld, user time = %ld sec, %ld msec\n",
       fib, c1_virtt_secs,
       elapsed_usecs(c1_virtt.it_value.tv_sec,
               c1_virtt.it_value.tv_usec) / 1000);
   printf("Child 1 fib = %ld, kernel time = %ld sec, %ld msec\n",
       fib, c1_proft_secs - c1_virtt_secs,
       (elapsed_usecs(c1_proft.it_value.tv_sec,
               c1_proft.it_value.tv_usec) / 1000) -
       (elapsed_usecs(c1_virtt.it_value.tv_sec,
               c1_virtt.it_value.tv_usec) / 1000));
   fflush(stdout);
   exit(0);
 }
else {
  pid2 = fork();
  if(pid2 == 0) {
  // Enable the child 2 signal handlers (disable parent handlers)
    ...
  // Set the child 2 itimers
    ...
```

```
    // Start the child 2 on the Fibonacci program
      fib = fibonacci(fibarg);
    // Read the child 2 itimer values and report them
      ...
    }
  else { /* This is the parent */
    // Start the parent on the Fibonacci program
      fib = fibonacci(fibarg);

  // Wait for the children to terminate
      waitpid(0, &status, 0);
      waitpid(0, &status, 0);

  // Read the parent itimer values, and report them
      ...
  }
   printf("this line should never be printed\n");
  }

  long unsigned int fibonacci(unsigned int n) {
   if(n == 0)
     return 0;
   else if (n == 1 || n == 2)
     return 1;
   else
     return(fibonacci(n-1) + fibonacci(n-2))
  }
```

3

four

Kernel Modules

Exercise Goal: You will study the *module*, a mechanism unique to Linux. Modules can be used to dynamically add functionality to the kernel. You will write a module that executes as a kernel-space extension of Linux to report the values of the kernel's **xtime** variable.

Introduction

A Linux *module* is a set of functions and data types that can be compiled as an independent program (with appropriate flags to indicate that it is kernel code). It is then linked into the kernel when the module is *installed*. Linux modules can be installed when the kernel is started—called *static loading*. They can also be installed while the kernel is running, called *dynamic loading* . If a function in a dynamic module is called before the module has been installed, then the call will fail. But if the module has been installed, then the kernel will field the system call and pass it on to the corresponding function in the module.

Linux systems typically have several modules loaded during normal kernel initialization (though the kernel can be built so that modules cannot be used with it). You can easily determine which, if any, modules (static or dynamic) are running on your Linux machine by reading the file /proc/modules.

Modules are generally used to implement device drivers. UNIX systems, however, have a traditional static mechanism for defining and adding device drivers at kernel configuration (you will learn more about device drivers in Exercise 10). One consequence of this is that the module API generally conforms to the API for a device driver. Even so, modules can be used to implement any desired function.

Module Organization

A module, once installed, will be executed in supervisor mode in the kernel's address space. Thus the module can read and write kernel data structures, provided that it knows their addresses. Because Linux is implemented as a monolithic kernel, a common problem is functions implemented in one file possibly needing to reference data that is defined in another file. In conventional programs, this problem is handled by using external (global) variables that the link editor can resolve when it builds the program executable object file.

Because modules are designed and implemented independently of the kernel, they cannot reference kernel data structures by variable names by relying on static linking. Instead, the Linux kernel incorporates a mechanism by which files that implement a data structure can *export* the symbolic name of the structure so that the structure can be used at runtime. Debuggers rely on this kind of runtime variable binding to allow users to reference data structures by symbolic name, so it was not necessary to invent the technique just to support modules.

Recall that you need to instruct the compiler to export symbols when it compiles a source file if a debugger will be used with the file; the same is true for the kernel. When the kernel is built, kernel public symbols are exported by using the file's header file. In general, to find out what kernal functions are exported, and hence are available for the module to use directly, read the file `kernel/ksyms.c`. When writing modules, be *very careful* when writing (changing the value of) an exported variable, since by writing a variable you will change the kernel's state in a way that its designers probably did not anticipate. Until you are certain that you know the effect of writing a kernel variable, you should only read them.

A modules is treated as a dynamic abstract data type that has an interface that can be interpreted by the static kernel. The minimum module interface must include two functions that the kernel will call when it installs and removes the module: respectively, `init_module()` and `cleanup_module()`. Thus the file that defines the module has the following form.

```
#include <linux/kernel.h>
#include <linux/module.h>
...
int init_module() {
/* Code to initialize the module when it is installed */
   ...
}

void cleanup_module() {
/* Code to clean up when the module is removed
   ...
}
```

4

You can write a module that contains only these two routines. Then, the only functions in the module would be the one called when the module is installed (**init_module()**) and the one called when the module is removed (**cleanup_module()**). This is not completely useless, however, since you could use **init_module** to start an activity that would continue as long as the module is installed and **cleanup_module** to halt the activity (for example, see Pomerantz [1999]).

Because a module can implement relatively complex functions, Linux includes a mechanism for defining a new API for the module, one that has more functions than **init_module()** and **cleanup_module()**. For example, suppose that the module is designed to allow an application program to increment an internal module value. For it to do this, the designer might provide, say, a function named **increment()**. The module implementers can define any new function for the module's API, so they need some way to inform the OS that these new functions exist. Then when an application program wants to invoke the module's functions, it makes a system call; the kernel forwards the call to the specified function in the module. Each new function that is added to the module must be *registered* with the kernel when the module is installed in the kernel. If the module is statically loaded, then all of its functions are registered when the kernel is booted. If the module is dynamically loaded, then the functions must be dynamically registered with the kernel when the module is installed. Of course, if the module is dynamically *removed* then its functions must be *unregistered*. In this way, the module functions do not get called when the module is no longer loaded. Registration is usually done in **init_module()**, and unregistration is done in **cleanup_module()**.

Two types of interfaces are available to the designer to use with the module: device driver and **/proc** file. The device driver interface is more general than the **/proc** file interface (for example, **/proc** files can be read but they cannot be written). You will not study the device driver interface until Exercise 10, but the **/proc** file system interface was introduced in Exercise 1, so this discussion of the module interface focuses on that interface.

When the module uses the **/proc** interface, its implementation file will be saved in the **/proc** directory and referenced via **/proc**-style file operations. (You can read about using **/proc** pseudo files in Exercise 1 now if you have not already done that exercise.) The module is registered and unregistered with, respectively, the **proc_register()** and **proc_unregister()** functions. These functions reference a **struct proc_dir_entry** data structure that is defined in **include/linux/proc_fs.h**, as follows.

```
struct proc_dir_entry = {
   unsigned short low_ino;    // inode #
   unsigned short namelen;    // Length of the filename
   const char *name;          // The filename
   mode_t mode;                    // File mode
   nlink_t nlink;             // Number of links to this file
   uid_t uid;                 // uid for the file
   gid_t gid;                 // gid for the file
   unsigned long size;
                              // The size of file as it will be
reported by ls
   struct inode_operations *ops; // Functions to manipulate inode
   int (*get_info)(char *, char  **, off_t, int, int);
                              // Read the function entry point
   void (*fill_inode)(struct inode *);
                              // Fct to change permissions, etc.
   struct proc_dir_entry *next, *parent, *subdir;
                              // Optional links if in a list
   void *data                 // Unused
   int (*read_proc) (char *page, char **start, off_t off,
                              int count, int *eof, void *data);
   int (*write_proc)(struct file *file, const char *buffer,
                              unsigned long count, void *data);
   int (*readlink_proc)(struct proc_dir_entry *de, char *page);
   unsigned int count;        /* use count */
   int deleted;               /* delete flag */
};
```

struct proc_dir_entry specifies the characteristics of the new pseudo file that will appear in **/proc** after the module has been registered. The **low_ino** field is set to zero to tell the system to assign this value. If the name of the pseudo file is to be `my_module`, then **namelen** would be set to 9 and **name** would be **my_module**. The **mode** field describes the mode of the resulting pseudo file. This mode may have the values described for the mode argument for **stat(2)**; see **man 2 stat** for the values. The **nlink** field is the number of links that reference this pseudo file, usually one. The **uid** and **gid** fields are the user and group IDs for the pseudo file; if they are set to zero, root is the owner. When **ls** is applied to the pseudo file, it returns a length; however, this could, of course, be meaningless, since the pseudo file is really a module. The value of the **size** field is returned as the size of the file by the **ls** command. The **ops** field is a pointer to a list of functions to manage the pseudo file inode (see Part 1, Section 7.2). Unless you intend to do something particular to the inode, set this field to **NULL**.

4

Usually, a **/proc** pseudo file is a program in memory that responds to a **read()** system call on that pseudo file. The **read_proc** field in **struct proc_dir_entry** is a pointer to the function that should be called by the kernel in response to the **read()** system call. The module **read_proc** function has a prototype of the following form.

```
read_proc(
   char *page,
   char **start,
   off_t off,
   int count,
   int *eof,
   void *data
);
```

The system reserves buffer space for the pseudo file; the **page** field addresses the system space. The module programmer also can reserve system space and then use an application space pointer, **start**, to reference the reserved area using the pointer. The **off** field is the pseudo file offset position; this field might be meaningless in the module. The **count** field is the number of bytes allocated for **my_buffer**. The **@of** flag is set by **read_proc()** when it encounters an end of file condition. The last argument is not used at this time. In earlier versions of Linux the **get_info()** function was called the **read()** system call. To make the old code compatible with the new declaration, the default value for **read_proc** is **get_info** (meaning that if no **read_proc** is declared, the system will use the **get_info** function instead).

The following code fragment registers and unregisters a module named **my_module** with a supplementary function **my_read**.

```
#include <linux/kernel.h>
#include <linux/module.h>
#include <linux/proc_fs.h>
...
int my_read(char *, char  **, off_t, int, int) {
   ...
}

struct proc_dir_entry my_mod_proc_file = {
   0,
   9,
   "my_module",
   S_IFREG | S_IRUGO,
   1,
   0,
   0,
   BUF_LEN,
   NULL,
   my_read,
   NULL,
   NULL,
   0,
   0
};

int init_module() {
/* proc_root is the root of /proc */
   return proc_register(&proc_root, & my_mod_proc_file);
}

void cleanup_module() {
   proc_unregister(&proc_root, my_mod_proc_file.low_ino);

}
```

Module Installation and Removal

A module is compiled in user space (with appropriate flags), with the result being a file in an executable format. As mentioned in the previous subsection, a module can reference kernel variables, provided that the kernel code has been written so that the variables can be referenced from another module. Similarly, a module can export its own symbols so that other modules can use them.

When you install a module by using **insmod** (see Attacking the Problem that follows), the following happens.

1. The new module is added to the kernel address space (via a kernel function, **create_module()**).
2. Another kernel function, **get_kernel_syms()**, resolves the external symbol references in the module by searching the exported kernel symbols, followed by the list of other modules that have already been loaded. This means that if one module references symbols that are defined in other modules, then the module that defines the symbol must be loaded before the one(s) that reference it.
3. **create_module()** allocates memory space for the module.
4. The module is loaded by the **init_module()** system call. Here is when the symbols defined by this module are exported for use by other modules that might be loaded later.
5. **insmod** calls the **init_module()** function for the newly loaded module.

When the module is to be removed (by using **rmmod**; see Attacking the Problem), **cleanup_module()** is called. Then the space used by the module is released and the virtual addresses unmapped.

Note that if a module has been installed and then another module is installed after it that uses symbols from it, removing the first module will cause an error in the second. Because the second module uses variables declared in the first, the first module must remain loaded as long as the second still needs to reference those variables.

Problem Statement

Design and construct a module that implements a **clock** file in **/proc**. The file should support only the file **read()** operation. When **read()** is called, it should return a single ASCII string with two numerical substrings separated by a single space. For example, it must return a string of the form

```
934380108 184263
```

if the system time variable, **xtime**, was set to

```
xtime.tv_sec = 934380108
xtime.tv_usec = 184263
```

Also provide an application program that demonstrates your module. As one particular test of your program, write a tight loop of the following form.

```
#include <stdio.h>
#include <sys/time.h>
#define N ...

  struct timeval gtodTimes[N];
  char *procClockTimes[N];
  ...
  my_clock = fopen("/proc/...", "r");
  for(i = 0; i < N; i++) {
    gettimeofday(&gtodTimes[i], 0);
    fgets(procClockTime[i], LENGTH, my_clock);
  }
  for(i = 0; i < N; i++) {
    printf("...", gtodTimes[i], procClockTime[i]);
  }
```

Use **gettimeofday()** to determine the apparent resolution of the clock values that you read and of the values read from the kernel variable. Explain why **gettimeofday()** has a much finer resolution than the 10 millisecond time between timer interrupts.

Attacking the Problem

Several small items can cause problems while you are working on this exercise. This section provides hints—and in some cases, vital information—that you will find useful.

The read() *Procedure*

Write a module with the `get_info` field set to reference your read function—**my_read()** in the exercise introduction. You likely will want to reserve your own buffer inside of the **get_info()** routine and then return a pointer to it by using the second parameter. If you do this, you also must assure that after you allocate your buffer, it does not "disappear" when **get_info()**returns. You might want to use the file position parameter to determine how many characters have been read on previous operations.

The End-of-File Condition

The EOF (end-of-file) condition for a file in **/proc** requires some special handling. This is because when the file is read, your read function needs to know that it has encountered the end of the file. To handle this correctly, you must use buffers to read the entire file content into an array. Then you introduce your own **EOF** condition, specifically when the entire buffer has been consumed by read operations (you might want to use the value of the file position that is passed into your **read()** function). For this exercise, you may take liberties with handling the **EOF** condition (to avoid writing a lot of buffer-handling code). For example, you can assume that every read consumes the entire contents of the file (and returns an **EOF**; study the man page for the **read()** system call carefully).

Compiling a Module

Once you have designed and coded your module, you must compile it into an object file suitable for loading by the kernel. You need to instruct the compiler to compile this as kernel code rather than as normal user code; do this by passing the flag _ _KERNEL_ _ to the compiler (notice the two underbar characters preceding and following KERNEL). Use the MODULE compile-time flag to tell the compiler that the file is a module rather than an ordinary file. Use the `-W` compiler option to pass `all` to the loader and the `-c` switch to tell the compiler not to call the linker after it compiles the file.

A command line to compile a file **foo** that contains a module might look like this:

```
gcc –c –Wall –D_ _KERNEL_ _ -DMODULE foo.c
```

The mandrake Kernel distribution requires an additional argument ,–D_Loose_Kernel_Names before it will handle kernel symbols properly.

Installing and Removing a Module

Anyone with superuser permission can install and remove a module from the command line. The command /sbin/insmod <module_name> will perform the work described earlier in the exercise to complete the module installation. So that you can check to ensure that insmod worked, print /proc/modules before you install and then again after. After you have finished using the module, be sure to remove it with /sbin/rmmod.

The Clock Resolution Question

To answer the upcoming clock resolution question, read the Linux source code. Start with .../linux/kernel/time.c, but also be sure to look at .../linux/arch/i386/kernel/time.c.

More Help

More detailed information about modules is available. The main source for this exercise is the article on modules by Ori Pomerantz that appears at

http://metalab.unc.edu/mdw/LDP/lkmpg/mpg.html in the Linux Documentation Project. *Dr. Dobb's Journal* (May 1995) [Welsh, 1995] contains another good description of modules that also can be accessed on the Web at **http://www.ddj.com/articles/1995/9505/9505a/9595a.htm**. Also read Beck, et al. [1998] Chapter 9 for background information, though it does not provide as many details as Pomerantz's article.

five

System Calls

Exercise Goal: You will learn how to make a system call and about reading/writing user space from the kernel by adding a new function to the kernel. The function itself is trivial—it simply returns the value of **xtime**.

Introduction

A system call is the name of a kernel function that is exported for use by user-space programs. In Part 1, Section 3.2, you learned that kernel functions that appear on the system call interface cannot be called directly like an ordinary function. Instead, they must be called indirectly via the trap table. Thus if you write a new kernel function, then you need to create a new entry in the kernel trap table to reference your new function. If user-space programs are to call the program like they do any other system call, then you also need to provide a system call stub function (that contains a trap instruction). Strictly speaking, you can avoid creating the system call stub by using the **system_call()** routine, as explained in Section 5.1.3 that follows.

In the remainder of these introductory remarks, you can read the details of how system calls are set up in the kernel, how a kernel function generally is organized, and how your new kernel function can read and write user-space variables. However, to do the exercise, you will probably need to explore various parts of the kernel source code (use Linux text searching tools to do this, such as **find** and **grep**).

The System Call Linkage

A user-space program calls a system call stub, which contains a trap instruction. As a result, the CPU switches to supervisor mode and begins to execute at a specified location in kernel space. In the i386 hardware, the trap instruction actually causes interrupt **0x80** to occur, with the ISR address pointing at the entry point of the **system_call()** assembler routine (see **arch/i386/kernel/entry.S**). This code uses an argument as the offset into the **sys_call_table** (also defined in **arch/i386/kernel/entry.S**). In the Version 2.2.12 source code, the table is defined as follows.

```
.data
ENTRY(sys_call_table)
   .long SYMBOL_NAME(sys_ni_call)                    /* 0 */
   .long SYMBOL_NAME(sys_exit)
   .long SYMBOL_NAME(sys_fork)
   .long SYMBOL_NAME(sys_read)
   .long SYMBOL_NAME(sys_write)
   .long SYMBOL_NAME(sys_open)                       /* 5 */
   ...
   .long SYMBOL_NAME(sys_signalstack)
   .long SYMBOL_NAME(sys_sendfile)
   .long SYMBOL_NAME(sys_ni_call)
   .long SYMBOL_NAME(sys_ni_call)
   .long SYMBOL_NAME(sys_fork)
   /*
   *NOTE!! This doesn't have to be exact—we just have
   *to make sure we have_enough of the "sys_ni_call"
   *entries. Don't panic if you notice that this hasn't
   *been shrunk every time we add a new system call.
   */
   .rept NR_syscalls_190

   .long SYMBOL_NAME(sys_ni_call)
   .endr
```

Entry 1 contains the address of the **exit()** system call (the kernel function named **sys_exit**), 2 is for **fork()**, and so on.

Under usual processing, the **system_call()** function saves the context of the calling process, checks to be sure that the function number is in range, and then calls the kernel function. The flow of control differs if kernel tracing is enabled by using the **syscall_trace()** function. In this case, **system_call()** invokes **syscall_trace()** before and after the function call.

Part 1, Section 4.1 describes **ret_from_sys_call** processing used to process the bottom halves of ISRs and to call the scheduler. This block of code actually appears in the **arch/i386/kernel/entry.S** file.

In ANSI C programs, the compiler uses function prototypes to check that a function call agrees with the target function header. The function call is compiled only if it provides the correct number and types of arguments according to the prototype definition. The system call linkage is dynamic, meaning that it does not use the compiler's type checking mechanism. Instead, when the kernel function begins to execute, it presumes that the correct number and type of arguments have been placed on the stack when the function is called. In several cases, the kernel function checks for obvious error values (such as, an attempt is made to dereference a null pointer), but you have no assurance that bad parameter values will be caught by the kernel function.

5

Defining the System Call Number

System calls are defined in **sys_call_table**. Thus when you add a new system call, you need to add an entry to the table. You do this by editing the table in the **arch/i386/kernel/entry.S** file, as follows.

```
.data
ENTRY(sys_call_table)
   .long SYMBOL_NAME(sys_ni_call)          /* 0 */
   .long SYMBOL_NAME(sys_exit)
   ...
   .long SYMBOL_NAME(sys_ni_call)          /*190*/
   .long SYMBOL_NAME(sys_my_new_call)      /* 191 */
   ...
   .rept NR_syscalls-191
   .long SYMBOL_NAME (sys_ni_call)
   .endr
```

This editing allows a trap (interrupt 0x80) with an argument of 191 to invoke a new kernel function, **sys_my_new_call()**. Notice that by editing this file, you change your original copy of the kernel source code. Therefore *you should make two copies of the original* **entry.S** *in a user-space directory in which you are developing your solution.* Retain one copy to ensure that you have a copy of the original, and use the other as your experimental version. Edit the experimental version, and copy it into **arch/i386/kernel**, to replace the kernel version. Note, you need superuser (**su**) permission to complete this copy operation because you are placing a new version of the file in the directory that contains the kernel source code.

This new system call can be invoked by using the system call **syscall()**. **syscall()** takes the system call table entry number and arguments as parameters and then traps to the kernel.

To generate a system call stub so that an ordinary C function call will invoke the new system call, you also need to edit the **include/asm/unistd.h** file, as follows, so that it can be used.

```
#define __NR_exit                    1
#define __NR_fork                    2
#define __NR_read                    3
#define __NR_write                   4
#define __NR_open                    5
   ...
#define __NR_sched_get_priority_min  160
#define __NR_sched_rr_get_interval   161
#define __NR_nanosleep               162
#define __NR_mremap                  163
#define __NR_poll                    168
#define __NR_getpmsg                 188
#define __NR_putpmsg                 189
#define __NR_vfork                   190
#define __NR_my_new_call             191
```

Finally, you need to generate the system call stub. These constant definitions are used to create the system call stub function for use with C programs for no arguments, one argument, and so on.

Generating a System Call Stub

The system call stub is generated by using a macro call from a user-space program. Macros are available for generating a stub with zero to five parameters. For example, the macro for generating a stub with two arguments has the form

```
_syscall2(type, name, type1, arg1, type2, arg2);
```

In this macro, **type** is the type of the return value of the system call stub, **name** is the name of the stub, **type1** is the type of the first argument, **arg1**, and **type2** is the type of the second argument, **arg2**. These macros are defined in **include/linux/unistd.h** (which includes the file **include/asm/unistd.h**).

You can generate the stub by making the following macro call in your user program.

```
#include        <linux/unistd.h>
...
/* Generate system call for int foo(char *baz, double bar) */
   _syscall2(int, foo, char *, baz, double, bar);
...
```

Also, a system function, **system_call()**, defined in **arch/i386/entry.S**, can be used to invoke a kernel function (without generating a stub). For example, if the index in the **sys_call_table** for **foo()** is **193**, then you can call the imaginary **foo()** function with the following.

5

```
#include        <sys/syscall.h>
...
   syscall(193, &baz_arg, bar_arg);
...
```

Kernel Function Organization

A kernel function is an ordinary C function compiled to execute in supervisor mode with the rest of the kernel. Other than its header, it requires no particular organization, since it can perform any task that its author chooses.

Consider the simplest kind of kernel function, one that performs some action without accepting a parameter or returning a value (this function is hypothetical, since the kernel contains no such functions).

```
asmlinkage void sys_foo(void) {
   /* Write a value to the console */
}
```

Suppose that **sys_foo()** is a real kernel function (it is not). If a user program calls it by using **system_call()**, then **sys_call_table[NR_foo]** will have an entry and will contain the entry point address for **sys_foo()** (see Part 1, Section 3.2). **NR_foo** will be set in **include/asm/unistd.h**, and the **sys_call_table** entry will be set to the address of **sys_foo()** in **arch/i386/kernel/entry.S**. If a stub had been created, then when a user program called **void foo(void)** the kernel would begin executing at the entry point for **asmlinkage void sys_foo(void)**. After the function finished, the kernel would return to the user program (via the **ret_from_sys_call** sequence).

A slightly more complex function, such as **sys_getuid()**, returns a value, as follows.

```
asmlinkage int sys_getuid(void) {
    return current->uid;
}
```

In this case, the **uid_t getuid()** stub traps to **sys_call_table[NR_getuid]** (that is, to **sys_call_table[24]**, which points to the entry point for **asmlinkage int sys_getuid(void)**). The **current** variable is global to the kernel and references the **struct task_struct** of the currently executing process, so **current->uid** is the user id for the current process. When the **sys_getuid()** function returns, its return value is placed on the user-space stack so that the user process can receive the result.

Now consider a kernel function that takes one or more arguments, such as this one.

```
asmlinkage int sys_close(unsigned int fd) {
    int error;
    struct file *filp;
    struct files_struct *files;

    files = current->files;
    error = -EBADF;
    if(fd < NR_OPEN && (filp = files->fd[fd]) != NULL) {
        ...
    }
    return error;
}
```

The **fd** input parameter is passed to **sys_close()** by the **system_call()** function, simply by passing the argument value that it received on the stack when the system call stub was called. As mentioned in a previous section, kernel functions are called indirectly (via the **sys_call_table**), so the C compiler does not check the type and number of actual parameters. Therefore it is prudent for the kernel function to perform runtime checks on the values that are passed to determine whether they are reasonable. (**sys_close()** does not check **fd** before using it). Thus if it gets a bad parameter, then it will attempt to reference an element of the **files->fd** array. However, it passes **fd** on to other routines that can check it before real harm is done.) If you write a kernel function and do *not* check the parameters prior to using them, you might crash the system.

Referencing User-Space Memory Locations

Your function might have a call-by-reference argument in which the kernel function needs to write information into a user-space address. That is, the argument is a pointer to a variable that was declared in the calling function. Kernel functions execute in the kernel data segment (see Part 1, Section 5), so the memory translation mechanism does not allow a process that is executing in kernel space to write into a user segment without changing the state of the protection mechanism. To read or write user-space memory from the kernel, the kernel first should check to see whether the address is legitimately defined in the user virtual address space by using the following function:

```
verify_area(int type, const void *addr, unsigned long size);
```


This function checks the validity of a read operation (**type** is set to VERIFY_READ) or a write operation (**type** is set to VERIFY_WRITE). The **addr** argument specifies the address to be verified, and the **size** argument is the number of bytes in the block of memory to be verified. **verify_area()** returns zero if the operation is permitted on the memory area, and nonzero otherwise. Following is a typical code fragment to verify the kernel's ability to read a memory block named **buf** of length **buf_len**.

```
flag = verify_area(VERIFY_READ, buf, buf_len);
if(flag) {
        // Error—unable to read buf
}
```

"If a block of user-space memory is to be written by the kernel, it is necessary to use the **put_user(int x, void *ptr)** function to write the information. The x parameter is the number of bytest to be written, and the ptr pointer is the address to be written. The **verify_area()** and **put_user()** function prototypes and related manifest constants are defined in **include/asm/uaccess.h**, so you must have **#include <asm/uaccess.h>** in your program that references user memory."

Problem Statement

Part A

Design and implement a new kernel function, **pedagogictime()**, that returns the current system time via a call by reference argument. If the flag argument is

TRUE, then your kernel function should also print the current system time on **stdout**. Your function should have the following prototype:

```
int pedagogictime(int flag, struct timeval *curent_time);
```

Your new function should be almost the same as **gettimeofday()**, though it should ignore the time zone parameter and have the flag to control printing the time to the console. Your function should return **TRUE** if the function succeeds, and **FALSE** otherwise.

Part B

Write a user-space program to test **pedagogictime()**. The program also should create a stub for your new system call function.

Attacking the Problem

The Kernel printk() *Function*

When writing kernel code, you often will want to print messages to **stdout** as you develop and debug it. (Note that if your program is using **printk()**, then the process that executes the code must be running with root's user id.) Of course, software that implements the kernel does not have the **stdio** library available to it; thus you cannot necessarily use **printf()** to write to **stdout**. Kernel programmers decided many years ago that they could not live without a print statement and also that they did not want to rely on **printf()**'s working in the kernel, so they developed their own kernel version of **printf()**, called **printk()**. **printk()** behaves the same as **printf()**; it actually is implemented by using **printf()** in Linux (see **include/linux/kernel.h**). If **printk()** is not printing to your console, you can find the messages embedded in the system log — **/var/log/messages**.

Organizing a Solution

You need to learn many small details in order to get your first kernel function to work properly. So you are advised to use a conservative, incremental strategy for developing your first kernel function. Here are some guidelines.

- For your first debug version, focus on getting the system call interface to work properly. It should not take any arguments or return any values. Instead, simply do a **printk()** within the function body so that you can see that you have successfully implemented a complete function in the kernel and that the system call interface is working properly.

- Next, create a dummy version that passes an argument into the kernel (call-by-value) but that does not expect the kernel to write anything back into the user space.
- Your third version should be a simple call-by-reference call. You will have to use **verify_area()** to reference user space, **memcpy_fromfs()** to read information from the user space, and **memcpy_tofs()** to write data when it is returned by reference.

Here is a code skeleton for your kernel function.

```
#include <sys/time.h>
#include <linux/kernel.h>
#include <linux/mm.h>
#include &ltasm/uaccess.h>

asmlinkage int sys_pedagogictime(int flag, struct timeval *thetime)
{
   int write_failed;

/* Get the system time from the exported kernel variable, xtime.
 * Reading xtime will probably not cause a race condition
 * with another part of the kernel, but you will be conservative and
 * block interrupts while reading the shared variable.
 */
   cli();                        /* Disable interrupts */
      ...
   sti();                        /* Enable interrupts */

/* Load encoded time into the time */

   write_failed = verify_area(VERIFY_WRITE, ...);
   if(write_failed){
      printk("skelcall: Cannot write into user space\n");
      return;
   }
   ...
/* Print the time if the flag is TRUE */
   printk(...);

   return 0;
}
```

After you complete your implementation of **sys_pedagogictime()**, you can put it in **time.c**. Be sure to save the original so that you can restore it after you have completed this exercise. Alternatively, you can put the new function in your own new file. In this case, you will need to edit the **Makefile** in the kernel directory in which the new file is placed. Add the name of the new file to the O_OBJS list in the **Makefile**.

Rebuilding the Kernel

Ultimately, the kernel is just another program that must be compiled and then linked into its runtime environment in preparation for execution. Unlike other programs, however, its environment is determined by the *logical configuration*—the configuration dictated by the hardware and the system administrator's parameter choices. Thus it cannot depend on the existence of other software in its runtime environment.

Software engineers have spent many years refining the technique for building UNIX. Linux uses those accumulated tools in its *build environment*. Because you are using a running Linux machine that has the source code, the build environment should already be in place on the machine (it is installed with the source code).

The build procedure takes place from the base directory of the Linux source, typically in **/usr/src/linux**, though your **linux** source directory might be installed elsewhere. **/usr/src/linux** is the source subtree described in Exercise 3. The **linux** directory contains the directories that have source code, include files, and library routines. It also includes the files **README** and **Makefile**. You should read the **README** file, even if you cannot understand all of it at this point. It provides information regarding, for example, where the build environment should be installed (in **/usr/src**) and what to do if things break badly while you are doing kernel work.

The **Makefile** in the **linux** root directory is the top-level makefile for building the Linux kernel. As you might expect, it is relatively complex, as it is designed to automate most of the details of building and installing a new kernel. It does this by invoking various other tools and by using other makefiles in subdirectories. In a properly installed build environment, the kernel is rebuilt with only five commands (executed by a superuser):

```
# make clean
# make <config_opt>
# make depend
# make
```

make <boot_opt>

All of these commands use **linux/Makefile** to create a new kernel and store it in **linux/arch/<arch_type>/boot/zImage**.

Next, you will examine each command more closely. Assume that <arch_type> is **i386**.

- **make clean**: Removes old relocatable object files and other temporary files so that your build will have a clean environment in which it can be built.
- make **<config_opt>**: Defines the logical environment in which the new kernel should exist. Generally, the **<config_opt>** parameter can be set to **config**. In this case, **make** will run a bash script named **Configure**, which reads a configuration file, **linux/arch/i386/config.in**. Then it queries the system builder regarding kernel options to be installed in the new kernel. You usually will not want to change the **config.in** file, though you should inspect it to get an idea of how it works. (If you decide to change the **config.in** file, you will need to dig deeper into the tools and configurations than you will in this manual. Start your exploration by reading Section 2.3 of Beck et al. [1998].) To use the existing **config.in**, as well as the default options for making the kernel configuration, use the **oldconfig** value for **<config_opt>** rather than the **config** value for this step. This part of **Makefile** creates **linux/.config** and **linux/include/linux/autoconf.h** files. The **.config** file captures the responses from the interactive dialog that determines the exact configuration; if you run **make config** again, it will use the responses from **.config**. The **autoconf.h** file is a header file that is used to invoke compile-time options that correspond to the choices made in the interactive dialog with **make**.
- **make depend**: Many files must be compiled and in a particular order. **make depend** creates a file, **linux/.depend**, that specifies the compile-order dependencies. Specifying dependencies is a simple, but laborious, task that is automated in the **depend** option of **Makefile**.
- **make**: Compiles all of the kernel source code, producing **linux/vmlinux**, the kernel executable file. If you have written new kernel code, or modified existing files, then this step will compile that code (therefore this is probably where you will encounter your first problems in building a new kernel). This is the most complex part of **Makefile**. It invokes **make** on all of the subdirectories and then ultimately links the results together to form the kernel executable.

- make <boot_opt>: Compresses the **linux/vmlinux** file to create a bootable kernel image and installs it in **linux/arch/i386/boot/zImage**. This can be done with **<boot_opt>** set to **boot**. To make a copy of the bootable kernel image on a floppy disk, use **zdisk** instead of **boot** as the <boot_opt> parameter. In Version 2.2.x, a kernel that you generate might be too large. If you set **<boot_opt>** to **bzdisk**, you should be able to generate a boot floppy disk.

Performing the steps to build a new kernel is relatively easy because the detailed work has been encapsulated in the **linux/Makefile**, the subdirectory makefiles, and the configuration files. Before you attempt to create a new bootable kernel, be sure to save **zImage** so that you can restore it when needed. See the README file in the **linux** directory for more information.

Leaving a Clean Environment

You will be changing the files and file contents in kernel directories. After you finish a debugging session, you should always restore the environment to the state in which you found it. If you begin to work in an environment and it seems not to be correct, then someone might have polluted it. If you attempt to work in a polluted environment, then you will probably have trouble with your solution. You will have to restore the environment to its original state before you can do your own work.

Shared Memory

Exercise Goal: You will learn how the existing System V shared memory facility is implemented in the kernel. Then, you will modify the standard kernel so that it uses a dynamic data structure for managing memory segments.

Introduction

Shared memory is a common block of memory that is mapped into the address spaces of two or more processes. Information that a process writes to a location in the shared memory can be read with a memory read operation in any other process that is using the shared memory. Within an individual computer—either uniprocessor or multiprocessor—shared memory is usually the fastest way for two processes to share information.

Linux's shared memory feature is derived from the form of shared memory introduced in System V UNIX. Even though the shared memory mechanism allows multiple processes to map a common memory segment into their own address spaces—the segment is logically a part of the memory manager—it was designed and implemented in System V UNIX as a part of the IPC (interprocess communication) mechanism.

The Shared Memory API

You can use shared memory to allow any process to dynamically define a new block of memory that is independent of the address space created for the process before it began to execute. As explained in Part 1of this manual, every Linux process is created with a large virtual address space, only a portion of which is used to reference the compiled code, static data, stack, and heap. The remaining addresses in the virtual address space are initially unused. A new block of shared memory, once defined, is mapped into a block of the unused virtual addresses, after which the process can read and write the shared memory as if it were ordinary memory. Of course, more than one process can map the shared memory block into its own address space, so code segments that read or write shared memory are normally considered to be *critical sections*.

The following four system calls define the full kernel interface to support shared memory.

```
#include <sys/types.h>
#include <sys/ipc.h>
#include <sys/shm.h>
int shmget(key_t key, int size, int shmflg);
void *shmat(int shmid, char *shmaddr, int shmflg);
void *shmdt(char *shaddr);
int shmctl(int shmid, int cmd, struct shmid_ds *buf);
```

- **shmget()** creates the shared memory block.
- **shmat()** maps an existing shared memory block into a process's address space.
- **shmdt()** removes (unmaps) a shared memory block from the process's address space.
- **shmctl()** is a general-purpose function (in the style of **ioctl()**) used to perform all other commands to the shared memory block.

To create a new block of shared memory, the process must call **shmget()**. If **shmget()** successfully creates a new block of memory, then it returns a *shared memory identifier* of type **int**. The shared memory identifier is a handle into a kernel data structure. The next section discusses how shared memory is implemented, illustrating that it is actually an index into a kernel array. If **shmget()** can create the new block of shared memory, then the kernel array whose index is returned references an instance of the **struct shmid_kernel** data structure, which includes a field, as follows.

```
struct shmid_kernel
{
   shmid_ds u;
   ...
};
```

The arguments to **shmget()** are **key_t key**, **int size**, and **int shmflg**. The **size** argument specifies the size of the new block of memory. All memory allocation operations are in terms of pages. That is, if a process requests 1 byte of memory, then the memory manager allocates a full page (PAGE_SIZE = 4,096 bytes on i386 machines). Thus the size of the new shared memory block will be the value of the **size** argument rounded up to the next multiple of the page size. A **size** of 1 to 4,096 results in a 4K (one-page) block, 4,097 to 8,192 results in an 8K (two-page) block, and so on.

The **key** argument may be either the key of an existing memory block, **0**, or IPC_PRIVATE. When it is IPC_PRIVATE, the **shmget()** call creates a new block of shared memory. When it is **0**, and the IPC_CREAT flag is set in the **shmflg** argument, then **shmflg** also can cause a new block to be created.[1] A process that wants to reference a shared memory block that was created by another process (such as a parent or server) usually will obtain the **struct shmid_kernel** reference from the creator. However, it also can set the **key** argument to the **key** value of an existing memory block. If **key**'s value is so set, and **shmflg** is set with IPC_CREAT | IPC_EXCL, then **shmget()** will fail. **shmflg** also must define the access permissions for user, group, and world accesses to the memory block as its lower 9 bits (by using the same bit pattern as for file protection).

When a shared memory region is successfully created, **shmget()** returns an integer reference to its **struct shmid_ds**.

```
struct shmid_ds {
   struct ipc_perm shm_perm;        /* operation perms */
   int shm_segsz;                   /* size of segment (bytes) */
   __kernel_time_t shm_atime;       /* last attach time */
   __kernel_time_t shm_dtime;       /* last detach time */
   __kernel_time_t shm_ctime;       /* last change time */
   __kernel_ipc_pid_t shm_cpid;     /* pid of creator */
   __kernel_ipc_pid_t shm_lpid;     /* pid of last operator */
   unsigned short shm_nattch;       /* no. of current attaches */
   unsigned short shm_unused;       /* compatibility */
```

[1] The **shmflg** argument is a set of single-bit flags. Setting multiple flags in **shmflg** involves combining them with a logical OR operator ("|") and then assigning them to **shmflg**.

6

```
    void  shm_unused2;        /* ditto – used by DIPC */
    void  shm_unused3;        /* unused */
};
```

You use the **struct ipc_perm shm_perm** field to define the owner of the shared memory block and the permissions for other processes to use the block. It contains fields in which to specify the owner's user and group ids, the creator's user and group ids, the access mode (read or write), and the key value for the memory block. (The **man** page for **shmget()** describes the **shmid_ds** and **ipc_perm** structure fields.)

The **void *shmat(int shmid, char *shmaddr, int shmflg)** system call maps the memory block into the calling process's address space. The **shmid** argument is the result returned by the **shmget()** call that created the block. The **shmaddr** pointer is the virtual address to which the first location in the shared memory block should be mapped. If the calling process does not wish to choose the address to which the memory block will be mapped, it should pass a value of **0** for **shmaddr**. **shmaddr**'s value should be aligned with a page boundary. If **shmaddr** is specified, and **SHM_RND** is asserted in **shmflg**, then the address will be rounded down to a multiple of the **SHMLBA** constant. **shmflg** is used in the same way as the corresponding flag in **shmget()**, that is, to assert a number of different 1-bit flags to the **shmat()** system call. In addition to asserting the **SHM_RND** flag, the calling process can assert **SHM_RDONLY** to attach the memory block so that it can be only read, and not also written.

When a process finishes using a shared memory block, it calls **void *shmdt(char *shaddr)**, where **shaddr** is the address used to attach the memory block. The kernel then updates the corresponding **struct shmid_kernel** to reflect that this process is no longer using the memory block.

The final shared memory call is **int shmctl(int shmid, int cmd, struct shmid_ds *buf)**. This call performs control operations on the shared memory block descriptor. The **shmid** argument identifies the shared memory block, and the **cmd** argument specifies the command to be applied to the descriptor. If **cmd** is set to **IPC_STAT**, then the calling process must provide a buffer, **buf**, that is at least as large as a **struct shmid_kernel**. **shmctl()** fills in the current values of the **shmid_ds** and returns them in **buf**. If **cmd** is set to **IPC_SET**, then the data structure will be updated, provided that the calling process is an owner or creator (or has superuser permission). A call with **cmd** set to **IPC_RMID** causes the memory segment to be destroyed (it will not otherwise be destroyed, even when no process is attached to it). A superuser can lock or unlock the block.

Here is a simple example of a parent process that creates a shared memory block and then creates a child process that also can use the block.

```
#include    <sys/types.h>
#include    <sys/ipc.h>
#include    <sys/sem.h>
#include    <sys/wait.h>

#define     SHM_SIZE   ...

void run_child(int, int);

int main() {
   int pid, shm_handle, status;
   char *my_shm_ptr;

/* Create the shared memory */
   shm_handle = shmget(IPC_PRIVATE, SHM_SIZE, IPC_CREAT |
      0x1C0);
   if(shm_handle == -1) {
            printf("Shared memory creation failed\n");
            exit(0);
   }

/* Start the child */
         if((pid = fork()) == 0) {
                  run_child(childNum, shm_handle);
                  exit(0);
   }
/* Do work, share results with child via shared memory */
   my_shm_ptr = (char *) shmat(shm_handle, 0, 0);
   if(my_shm_ptr == (char *) -1) {
            printf("Shared memory attach failed\n");
            exit(0);
   }
   ...
/* Wait for the children to finish */
   wait(&status);
   shmctl(shm_handle, IPC_RMID, 0);   /* Remove shared
```

6

```
        memory */
    printf("Parent: Terminating\n");
}

void run_child(int me, int shm_handle) {
    char *my_shm_ptr;
    int i;
    unsigned int shm_flag  = 0;

/* Attach the shared memory */
    my_shm_ptr = (char *) shmat(shm_handle, 0, 0);
    if(my_shm_ptr == (char *) -1) {
     printf("Shared memory attach failed\n");
     exit(0);
    }
 *(my_shm_ptr+64+i) = ...; /* Write shmem location i */
 ... = my_shm_ptr+i);              /* Read shmem location i */
 ...
}
```

The Implementation

Shared memory is implemented entirely within the file **ipc/shm.c**. The four system calls described in the previous section appear in this file.

```
asmlinkage int sys_shmget (key_t key, int size, int shmflg)
asmlinkage int sys_shmat (int shmid, char *shmaddr, int shmflg,
ulong *raddr)
asmlinkage int sys_shmdt (char *shmaddr)
asmlinkage int sys_shmctl (int shmid, int cmd, struct shmid_ds
      *buf)
```

The **shm_init()** function initializes the shared memory data structures. It is called by **ipc_init**, which is called by **start_kernel()** during the general startup procedure.

```
void __init shm_init (void)
{
    int id;

    for (id = 0; id < SHMMNI; id++)
        shm_segs[id] = (struct shmid_kernel *) IPC_UNUSED;
    shm_tot = shm_rss = shm_seq = max_shmid = used_segs = 0;
```

```
    shm_lock = NULL;
    return;
}
```

The shared segment table, **shm_segs[]**, is the kernel data structure that is filled in whenever a new shared memory block (or segment) is created by **shmget()**. The **shmid** value returned by **shmget()** is the index into **shm_segs[]**. This routine initializes the array by setting each entry in the static array to IPC_UNUSED. It then initializes various global variables that represent the number of segments, and so on.

The **sys_shmget()** system call is shown next in its entirety.

```
asmlinkage int sys_shmget (key_t key, int size, int shmflg)
{
    struct shmid_kernel *shp;
    int err, id = 0;

    down(&current->mm->mmap_sem);
    lock_kernel();          // New in Version 2.2 for SMP support
    if (size < 0 || size > shmmax) {
        err = -EINVAL;
    } else if (key == IPC_PRIVATE) {
        err = newseg(key, shmflg, size);
    } else if ((id = findkey(key)) == -1) {
        if (!(shmflg & IPC_CREAT))
            err = -ENOENT;
        else
            err = -EACCES;
        else
            err = (int) shp->u.shm_perm.seq * SHMNI + id;
    }
    unlock_kernel();        // New in Version 2.2 for SMP support
    up(&current->mm->mmap_sem);
    return err;
        return newseg(key, shmflg, size);
    }
}
```

Most of the work is done in the **newseg()** function. Notice that when the key is set to IPC_PRIVATE, the system call only checks to see that the size is positive and not too large and then it calls **newseg()**. If another option is chosen, then the **findseq()** function is called to determine whether the segment currently exists.

An interesting race condition can happen between **findseq()** and **newseg()** that is resolved by their code using the value of the **shm_segs[i]** entry. See the code for these functions in **ipc/shm.c** and further discussion in the following Attacking the Problem.

The **shmat()** system call maps a shared memory segment into the calling process's address space. Following is a skeleton of the code. (Most of the error checking has been removed so that you can focus on the function's essential parts.)

```
asmlinkage int sys_shmat (int shmid,
                    char *shmaddr, int shmflg, ulong *raddr)
{
   struct shmid_kernel *shp;
   struct vm_area_struct *shmd;
   int err = -EINVAL;
   unsigned int id;
   unsigned long addr;
   unsigned long len;

   shp = shm_segs[id = (unsigned int) shmid % SHMMNI];

   if (!(addr = (ulong) shmaddr)) {
      if (shmflg & SHM_REMAP)
         goto out;
      err = -ENOMEM;
      addr = 0;
   again:
      if (!(addr = get_unmapped_area(addr, shp->u.shm_segsz)))
         goto out;
      if (addr & (SHMLBA - 1)) {
         addr = (addr + (SHMLBA-1)) & ~(SHLBA – 1);
         goto again;
      }
   } else if (addr & (SHMLBA-1)) {
      if (shmflg & SHM_RND)
         addr &=~(SHLBA-1);       /* round down */
      else
         goto out;
```

```
    }
    /*
     *Check if addr exceeds TAX_SIZE (from do_mmap)
     */
    len = PAGE_SIZE*shp->shm_npages;
    err = -EINVAL;
    if (addr >= TASK_SIZE || len > TASK_SIZE
                    || addr > TASK_SIZE - len)
        goto out;
/*
 * If shm segment goes below stack, make sure there is some
 * space left for the stack to grow (presently 4 pages).
 */
    if (addr < current->mm->start_stack &&
        addr > current->mm->start_stack –
                PAGE_SIZE*(shp->shm_npages + 4))
    {
        goto out;
    }

    err = -EACCES;
    if (ipcperms(&shp->shm_perm, shmflg &
                SHM_RDONLY ? S_IRUGO : S_IRUGO|S_IWUGO))
        goto out;
        err = -EIDRM;
    if (shp->u.shm_perm.seq != (unsigned int) shmid / SHMMNI)
        gotoOUT;

    shmd = kmem_cache_alloc(vm_area_cachep, shmd);
    shmd->vm_pte = SWP_ENTRY(SHM_SWP_TYPE, id);
    shmd->vm_start = addr;
    shmd->vm_end = addr + shp->shm_npages * PAGE_SIZE;
    shmd->vm_mm = current->mm;
    shmd->vm_page_prot =
        (shmflg & SHM_RDONLY) ? PAGE_READONLY : PAGE_SHARED;
    shmd->vm_flags = VM_SHM | VM_MAYSHARE | VM_SHARED
            | VM_MAYREAD | VM_MAYEXEC | VM_READ | VM_EXEC
            | ((shmflg & SHM_RDONLY) ? 0 : VM_MAYWRITE | VM_WRITE);
    shmd->vm_file = NULL;
    shmd->vm_offset = 0;
    shmd->vm_ops = &shm_vm_ops;
```

```
    shp->shm_nattch++; /* prevent destruction */

    insert_attach(shp,shmd); /* insert shmd into shp->attaches */

    shp->u.shm_lpid = current->pid;
    shp->u.shm_atime = CURRENT_TIME;

    *raddr = addr;
    err = 0;
out:
    unlock_kernel();
    up(&current->mm->mmap_sem);
    return err;
}
```

The routine first looks up the **struct shmid_ds** for the given id, **shmid**, saving the pointer in **shp**. It then checks **shmaddr**, adjusting it as required (page or SHMLBA boundary). Next, the segment is checked to determine whether it will fit into the virtual address space, starting at **shmaddr**. In the next part of the code, the process descriptor (**current**) is checked to determine whether the block interferes with the stack. If permissions are acceptable, then the function allocates a new instance of a virtual memory structure, **struct vm_area_struct *shmd**, and fills it in so that it indicates that a shared memory block has been added to the virtual address space.

A currently attached shared memory segment is released by the **shmdt()** system call, shown as follows.

```
asmlinkage int sys_shmdt (char *shmaddr)
{
    struct vm_area_struct *shmd, *shmdnext;

    down(&current->mm->mmap_sem);
    lock_kernel();
    for (shmd = current->mm->mmap; shmd; shmd = shmdnext) {
      shmdnext = shmd->vm_next;
      if (shmd->vm_ops == &shm_vm_ops
        && shmd->vm_start - shmd->vm_offset == (ulong) shmaddr)
          do_munmap(shmd->vm_start, shmd->vm_end -
          shmd->vm_start);
    }
```

```
    unlock_kernel();
    up(&current->mm->mmap_sem);
    return 0;
}
```

This code steps through the **struct vm_area_struct** instances, which are added to the **current->mm-mmap** list by the **insert_attach()** call in **shmat()**. It then releases the block that contains **shmaddr**. The fields in the **for** statement qualify as "tricky code."

The final system call is the **shmctl()** function. The following code skeleton shows only the code that implements the IPC_STAT command (some of the error checking code was removed).

```
asmlinkage int sys_shmctl (int shmid, int cmd, struct shmid_ds
*buf)
{
    struct shmid_ds tbuf;
    struct shmid_kernel *shp;
    struct ipc_perm *ipcp;
    int id, err;

    lock_kernel();

    switch (cmd) { /* replace with proc interface ? */
    case IPC_INFO:
        ...
    case SHM_INFO:
        ...
    case SHM_STAT:
        ...
    }

    shp = shm_segs[id = (unsigned int) shmid % SHMMNI];
    ipcp = &shp->u.shm_perm;

    switch (cmd) {
    case SHM_UNLOCK:
            ...
    case SHM_LOCK:
            ...
    case IPC_STAT:
```

```
            err = -EACCES;
            if (ipcperms (ipcp, S_IRUGO))
                goto out;
            err = - EFAULT;
            if (copy_to_user (buf, &shp->u, sizeof(shp->u)))
                goto out;
            break;
        case IPC_SET:
            ...
        case IPC_RMID:
            ...
        default:
            return -EINVAL;
    }
    err = 0;
out:
    unlock_kernel();
    return err;
}
```

After checking the input parameters, **shmctl()** uses a **switch** statement to check for commands that the **ipcs(8)** shell command uses (IPC_INFO, SHM_STAT, and SHM_INFO). Next, it retrieves the **struct shmid_ds** for the specified **shmid** and enters a second **switch** statement that contains a case for IPC_STAT. It then determines whether the calling process has permission to read the status and permission to write the result back into the user space (in the area referenced by the **buf** parameter). Finally, it copies the data into a temporary buffer; the data is then copied into user space.

This introduction to memory management did not discuss how the memory manager implements virtual memory. That is the main topic of the next exercise.

Problem Statement

Part A

Write a program that creates and uses — reads and writes — multiple blocks of shared memory.

Part B

The file **ipc/shm.c** implements the normal version of System V shared memory. It uses a static array, **shm_segs[]**, to keep track of each shared memory segment that is created. UNIX kernels traditionally have used static arrays for multirecord data structures (for example, the process descriptors are usually implemented as a static array). Your task is to modify the existing version of **ipc/shm.c** so that it uses a list, rather than a static array, to keep track of shared memory segments. This is a pedagogic exercise rather than an actual improvement to the kernel. That is, although it allows an arbitrary number of memory segments to be created, list manipulation will be much slower than array dereferencing would be.

Attacking the Problem

First, you should write a simple driver program that uses the standard form of shared memory. Doing this will help you to understand how the facility works, as well as provide you with a program for testing your new version of **ipc/shm.c**. Be sure that the test program uses multiple shared memory segments.

You can edit and compile your new version of **ipc/shm.c** in user space (in your own development directory). Make two copies of **ipc/shm.c** in your development directory, one to be the original version that is stored in the Linux source tree and the other to be your new version. Study **ipc/shm.c** carefully to understand how it interacts with the **shm_segs[]** array.

You will discover an interesting race condition that is resolved by using special pointers in the **shm_segs[]** array (the **IPC_NOID** and **IPC_UNUSED** pointers). The race condition can occur if **findkey()** is called when **newseg()** is in progress. That is, the data structure that **newseg()** creates may be only partially filled when **findkey()** runs; it might then return an **id** for an inconsistent data structure. The code uses **IPC_NOID** as a flag to block **findkey()** if it begins to run when **newseg()** is in progress. **newseg()** wakes the blocked **findkey()** process, if it became blocked on the **IPC_NOID** value for the segment pointer. Now read the code to see exactly how this works. When you modify the code, you will probably remove this race condition. However, you will add a new one, linking/unlinking a node in a list. Of course, you will need to protect this new race condition.

Design your list, and modify the code in your experimental version of **ipc/shm.c** in your development directory. Compile the code by using the compile flags **–D__kernel__** and **–Wall**.

In designing your solution, you need to find all parts of the existing code that reference the **struct shmid_kernel shm_segs[]** data structure and then change those references so that they access the individual data structures from a list rather than from an array. First, observe that the existing file allocates **shm_segs[]** as a static, global array:

```
static struct shmid_kernel *shm_segs[SHMMNI];
```

You need to replace this declaration with your new list descriptor—a static variable that points to the list of **struct shmid_kernel** entries. Next, you need to find each place at which the code references the array and ensure that it references a list entry. You will probably have to change the **shm.h** file as well (it is located in **include/linux/shm.h**).

You should not change any parts of **ipc/shm.c** that do not manipulate **shm_segs[]**. You should change only the way that the **struct shmid_kernel** data structure is retrieved from the collection of such data structures.

Once your code compiles successfully, and you are sure that your solution is correct, place your new version of **shm.c** into the Linux source directory, replacing the original **ipc/shm.c**. You will have copies of your experimental version and the original version in your development directory. Recompile the kernel, and make a new boot floppy disk. Test your code by rebooting from the floppy disk and running your test code that worked with the original version of **ipc/shm.c**.

seven

Virtual Memory

Exercise Goal: You will study how Linux implements virtual memory. A general architecture-independent memory model is the basis of all Linux virtual memory implementations, though any specific implementation depends on the particular hardware platform. This discussion focuses on the i386- implementation. The introduction explains the memory manager design. You also will study the code details so that you can instrument the virtual memory code to detect the rate at which the system is incurring page faults.

Introduction

Part 1, Section 4 introduced the operation of the virtual memory system. Briefly, each process is created with a 4GB virtual address space, 1GB of which is mapped to the kernel for its use (this enables a user program to reference kernel addresses, though it does not give the program the *permission* to do so). No address can be used until it is mapped. The loader maps the addresses generated by the compiler and linkage editor into the lower 3GB user portion of the virtual address space. When a process is defined, the contents of virtual addresses are defined by mapping information to specific blocks of virtual addresses; unused portions of the virtual address space also can be mapped at runtime. The mapped portions of the virtual address space are divided into equal-sized pages, 4K per page. The contents of mapped pages can be in the swap space (either a file or disk).

Not all virtual address contents are defined when the virtual address is defined. For example, the compiler can cause space to be reserved but not initialized; examples of this are the space for the stack and heap. Mapped blocks of the virtual address space that have no initial content definition are called *anonymous memory blocks*. They are handled a little differently than those blocks whose contents are defined in the swap space.

Figure 2.7 summarizes the components of the virtual memory manager. The process is ready to execute once the information that is located in the swap space has been mapped into the virtual address space (see **do_mmap()** in the figure). To fetch its first instruction, the process references the part of the virtual address space that contains the entry point for the program. If the page address translation hardware detects that the page is not loaded, then it will cause a page fault interrupt. The kernel interrupt processing mechanism typically fields the page fault interrupt, performs standard processing (see Part 1, Section 3), and then calls the page fault handler (**do_page_fault()**). This handler is responsible for determining if the virtual address reference is within the virtual address space and, if it is, for retrieving the missing page from the swap space.

Loading the page requires that the page fault handler find a place to load the page in the primary memory, swap the page into the primary memory, and

Figure 2.7
Virtual Memory Components

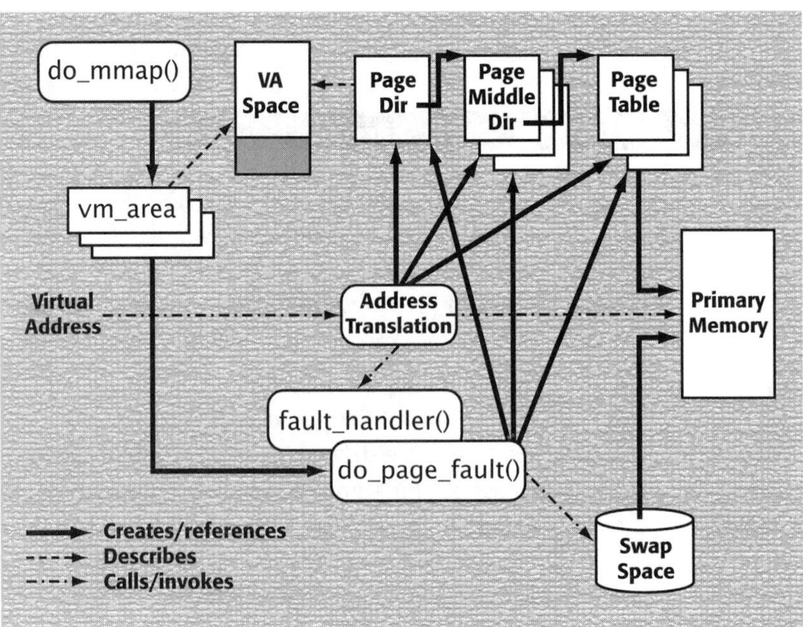

then update the page directory, page middle directory, and page table. After the page is loaded—the page fault handling has been completed—the instruction that caused the interrupt is executed again, this time assured that the missing page has been loaded. As the process continues to execute, it references different pages that contain its program as well as the data on which the program is executing. Each time that a process references a virtual address in a page not currently loaded in the primary memory, a page fault occurs.

The Virtual Address Space

When a process is created, it inherits a 32-bit (4GB) virtual address space from its parent. It uses locations **0x0** to **0xBFFFFFFF** when it executes in user space and locations **0xC0000000** to **0xFFFFFFFF** when it executes in supervisor mode. The last 1GB references kernel components, so this portion of the address space has the same mapping for every process. In terms of the architecture-independent model introduced in Part 1, Section 5, every process uses the same page table to reference the addresses used by the kernel (meaning that the page middle directory entry for this part of the address space references the same page table in every process).

A virtual address includes a segment, specified by a *segment selector*, and an offset within the segment. The kernel addresses and user space addresses have different segment names. Each segment is subdivided into segments that hold

data (that can be read or written) and code (that can only be executed and read). User code has the segment selector implicitly set to **user**, so the code provides only offsets within the user segment. Each segment has its own page table (the collection of page tables for the process is kept in the page middle directory). The memory translation mechanism can then prevent the user-space process from referencing locations in the kernel segment, and it warns the kernel when it is referencing user-space locations (to prevent inadvertent reading or writing). Various macros are provided to manipulate the different segments defined in **include/asm/segment.h**. The **put_user_byte/word/long()** and **get_user_byte/word/long()** macros allow kernel-space software to bypass the protection mechanism to write or read 1 byte, 2 bytes (**word**), or 4 bytes (**long**) in a user segment. The file also defines other macros to copy and manipulate segment contents.

The organizations of the use-space segments are specific to the version of Linux and the loader format (**a.out**, COFF, or ELF). Figure 2.8 illustrates the layout of ELF in Version 2.0 [Beck, et al., 1998]. The heap grows in increasing address direction above the BSS area, whereas the stack grows toward lower addresses from the arguments and environment. Shared C libraries (each a group of

Figure 2.8
User-Space Format

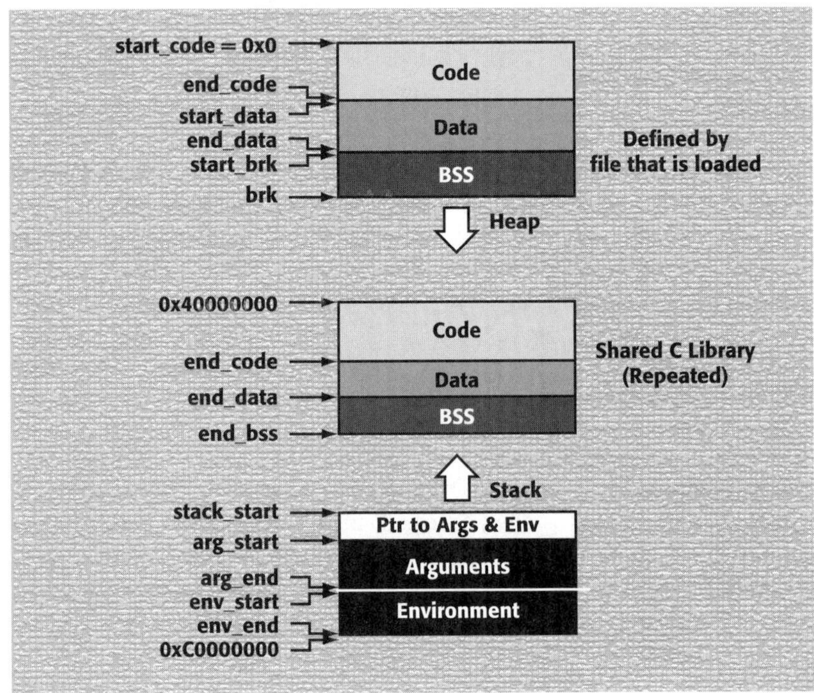

code, data, and BSS) are mapped into the address space at location 0x40000000 toward higher addresses. Whenever the loader (or any form of an exec() system call) is run, the portion of the address space between start_code and brk is (re)mapped so that the new memory image is bound to specific virtual addresses. These virtual addresses are saved in the mm field of the process descriptor by the loader.

```
struct task_struct {
   ...
/* Memory management info */
   struct mm_struct *mm;
   ...
   };

struct mm_struct {
   ...
   unsigned long start_code, end_code, start_data, end_data;
   unsigned long start_brk, brk, start_stack;
   unsigned long arg_start, arg_end, env_start, env_end;
   ...
```

```
};
```

The kernel function **do_mmap()** in **mm/mmap.c** is the function that actually performs the mapping, as follows.

```
unsigned long do_mmap(
    struct file * file,
    unsigned long addr,
    unsigned long len,
    unsigned long prot,
    unsigned long flags,
    unsigned long off
);
```

The **file** parameter identifies a file in loadable format of length **len**. If the target address, **addr**, and the length, **len**, are compatible with the address space, then **do_mmap()** will relocate the file so that its contents are bound to virtual addresses **addr** to **addr+len**. The **prot**, **flags**, and **off** parameters specify various options to control the binding (read-only access, write access, and so on). No direct system call is made to map portions of the address space—only indirect calls via normal calls such as **exec()**.

The **brk()** system call, too, can cause addresses to be mapped. **brk()** extends the size of the virtual address space being used by the process. The value representing this size is set at load time by the loader or **exec()** and can be modified at runtime by **brk()**. When **brk()** (see **mm/mmap.c**) is called, it performs various error checking and then calls **do_mmap()**.

Virtual Memory Areas

The memory manager must be able to accommodate dynamic mapping without allocating space in the various page tables (since the space might never be used even though it has been mapped). Each time that a new block of information is mapped into the virtual memory, the memory manager determines if it will overlap some existing memory addresses before it actually performs the mapping. It also must check several other things for the new block, for example its protections. Further, some of these blocks are shared among address spaces, meaning that they must be treated differently than the other blocks in the virtual address space. Within the kernel, each of these blocks is called a *virtual memory area*. Whenever a virtual memory area is to be mapped, a new **struct vm_area_struct** (virtual memory area descriptor, abbreviated to **vm_area** in Figure 2.7) is created and filled in by **do_mmap()**. Then the information can be referenced and updated by different parts of the kernel, such as the page fault handler. You can inspect the **struct** definition in **include/mm.h**.

```
struct vm_area_struct {
    struct mm_struct * vm_mm; /* VM area parameters */
    unsigned long vm_start;
    unsigned long vm_end;
/* Linked list of VM areas per task, sorted by address */
    struct vm_area_struct * vm_next;
    pgprot_t vm_page_prot;
    unsigned short vm_flags;
    ...
    struct vm_operations_struct * vm_ops;
    ...
};
```

The new **struct vm_area_struct** contains a **struct mm_struct** descriptor to specify the code, data, and other parts of the area. The **vm_start** and **vm_end** addresses specify the range of the area. The **vm_page_prot** field specifies the protection mode—read, write, or execute—for the pages in the area, and the **vm_flags** field contains information about the type of the area, for example code or data. The **vm_next** field is a pointer to a list of areas used by this task.

The **vm_ops** field is used when the memory mapping mechanism causes a page fault. The page fault handler will use functions defined in this field to determine the pages in the secondary memory that should be bound to the area. The most important aspects of the **struct vm_operations_struct** are defined in **include/mm.h** by the following.

```
struct vm_operations_struct {
    void (*open)(struct vm_area_struct * area);
    void (*close)( struct vm_area_struct * area);
    ...
    int (*swapout)(
        struct vm_area_struct *,
        struct page *
    );
    pte_t (*swapin) (
        struct vm_area_struct *,
        unsigned long,
        unsigned long
```

```
    );
};
```

open() is called when the area is mapped into the virtual address space, and **close()** is called when it is removed from the virtual address space. **swapout()** copies a loaded page back to the swap space. The page fault handler calls **swapout()** when it decides to remove a page from the primary memory. **swapin()** copies a page from the swap space into the primary memory and then adjusts the page table so that it points at the newly loaded page. The page fault handler calls it when it decides to load a page.

Address Translation

Whenever a process references the primary memory, the hardware generates a virtual address and sends it to the memory mapping mechanism so that it can be translated into the physical address of the information in the machine's primary memory (see Figure 2.7). The address translation mechanism is hardware that converts the virtual address according to the strategy described in Part 1, Section 5.4. The process has a page directory. Part of the address selects the page directory entry for the address, another part selects the page middle directory entry (not used in the i386), the third part selects the page table entry, and the fourth specifies the byte address offset within the page. Because of cost considerations, the page mapping hardware usually employs a part of the primary memory system to cache parts of the various page-related tables into a *translation lookaside buffer* (TLB). References to the cached parts of the page tables use the TLB rather than the actual page tables. Of course, the page fault handler must also participate in the TLB management whenever it loads or unloads pages. Address translation is performed by very low-level software (often written in assembly language) or by hardware. A collection of macros to manipulate the page tables is defined in **include/asm/pgtable.h**.

If address translation fails because the target page is not loaded, then the address translation mechanism forces a page fault interrupt. This interrupt initially is handled like all other interrupts (see Part 1, Section 5.4) before it is determined to be a missing page fault. The general interrupt handler will then call **do_page_fault()**, which will complete the handling of the missing page interrupt.

The Page Fault Handler

The page fault handler is responsible for

- finding a page frame in the physical memory (possibly swapping an existing page back to the swap space),
- swapping the missing page into the page frame, and
- adjusting the page tables.

Recall that Linux uses the copy-on-write strategy for sharing pages among address spaces. Thus whenever any process attempts to write to a page that is marked to be copied on a write operation (that is, it is marked as read-only), the write operation will cause a page write violation fault. Figure 2.9 summarizes the kernel functions that accomplish this work (though this discussion omits most of the details). The address translation mechanism raises interrupt **0x80** when it detects a missing page or other page fault (such as a protection violation). The system interrupt handler dispatches **do_page_fault()** to handle the interrupt.

The **do_page_fault()** function is architecture-specific code located in **arch/i386/mm/fault.c**. The following abstraction of the code highlights the critical aspects of the page fault handler.

```
asmlinkage void do_page_fault(
    struct pt_regs *regs, unsigned long error_code)
```

Figure 2.9
Page Fault Handler

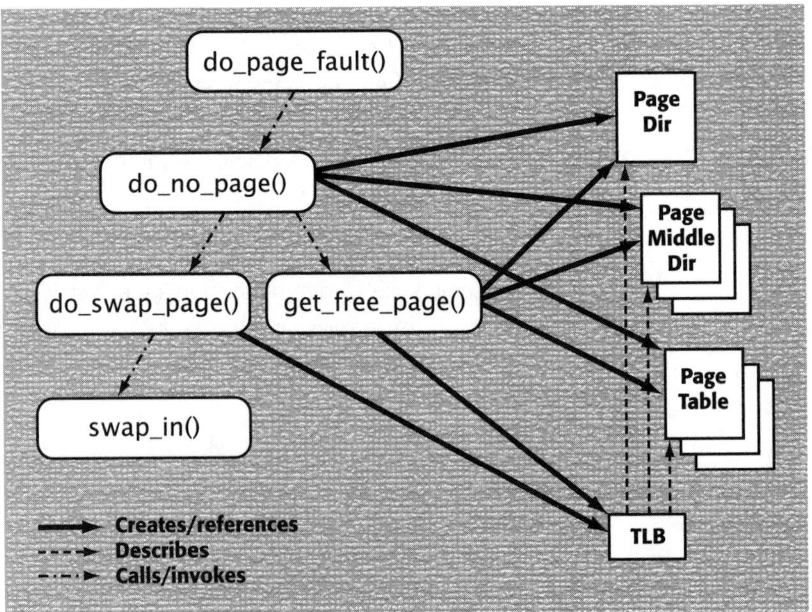

```
{
    struct task_struct *tsk;
    struct mm_struct *mm;
    struct vm_area_struct * vma;
    ...
    /* Get the address */
    ...
    tsk = current;          // current is the task_struct of the task
                                    // that calls this function
    mm = tsk->mm;
    vma = find_vma(mm, address);
    // Various checks on the task state and address
    ...
    /*
     * Ok, you have a good vm_area for this memory access, so
     * you can handle it . . .
     */
good_area:
    write = 0;
    switch (error_code & 3) {
    default: /* 3: write, present */
        ...
        /* Fall through */
    case 2: /* write, not present */
        ...
        write++;
        break;
    case 1: /* read, present */
        goto bad_area;
    case 0: /* read, not present */
        if (!(vma->vm_flags & (VM_READ | VM_EXEC)))
            goto bad_area;
    }
    /*
     * If for any reason at all we couldn't handle the fault,
     * make sure we exit gracefully rather than endlessly redo
     * the fault.
     */
survive:
    {
```

7

```
        int fault = handle_mm_fault(tsk, vma, address, write);
        if (!fault)
            goto do_sigbus;
        if (fault < 0)
            goto out_of_memory;
    }

    ...
    return;

    /*
     * Something tried to access memory that isn't in our
     * memory map.. Fix it, but check if it's kernel or user first..
     */
bad_area:
    /* (various attempts at recovery or reporting */
    ...
}
```

The kernel code often includes labels (such as **good_area** and **bad_area**) coupled with **goto** statements in order to generate highly efficient code. As you can see from the code abstract, **do_page_fault()** will call **handle_mm_fault()** if the request results in a page miss.

The **handle_mm_fault()** function is defined in **mm/memory.c**. It sets a few parameters and then checks to see whether the request is for a write to a page that is present. An affirmative means that this is a copy-on-write situation that requires that a copy of the target page be made for the calling task, so **handle_mm_fault()** calls **do_wp_page()** (in **mm/memory.c**). Otherwise—this is the normal case—the page fault will be handled by **do_no_page()**. The Version 2.2.12 code for **do_no_page()** is messy; it was changed in Version 2.2.14 to have far less complicated control flow.

handle_mm_fault() first adjusts the page tables by using the macros from **include/asm/pgtable.h** and then handles the following specific cases.

- **Anonymous**: The **vm_area** definition does not have a file to define memory content—the memory content is **NULL** (anonymous). If the page is write-accessible, then a new page frame must be allocated (by using **__get_free_pages()** from **mm/page_alloc.c**). The new page is then loaded and the page table entry is updated.
- **Swap in a page**: Load the new page by using the **do_swap_page()** function; see **mm/memory.c**. **do_swap_page()**updates the TLB. It

then calls the swap_in() function in mm/page_alloc.c, which next calls other lower-level functions to perform the actual disk input operation from the swap space.

- **Need more memory**: Call the out-of-memory kernel function and quit.

The do_wp_page() function also is called by do_page_fault() when a write operation to a write-protected page occurs. This is usually an indication that a write operation is being performed to a shared page. This part of the page fault handler replicates a shared page that is being written, thereby giving each process its own copy of the page. This is done because the respective copies should now differ, since one process has requested the write operation. The details of do_wp_page() differ from those of do_no_page(), but the general behavior is the same. (In fact, Version 2.2.14 generalizes and combines the two functions.) You should inspect mm/memory.c to see the details of do_wp_page().

Primary Memory Allocation

The memory manager uses a *dynamic page allocation strategy*, meaning that the number of page frames allocated to a process varies according to the behavior of that particular process and the overall activity in the system. Here, *process behavior* refers to the size of the process's *working set*—the number of different pages that the process is using at any given time. For example, the 7
process might be using 10 different pages that contain code and another 15 that contain data. The size of the working set would then be 25 pages. Another process might be using only 12 code pages and 6 data pages, or 18 total pages. When a process generates a page fault, the memory manager ordinarily tries to allocate an additional page frame in which to load the missing page (see the __get_free_pages() function in mm/page_alloc.c). Thus, when one process needs another page frame, some other process might lose one. Other pools of page frames are available from which the manager may tap—pages being used, for example, by shared library code, for memory-mapped files, or for device caching.

Problem Statement

Part A: Instrument the Virtual Memory Manager

Instrument the memory manager software so that you can determine the rate at which any particular process, or the whole system, is incurring page faults. You need to define a new page fault system call that can serve the following purposes.

- Initialize your page fault frequency parameters. For example, you could specify the size of the window on the reference stream that you will consider in computing the average number of page faults.
- Report the current page fault frequency in such a way that one could write a user program to use this data to create a performance meter.

Part B: Reporting the Performance

Write a user-space program that periodically calls your page fault system call to determine the current rate. Then, plot the page fault frequency rate versus time. Finally, read about the **vmstat** command to get ideas about how to design your reporting program.

Attacking the Problem

A problem that you will have to address in this exercise is debugging your program. The problem stems from two causes. One is the difficulty of comparing the output of your program with "the correct answer." This will require careful engineering on your part. You also need to address how to introduce enough load on the system so that it begins to page fault. Many contemporary machines have so much primary memory that very heavy computing load will be necessary in order to get the virtual memory system to incur faults.

eight

Synchronization Mechanisms

Exercise Goal: You will add a new synchronization mechanism to the kernel. This will require you to create a design for a new mechanism and then to add its implementation to the kernel.

Introduction

Every modern kernel provides one or more synchronization primitives to enable application programmers to coordinate the behavior of multithreaded software. Classic UNIX systems did not provide mechanisms for fine-grained multithread operation; the primary means for synchronizing processes was pipes (and files). System V UNIX provided semaphores as part of the shared memory implementation; these primitives are defined in POSIX and hence are supported by Linux.

Blocking a Task

As a *task* (a process executing in kernel space) runs, it might have to wait for some condition to become true before it can continue. For example, it might wait for an I/O operation to complete (an interrupt to occur). When a task decides to block itself, it changes its own state, by changing the **current->state** field in its descriptor from TASK_RUNNING to either TASK_INTERRUPTIBLE or TASK_UNINTERRUPTIBLE. Then it enqueues itself on a list of blocked processes and invokes the scheduler to run a different task. A task in the TASK_INTERRUPTIBLE state can be reactivated by a signal or an interrupt, whereas a task in the TASK_UNINTERRUPTIBLE state can be reawakened only if an interrupt occurs and changes something in the machine state so that the task can run again. For example, when a task starts an I/O operation, the device driver code places the task in the TASK_UNINTERRUPTIBLE state. The task can be awakened only by the interrupt that indicates that the I/O operation has completed.

As mentioned, when a task blocks itself, the kernel code links the process into a list of tasks, waiting for the given condition to become true. Thus you can think of each condition on which a task could block as defining a list of tasks. Whenever the corresponding condition becomes true, then one or more (depending on the semantics of the condition) of the blocked tasks in the list become unblocked. For example, the classic Dijkstra semaphore (see Chapter 8 in Nutt [2000]) is a form of condition that can block a task. A binary semaphore is an unsigned integer variable that has an initial value 1. For a semaphore, S, its value can be changed only by one of two functions, P(S) or V(S). Think of a semaphore as being like a C++ class or an abstract data type. That is, it has private data to represent the unsigned integer value and two public functions on its interface. The binary semaphore is the simplest form of semaphore; it can take on only values of 0 or 1. By contrast, general semaphores can take on arbitrary non-negative integer values. For a binary semaphore, when P(S) is called and S has the value 1, then S is decremented—changed to 0—and the calling process continues to execute. If S has the value 0, then the calling process is blocked until S is incremented to 1. The V(S) operation increments the semaphore.

The paradigm for using a semaphore is for a process to call P(S) before it begins to execute a *critical section*, code that could cause a race condition of the type described in Exercise 6. When the process completes executing the critical section code, it calls V(S) to increment the semaphore. Note that if one process is in a critical section—S will have been set to 0—then another process that attempts to enter its critical section by calling P(S) will be blocked until the first process executes V(S). The P() and V() functions are themselves critical sections, meaning that when they are being executed, they cannot be interrupted.

You can implement a semaphore by creating a kernel abstract data type that has an unsigned integer variable for the value of the semaphore and the two publicly accessible functions, **P()** and **V()**. You also can keep track of the tasks that are blocked on the semaphore by putting each blocked task in a list. If the value of the semaphore is **1**, then the list is empty. If one or more tasks are waiting for S, then each of these tasks is in the abstract data type's internal task list. When **V(S)** is called, exactly one task is removed from the list, thereby leaving the others still blocked. If no tasks are waiting when **V(S)** is called, then the value of the semaphore is changed to **1** with no further action. More details on how this works are provided after a discussion of kernel wait queues.

Wait Queues

The situation whereby a task/process must wait for some condition to become true occurs in many places in the kernel. This is another way of saying that the kernel has many critical sections in it. Therefore Linux provides a single, fundamental abstract data structure that can be used to maintain lists of tasks waiting on a condition, called wait queues. A *wait queue* is a circular list of elements in which each element contains a pointer to a **struct task_struct** process descriptor. These list implementations are not private—the kernel is implemented as a single monolithic block of code rather than as a collection of modules. However, the intent is that tasks be inserted into a wait queue only by using **__add_wait_queue()** and removed by using **__remove_wait_queue()**.

Following are the relevant definitions for a wait queue, taken from **include/linux/wait.h** for the data structure and macro and from **include/linux/sched.h** for the functions.

8

```
#define WAIT_QUEUE_HEAD(x) ((struct wait_queue *)((x)-1))

struct wait_queue {
   struct task_struct * task;
   struct wait_queue * next;
};

extern inline void __add_wait_queue(
      struct wait_queue ** p, struct wait_queue * wait)
{
   wait->next = *p ? : WAIT_QUEUE_HEAD(p);
   *p = wait;
}
```

```
extern inline void __remove_wait_queue(
      struct wait_queue ** p, struct wait_queue * wait)
{
   struct wait_queue * next = wait->next;
   struct wait_queue * head = next;
   struct wait_queue * tmp;

   while ((tmp = head->next) != wait) {
      head = tmp;
   }
   head->next = next;
}
```

This code is very compact. It does no error checking and uses a minimum amount of instructions to maintain the list. The **__add_wait_queue()** code simply places an element of type **struct wait_queue** * at the head of the wait queue (the argument of type **struct wait_queue** **). To enqueue a task, T, you create a wait queue instance, **newInstance**, set the task field, **newInstance->task** to reference the task, and then call **__add_wait_queue(targetWaitQueue, newInstance)**. The **__remove_wait_queue()** function works similarly to remove an element from the wait queue. Comments in the source code warn kernel programmers to be very careful about manipulating the lists without using these add and remove functions.

Using Wait Queues

The code in **kernel/sched.c** provides another set of functions that use wait queues for common forms of task management. The functions **sleep_on()** and **interruptible_sleep_on()** place the calling task on the specified wait queue. The first function **sets current->state** to TASK_UNINTERRUPTIBLE, and the second sets it to TASK_INTERRUPTIBLE.

```
#define SLEEP_ON_VAR \
   unsigned long flags; \
   struct wait_queue wait;

#define SLEEP_ON_HEAD \
   wait.task = current; \
   write_lock_irqsave(&waitqueue_lock,flags); \
   __add_wait_queue(p, &wait); \
```

```
    write_unlock(&waitqueue_lock);

#define SLEEP_ON_TAIL \
    write_lock_irq(&waitqueue_lock); \
    __remove_wait_queue(p, &wait); \
    write_unlock_irqrestore(&waitqueue_lock,flags);

void interruptible_sleep_on(struct wait_queue **p)
{
    SLEEP_ON_VAR

    current->state = TASK_INTERRUPTIBLE;

    SLEEP_ON_HEAD
    schedule();
    SLEEP_ON_TAIL
}

void sleep_on(struct wait_queue **p)
{
    SLEEP_ON_VAR

    current->state = TASK_UNINTERRUPTIBLE;

    SLEEP_ON_HEAD
    schedule();
    SLEEP_ON_TAIL
}
```

8

These functions are identical, except for the value that they assign to **current->state**. Notice that they also do not contain many statements (your solution to this exercise will not contain many lines of code either). The SLEEP_ON_HEAD macro adds the task to the wait queue. Then they call the scheduler, with the calling task being blocked (not eligible to be scheduled). When some other task awakens the sleeping task with **wake_up()** or **wake_up_interruptible()** (discussed next), the newly awakened task removes itself from the wait queue by using the SLEEP_ON_TAIL macro. The context in which the **sleep_on()** function may be called could allow interruption. Therefore the macro uses a lock for the critical section related to manipulating a wait queue.

Here are the corresponding functions to wake up the task, both based on __wake_up().

```
#define wake_up(x) __wake_up((x),TASK_UNINTERRUPTIBLE | \
      TASK_INTERRUPTIBLE)
#define wake_up_interruptible(x) __wake_up((x),TASK_INTERRUPT-
IBLE)
```

```
void __wake_up(struct wait_queue **q, unsigned int mode)
{
   struct task_struct *p;
   struct wait_queue *head, *next;

   if (!q)
      goto out;
   /*
    * this is safe to be done before the check because it
    * means no deference, just pointer operations.
    */
   head = WAIT_QUEUE_HEAD(q);

   read_lock(&waitqueue_lock);
   next = *q;
   if (!next)
       goto out_unlock;

   while (next != head) {
      p = next->task;
      next = next->next;
      if (p->state & mode) {
         /*
          * We can drop the read-lock early if this
          * is the only/last process.
          */
         if (next == head) {
            read_unlock(&waitqueue_lock);
            wake_up_process(p);
            goto out;
         }
         wake_up_process(p);
```

```
        }
    }
out_unlock:
    read_unlock(&waitqueue_lock);
out:
    return;
}
```

In Exercise 6, you studied the System V shared memory implementation. In your solution to the exercise problem, you had to change all array references of the form **shm_seg[]** to a list reference. In the functions **findkey()** in **ipc/shm.c**, you undoubtedly observed the following code segment.

```
...
for (id = 0; id <= max_shmid; id++) {
    while ((shp = shm_segs[id]) == IPC_NOID)
        sleep_on (&shm_lock);
        if (shp == IPC_UNUSED)
            continue;
        if (key == shp->u.shm_perm.key)
        return id;
}
...
```

And in **newseg()** in **ipc/shm.c**, you saw the following complementary code segment.

```
...
found:
    shp = (struct shmid_kernel *) kmalloc (...);
    if (!shp) {
        shm_segs[id] = (struct shmid_kernel *) IPC_UNUSED;
        wake_up (&shm_lock);
        return -ENOMEM;
    }
...
```

Now you can understand what is going on in this code. A race condition can occur when processes attempt to find a new key and is detectable by the **IPC_NOID** value in the **shm_segs[id]** variable. If the code detects the race, then the loser of the race puts itself to sleep on the **shm_lock** wait queue, to be awakened in the **newseg()** function by the **wake_up(&shm_lock)** function call.

Problem Statement

Part A

Design and implement a new kernel synchronization primitive that will allow multiple processes to block on an *event* until some other process signals the event. When a process signals the event, all processes that are blocked on the event are unblocked. If no processes are blocked on an event when it is signaled, then the signal has no effect. Implement the following new system calls.

```
int evntopen (int);          // Creates an event, returning ID
                             // arg=0  => new event; otherwise, uses
                             // an existing event; error accordingly
int evntclose(int);          // Destroy an event
int evntwait(int eventNum);          // Blocks thread until the event is
                                     // signaled
void evntsig(int eventNum);          // Unblocks all waiting threads
                                     // If no processes are blocked,
                                     // ignored
```

Part B

Write an application program to test your new kernel functions. Your test program should show that the kernel functions work for the usual cases, for example, with one process waiting, and also for boundary conditions such as

- no tasks waiting when **evntsig()** is called,
- multiple tasks waiting when **evntsig()** is called,
- multiple events open at one time, and
- processes waiting when **evntclose()** is called.

Attacking the Problem

You are to design a completely new facility to add to the kernel. When you add the facility, you will probably need to create a new implementation file (and change **Makefile** so that it compiles your new file). You also likely will need to change a few parts of the existing kernel, such as the initialization code. To do this, you should write a new **evnt_init()** function that can be called when the system is booted:

```
int evnt_init(int);                  // Initializes events__not a sys call
```

You also need to change the system initialization code to call this new **evnt_init()** function. (The initialization routine has an underbar between **evnt** and **init** because it is named by using the internal kernel function naming convention rather than the system call naming convention.) You can use this function to set up any internal structures that you require in your solution.

Begin by thinking carefully about the data structures that you will need to solve the problem. Your system will need to support several different events, so you need a set of descriptor data structures, one for each event. If you solved Exercise 6, then recall that each shared memory segment had its own descriptor; you will need the analog of a shared memory descriptor for an event. You can decide if you want a list or an array of such descriptors. Then your **evnt_init()** function can initialize that data structure.

If you use an array, you nevertheless should dynamically allocate the space for each entry (again, see the shared memory segment descriptors). This will require that you use **kmalloc()** and **kfree()**, two functions that allocate kernel memory dynamically.

You might want to work at the level of wait queues and the low-level manipulation routines. Your **evntwait()** code then might have a skeleton such as the following.

```
int evntwait(int eventNum)
{
    ...
    ...->state = TASK_INTERRUPTIBLE;
    add_wait_queue(...);
    schedule();
    ...
}
```

See the discussion in this exercise's introduction.

Similarly, your **evntsig()** function might have a skeleton such as that shown for the **wake_up()** implementation.

However, if you decide to use the **interruptible_sleep_on()/sleep_on()** and **wake_up()/wake_up_interruptible()** internal kernel functions, then your **evntwait()** function might have a skeleton such as this.

```
int evntwait(int eventNum)
{
```

```
    ...
    interruptible_sleep_on(...);
    ...
}
```

Similarly, your **evntsig()** function might have a skeleton such as this.

```
int evntsig(int eventNum)
{
    ...
    wake_up_interruptible(...);
    ...
}
```

nine

The Scheduler

Exercise Goal: You will learn more about how process management is designed, particularly how the scheduler is implemented. The scheduler is the heart of the multiprogramming system; it is responsible for choosing a new task to run whenever the CPU is available. Then, you will learn about an alternative approach called the *fair-share scheduling policy*. You will replace the standard scheduler with a fair-share scheduler. Finally, you will learn how to observe the behavior of the fair-share scheduler relative to the behavior of the standard scheduler.

Introduction

Process management is the part of the OS that creates and destroys processes, provides mechanisms to be used for synchronization, and multiplexes the CPU among runnable processes. You considered several aspects of process management in Exercises 1, 3, and 8. This exercise finishes the discussion of the process descriptor and process creation and then focuses on the scheduler.

Process Management

As suggested in Part 1, Section 3.4, Linux uses a different low-level view of how the OS is designed than the process model that appears at the system call interface. In this low-level view, when the hardware is started a single hardware process begins to run. After the Linux kernel has been loaded, the initial process is created (to use up all otherwise unused CPU cycles) and then Linux processes are started according to how the machine is configured to operate. For example, **getty** processes are started for each login port and daemons are started as specified. Thus, when the system is ready for normal operation, several processes are in existence, most of which are blocked on various conditions. The runnable tasks (those whose states are TASK_RUNNING) begin competing for the CPU. The kernel's view of this multiprogramming, summarized in Figure 2.10, is that the initial process never really creates any separate computational units (processes). Instead, a **fork()** command defines a new kernel **struct task_struct** data structure. The initial process simply multiplexes among the programs that are loaded in different address spaces as it sees fit (and as defined by the task descriptor). That is, within the kernel, only one thread of execution exists that jumps from one runnable task to another. At the system call interface, this behavior has the appropriate UNIX process semantics.

The **fork()** system call (the main work is performed in **do_fork()** defined in **kernel/fork.c**) performs the steps summarized in Part 1, Section 4.2. This code fragment omits portions that implement concepts not discussed here. The remaining code fragment are annotated with C++-style comments to highlight the most critical steps.

```
int do_fork(
      unsigned long clone_flags, unsigned long usp,
      struct pt_regs *regs
)
{
   int nr;
```

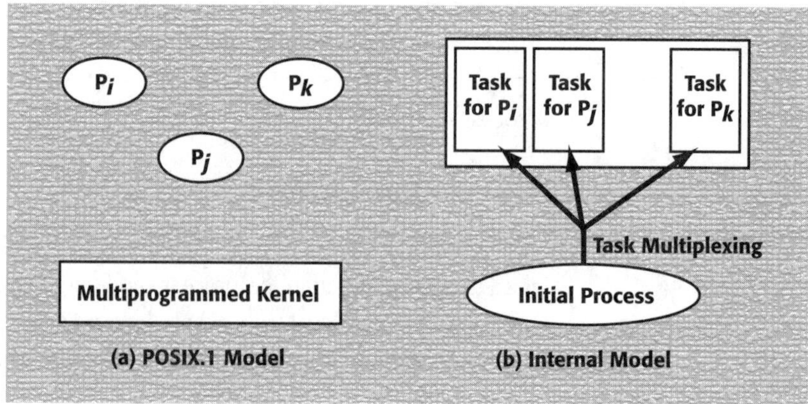

Figure 2.10 Kernel-Level Multitasking

```
...
struct task_struct *p;
...
if(clone_flags & CLONE_PID)
{
   /* This is only allowd from the boot up thread */
   if(current->pid)
      return -EPERM;
}

current->vfork_sem = &sem
// Allocate the task descriptor entry
p = alloc_task_struct();
...
// Copy the parent task descriptor entries to the child entry
*p = *current;
...
// Find an empty slot in the task structure
...
// Modify/initialize child-specific fields
...
p->swappable = 0;
*(unsigned long *) p->kernel_stack_page = STACK_MAGIC;
p->state = TASK_UNINTERRUPTIBLE;
copy_flags(clone_flags, p);
p->pid = get_pid(clone_flags);
p->state = TASK_RUNNABLE;
p->next_run = p;
p->prev_run = p;

p->p_pptr = p->p_opptr = current;
p->p_cptr = NULL;
init_waitqueue(&p->wait_chldexit);
// Set fields related to signals
...
p->it_real_value = p->it_virt_value = p->it_prof_value = 0;
p->it_real_incr = p->it_virt_incr = p->it_prof_incr = 0;
init_timer(&p->real_timer);
p->real_timer.data = (unsigned long) p;
...
p->times.tms_utime = p->itmes.tms_stime = 0;
```

```
    p->times.tms_cutime = p->times.tms_cstime = 0;
    ...
    p->start_time = jiffies;
    ...
    nr_tasks++;
    ...
    /* copy all the process information */
    if (copy_files(clone_flags, p))  // File table and files
        goto bad_fork_cleanup;
    if (copy_fs(clone_flags, p))     // User data segment
        goto bad_fork_cleanup_files;
    if (copy_sighand(clone_flags, p)) // Signals and handlers
        goto bad_fork_cleanup_fs;
    if (copy_mm(clone_flags, p))     // Virtual memory tables
        goto bad_fork_cleanup_sighand;
    retval = copy_thread(nr, clone_flags, usp, p, regs);
    if(retval)
        goto bad_fork_cleanup_mm;
    ...
    /* ok, now we should be set up.. */
    p->swappable = 1;
    p->exit_signal = clone_flags & CSIGNAL;
    ...

bad_fork_cleanup_mm:
    ...
bad_fork_cleanup_sighand:
    ...
bad_fork_cleanup_fs:
    ...
bad_fork_cleanup_files:
    ...
bad_fork_cleanup:
    ...
}
```

Each process descriptor has a link to parents and siblings. The **p_opptr** field points to the process's original parent process, and the **p_pptr** field points to the parent. The **p_cptr** field points to this process's youngest child (the last child process that it created), and the **p_ysptr** field points to this process's next younger sibling process. Finally, the **p_osptr** field points to the next older sibling process.

Process States

The **state** field in the task descriptor can have any of the following values:

TASK_RUNNING

TASK_INTERRUPTIBLE

TASK_UNINTERRUPTIBLE

TASK_ZOMBIE

TASK_STOPPED

As you go through the kernel code, you will often see statements of the form

```
current->state = TASK_...;
```

For example, in the **sleep_on()** code, **state** is set to TASK_UNINTERRUPTIBLE just before the process is placed on a wait queue. In **wake_up()**, **state** is set back to TASK_RUNNING after it is removed from the wait queue. Recall that the distinction between the TASK_INTERRUPTIBLE and TASK_UNINTERRUPTIBLE states relates to the sleeping task's ability to accept signals. TASK_ZOMBIE represents a state in which a process has terminated, but its parent has not yet performed a **wait()** system call to recognize that it has terminated. That is, the task does not disappear from the system until the parent is notified of its termination. The final possible value for the state field is TASK_STOPPED, which means that the task has been halted by a signal or through the **ptrace** mechanism. Thus most of the kernel code sets the **state** field to TASK_RUNNING, TASK_INTERRUPTIBLE, or TASK_UNINTERRUPTIBLE.

Outside of the kernel, a different set of process states is visible to users. These states are defined by the POSIX model rather than by the Linux implementation, though they are analogous to the internal states kept in the task descriptor. You can review these external states by inspecting the manual page for the STAT column in a **ps** command. The **ps** has three fields. The first field may be one of the following:

- R: The process is running or runnable (its kernel state is TASK_RUNNING).
- S: The process is sleeping (its kernel state is TASK_INTERRUPTIBLE).

- D: The process is in an uninterruptible sleep (its kernel state is TASK_UNINTERRUPTIBLE).
- T: The process is either stopped or being traced (its kernel state is TASK_STOPPED).
- Z: The process is in the zombie state (its kernel state is TASK_ZOMBIE).

The second field of **ps** is either blank, or W if the process currently has no pages loaded. The third field is either blank, or N if the process is running at a reduced priority. Most of the kernel code transitions the state of the process among TASK_RUNNING, TASK_INTERRUPTIBLE, and TASK_UNINTERRUPTIBLE. If you solved Exercise 8, you gained a strong intuition about the nature of these state transitions (otherwise, you might find it helpful to review the material in Exercise 8 before solving this exercise). Roughly speaking, whenever a process is to be blocked, it will be put on a queue (usually a wait queue) and its state will be changed to one of TASK_INTERRUPTIBLE or TASK_UNINTERRUPTIBLE and then the scheduler will be called. A task/process, when awakened, is removed from the wait queue and its state is changed to TASK_RUNNING. This leaves the scheduler as the final critical piece of process management that this manual considers.

Scheduler Implementation

The scheduler is a kernel function, **schedule()**, that gets called from various other system call functions (usually via **sleep_on()**) and after every system call and slow interrupt. Each time that the scheduler is called, it does the following.

1. Performs various periodic work (such as running device bottom halves).
2. Inspects the set of tasks in the TASK_RUNNING state.
3. Chooses one task to execute according to the scheduling policy.
4. Dispatches the task to run on the CPU until an interrupt occurs.

The scheduler contains three built-in scheduling strategies, identified by the constants SCHED_FIFO, SCHED_RR, and SCHED_OTHER. The scheduling policy for each process can be set at runtime by using the **sched_setscheduler()** system call (defined in **kernel/sched.c**). The task's current scheduling policy is saved in the **policy** field. The SCHED_FIFO and SCHED_RR policies are intended to be sensitive to real-time requirements, so they use scheduling priorities in the range [0:99], whereas SCHED_OTHER handles only the zero priority. Each process also has a **priority** field in its task descriptor. Conceptually, the scheduler has a multilevel queue with 100 levels (corresponding to the priorities from 0 to 99). Whenever a process with a priority that is higher than the currently running process becomes runnable, the lower-priority process is preempted and the higher-priority process begins to run. Of course, in the normal timesharing (**SCHED_OTHER**) policy, processes do not preempt one another, since they all have a static priority of zero.

Any task/process that uses the **SCHED_FIFO** policy must have superuser permission and have a priority of 1 to 99 (that is, it has a higher priority than all **SCHED_OTHER** tasks). Thus a **SCHED_FIFO** task that becomes runnable takes priority over every **SCHED_OTHER** task. The **SCHED_FIFO** policy does not reschedule on a timer interrupt. Once a **SCHED_FIFO** task gets control of the CPU, it will retain control until either it completes, blocks by an I/O call, calls **sched_yield()**, or until a higher priority task becomes runnable. If it yields or is preempted by another, higher-priority, task, it is placed at the end of the task queue at the same priority level.

The **SCHED_RR** policy has the same general semantics as the **SCHED_FIFO** policy, except that it uses the time-slicing mechanism to multiplex the CPU among tasks that are in the highest-priority queue. A running **SCHED_RR** task that is preempted by a higher-priority task is placed back on the head of its queue so that it will resume when its queue priority is again the highest in the system. The preempted process will then be allowed to complete its time quantum.

The **SCHED_OTHER** policy is the default timesharing policy. It uses the conventional time-slicing mechanism (rescheduling on each timer interrupt) to put an upper bound on the amount of time that a task can use the CPU continuously if other tasks are waiting to use it. This policy ignores the static priorities used to discriminate among tasks in the other two policies. Instead, a dynamic priority is computed on the basis of the value assigned to the task by the **nice()** or **setpriority()** system call and by the amount of time that a process has been waiting for the CPU to become available. The **counter** field in the task descriptor becomes the key component in determining the task's dynamic priority. It is adjusted on each timer interrupt (when the interrupt handler adjusts the various timer fields for the task).

The following annotated code fragment from **kernel/sched.c** represents the main flow of the scheduler; most error checking and obscure cases have been removed from this fragment. The C++-style annotations have been added as explanation in this manual and do not appear in the Linux source code. Beck, et al. [1998] note that the Version 2.*x* scheduling code has become much more complex than the Version 1 code, primarily for efficiency reasons. (You can inspect the version 1 code to get a good idea of what a scheduler has to do and the Version 2 code to see more efficient ways to do scheduling in a contemporary OS.)

```
asmlinkage void schedule(void)
{
   struct schedule_data * sched_data;
   int c;
   struct task_struct *prev, *next, *p;
   int this_cpu, c;

   ...
   prev = current;
   this_cpu = prev->processor;
   ...
// Here is where the bottom halves and task queues get executed
// Logically, this is part of ret_from_sys_call
   if (bh_active & bh_mask)
      goto handle_bh;
handle_bh_back:
   ...
   /* move an exhausted RR process to be last.. */
   if (prev->counter == SCHED_RR)
      goto move_rr_last;
move_rr_back:

   switch (prev->state) {
   case TASK_INTERRUPTIBLE:
      if (signal_pending(prev)) {
         prev->state = TASK_RUNNING;
         break;
      }
   default:
      del_from_runqueue(prev);
   case TASK_RUNNING:
   }
   prev->need_resched = 0;

repeat_schedule:

/* this is the scheduler proper: */

   p = init_task.next_run;
   c = -1000;
   if(prev->state == TASK_RUNNING)
```

```
        goto still_running;
still_running_back:
    ...
// This loop finds the task that has the highest counter (dynamic
// priority value; that is the task that will be dispatched
    while (p != &init_task) {
        if (can_schedule(p)) {
            int weight = goodness(p, prev, this_cpu);
            if (weight > c)
                c = weight, next = p;
        }
        p = p->next_run;
    }

    /* if all runnable processes have "counter == 0", re-calculate
     * counters
     */
    if (!c)
        goto recalculate;
...
// Finally, you are ready to dispatch task next
    kstat.content_swtch++;
    get_mmu_context(next);
    switch_to(prev, next, prev);
    __schedule_tail(prev)—;
    ...
    return;

recalculate:
    ...
    for_each_task(p)
        p->counter = (p->counter >> 1) + p->priority;
    goto repeat_schedule;

still_running:
    c = prev_goodness(prev, prev, this_cpu);
    next = prev;
    goto still_running_back;

handle_bh:
    do_bottom_half();
```

9

```
    goto handle_bh_back;
    ...
move_rr_last:
    if (prev->counter) {
        prev->counter = prev->priority;
        move_last_runqueue(prev);
    }
    goto move_rr_back;

    ...
}
```

Fair-Share Scheduling

Fair-share scheduling [Bach, 1986] is a more abstract strategy for scheduling than any of the three built-in strategies. The idea is that the CPU should be shared among sets of processes according to the groups that own those processes. For example, suppose that Tom, Dick, and Harry belong to different groups and are logged in to a machine that uses fair-share scheduling. Further suppose that Tom has only one runnable process, Dick has three, and Harry has six. Fair-share scheduling calls for ten runnable processes and instead of each process getting 10% of the CPU cycles, the three groups each get one-third of the CPU cycles to allocate to the processes that they own. So Tom's single process would get 33% of the available CPU cycles, each of Dick's three processes would get about 11% of the available CPU cycles, and each of Harry's six processes would get about 5.5% of the CPU cycles. If Betty belonged to Dick's group and she logged in to the machine and created two more processes, then Tom's group would have one process but still receive one-third of the CPU cycles. Dick and Betty would have five processes and would be allocated one-third of the CPU cycles, distributed equally among their five processes, with each receiving about 6.7% of the total machine cycles. Each of Harry's six processes would continue to receive about 5.5% of the available CPU cycles.

Problem Statement

You are to modify the Linux scheduler and then measure the performance of the system with and without the modified scheduler so that you can compare the effect of the new scheduler.

Part A

Add a new scheduling policy to support fair-share scheduling. To simplify the problem, have your new scheduler have all processes use fair-share scheduling on the basis of each process's UNIX group identification (as specified in its task descriptor). That is, when your system is running the fair-share scheduler the **sched_setscheduler()** system call will have no effect.

Part B

Insert instrumentation software into the kernel so that you can obtain detailed performance data regarding the scheduler's behavior. Add a new system call that enables or disables the instrumentation. Also, have the system call include an option to initialize the instrumentation and another to dump its internal statistics to a file. Study the behavior of your fair-share scheduler, and report on its performance.

Attacking the Problem

Planning a Solution

The introductory explanation of the scheduler gives you the background information that you need to solve this problem. You need to modify **kernel/sched.c** to implement your scheduler. You probably will need to modify other components, such as the task descriptor. Design your strategy for implementing the fair-share scheduler so that it has as little impact on the existing code and data structures as possible, even if you have to sacrifice some performance. After you get the new scheduler to work properly, you can reconsider the design from the performance perspective.

Comparing Scheduler Performance

In Exercise 1, you learned how to use the **/proc** file system to observe various facets of kernel performance. You should consider the **/proc** facilities to get your first measurements of the modified system. For example, set up an experiment using a few different groups with CPU-intensive processes (for example, processes that simply execute a very long **for** loop). Start several instances of the CPU-intensive process, and then use the **/proc** tools to see how the CPU time is distributed among the different processes.

Next, you can exploit the timer information that is available to each process (see Exercise 3). You can rewrite your CPU-intensive load generator program so that it reads the task timers and then report each timer value to a file. You can analyze the collective files after you have run your experiment.

The first technique will not provide you with very fine-grained performance data, and the second has the liability that it does not take all activity in the system into account. After you have exploited these approaches, you should insert new instrumentation code into the kernel sources, along with a new system call to enable and disable the instrumentation. This level of performance inspection requires that you again design and modify kernel code, so you must do it carefully.

ten

Device Drivers

Exercise Goal: You will focus on Linux device drivers, learning how all device drivers are organized. Then you will write your own device driver for a virtual device, a FIFO queue (pipe).

Introduction

Part 1, Section 6. introduced the device manager strategy for the Linux kernel. In summary, each physical peripheral device—keyboard, display, mouse, disk, serial port, parallel port, network adapter, and so on—has a software device driver specifically designed to control that device. The device driver software encapsulates these details of how to control the device and exports a canonical set of operations through a specific interface (see Figure 2.11). The kernel uses the canonical device interfaces (block and character interfaces) to export the device operations to user-space programs via the file system interface.

Each device driver may use a polling strategy or an interrupt strategy.

- A driver that uses *polling* starts the device and continuously reads the device's status until it completes the operation. Thus the user-space process

Figure 2.11 Interface, Driver, and Device

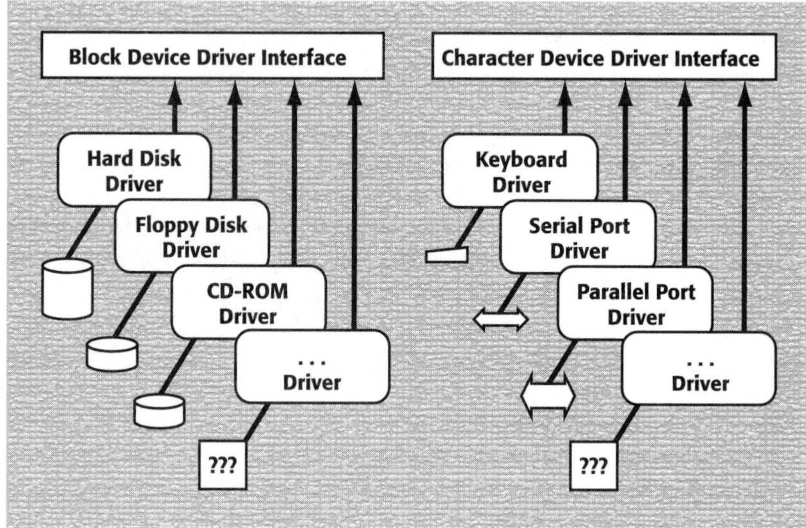

enters the kernel and begins executing the device driver. While the device is performing the I/O operation, the corresponding task is periodically polling the device's status register to determine when the operation has completed.

- A driver that uses *interrupts* starts the device and then suspends itself until the device completes and raises an IRQ. When the IRQ occurs, the ISR runs, possibly postponing certain aspects of the interrupt handling to a bottom half routine or to be a unit of work kept in the task queue. In this case, the user process uses the driver code to initiate the I/O operation and then blocks itself until the device completes the operation. Then the interrupt handler for the device runs, awakening the sleeping task and eventually resuming user-space processing.

Figure 2.11 shows a family of device drivers for *block devices* and another for *character devices*. In traditional UNIX systems, the interfaces for block devices differ substantially from those for character devices; this distinction is not as significant in Linux. I/O operations for block devices transfer multiple bytes to/from the primary memory cache on each hardware operation, whereas character devices transfer information byte-by-byte without using caching. As suggested by the figure, a disk is a block device and a serial port is a character device.

All UNIX systems are designed so that device drivers can be defined when the system is booted. At that time, the device drivers register their specific device interface implementation with the kernel. Linux differs from other versions of

UNIX in that it also allows device drivers to be implemented as loadable kernel modules (see Exercise 4). Thus the driver's implementation of the interface can be registered when the module is loaded, rather than just at boot time.

Driver Organization

A device driver is a collection of functions and data structures whose purpose is to implement a simple interface for managing a device. The kernel uses the interface to request the driver to manipulate its device for I/O operations. Alternatively, you can view a device driver as an abstract data type that creates a common function interface to every hardware device in the computer.

As mentioned in Part 1, Section 6, the kernel references a device driver by a major number and a minor number. The *major number* of a device normally identifies the class of devices that the driver can manage. The Linux community has agreed on a set of major numbers for device classes that are typically supported. For example, floppy disks have a major number of 2, IDE hard disks have a major number of 3, and parallel ports have a major number of 6. The file **include/linux/major.h** provides the full list of major numbers for the release of Linux on which you are working.

The *minor number* is an 8-bit number that references a specific device of a particular class (major number). Thus two floppy disks on a machine would have a major number of 2, with the first disk having a minor number of 0 and the second a minor number of 1.[1]

The kernel must be informed of the device's existence. When booted, the kernel creates a special file for each device in the system. A *special file* is an entry in **/dev** for the device that will be used to identify the device driver for that device. This can be done with the **mknod** command:

```
mknod /dev/<dev_name> <type> <major_number> <minor_number>
```

The **<dev_name>** parameter is the special file's name (you can view the list of special files in the **/dev** directory). The **<type>** parameter is **c** for a character device and **b** for a block device. The **<major_number>** and **<minor_number>** are the device's major number and minor numbers, respectively.

The interface to a device is intended to look the same as an interface to the file system. Recall from Part 1, Section 7 that each file system defines a fixed set of

[1] As discussed in Beck, et al. [1998], major devices 4 and 5 have minor number assignments to accommodate virtual consoles and pseudoterminals.

operations (functions) that can be applied to any of its files and directories. It does this by specifying a **struct file_operations** definition (see **include/linux/fs.h**). These same functions can be defined for any device driver, as follows.

```
struct file_operations {
  loff_t (*llseek) (struct file *, loff_t, int);
  ssize_t (*read) (struct file *, char *, size_t, loff_t *);
  ssize_t (*write) (struct file *, const char *, size_t, loff_t *);
  int (*readdir) (struct file *, void *, filldir_t);
  unsigned int (*poll) (struct file *, struct poll_table_struct *);
  int (*ioctl) (struct inode *, struct file *, unsigned int,
     unsigned long);
  int (*mmap) (struct file *, struct vm_area_struct *);
  int (*open) (struct inode *, struct file *);
  int (*flush) (struct file *);
  int (*release) (struct inode *, struct file *);
  int (*fsync) (struct file *, struct dentry *);
  int (*fasync) (int, struct file *, int);
  int (*check_media_change) (kdev_t dev);
  int (*revalidate) (kdev_t dev);
  int (*lock) (struct file *, int, struct file_lock *);
};
```

A device driver needs to define only functions that make sense for itself. For example, an input-only device probably does not have a **write()** function, and an output-only device might not have a **read()** function. The device driver designer decides which functions on the interface are required to operate the device, implements the desired functions, and then creates an instance of **struct file_operations**, with the appropriate entry points defined.

A conventional device driver for a device of type **foo** should also define an initialization function, **foo_init()**. This function should be called when the kernel is booted (loadable modules do not use the **init()** function, but **init_module()** can be used for initialization code). For example, the **tty_init()** function is for serial ports and the **hd_init()** function is for hard disks. Next, you must modify the kernel initialization code so that it calls the new **foo_init()** function. If the device is a character device, then you must modify the function **chr_dev_init()** in **drivers/char/mem.c.** Similarly, a block device is initialized in **blk_dev_init()**, which is stored in **drivers/block/ll_rw_bl.c**. Drivers for SCSI and network devices have their own initialization routines.

foo_init() allows the device driver to set up required data structures when the driver is installed (for example, when the machine is booted). Also, the initialization code should register the device driver interface—**struct file_operations**—with the kernel by using the **register_chrdev()** function for character devices or the **register_blkdev()** function for block devices. For example, if the imaginary **foo** device were a character device, then its driver would contain a function like the following.

```
foo_init()
{
   ...
   struct file_operations foo_fops = {
      NULL;          /* llseek – default */
      foo_read;      /* read */
      foo_write;     /* write */
      NULL;          /* readdir */
      NULL;          /* select */
      foo_ioctl;     /* ioctl */
      NULL;          /* mmap */
      foo_open;      /* open */
      NULL;          /* release */
   };
   ...
   register_chrdev(FOO_MAJOR, "foo", &foo_fops);
   /* Other initialization ... */
   ...
}
```

Once the driver has been initialized, the kernel can route a system call such as

```
open(/dev/foo, O_RDONLY);
```

to the **foo_open()** function in the driver. (You should inspect **sys_open()** in **fs/open.c** to get an idea of how the kernel can determine the entry point to call.)

In an interrupt-style device driver, each entry point is a part of the driver that performs an I/O operation. Once the device has been started, the calling process is changed to the TASK_UNINTERRUPTIBLE or TASK_INTERRUPTIBLE state. Then it is suspended (by a call to one of the two forms of **sleep_on()**) while it awaits the interrupt from the device. Therefore, when you write an entry point function that uses an interrupt, you also must write a separate device handler function. When the IRQ occurs, your device handler should be called. How does the kernel know which device handler to call? You register the device handler with the kernel by associating it with a particular IRQ using the kernel function **request_irq()**.

The interrupt may have bottom halves that it can mark for execution (or tasks that it can queue). To use a bottom half to finish any interrupt processing, you need to initialize the bottom half (see **init_bh()**) and then mark it for execution by using the **mark_bh()kernel** function.

Loadable Kernel Module Drivers

Loadable kernel modules (see Exercise 4) can be used to implement device drivers (see Pomerantz [1999] for a comprehensive discussion of modules). A driver implemented as a module can be loaded or unloaded at any time while the machine is executing (as opposed to being loaded only at boot time). If the device driver is implemented as a module, **mknod** must still have been used to create the special file in **/dev**. This differs from conventional drivers in that the driver can be registered when the module is installed, by using the **/sbin/insmod** command. The **/sbin/rmmod** command calls the **cleanup_module()**, which contains a kernel call to reverse the registration process. That is, it deletes the information that **/sbin/insmod** placed in the linkage tables of the driver entry point.

The driver module's **init_module()** function must be written to register the device driver entry points. This serves the same purpose as the **foo_init()** function in the previous subsection's example. A module may export one of two styles of interface: a **/proc** or a general **/dev**. The module example in Exercise 4 uses the **/proc**-style interface.

Here is a code fragment for the **foo** device driver for registering the driver.

```
/* Module device driver code fragment */
...
struct file_operations foo_fops = {
      NULL;           /* llseek – default */
      foo_read;       /* read */
      foo_write;      /* write */
      NULL;           /* readdir */
      NULL;           /* select */
      foo_ioctl;      /* ioctl */
      NULL;           /* mmap */
      foo_open;       /* open */
```

```
        NULL;              /* release */
    };
...
int init_module()
{
    int majorNumber;
    ...
    majorNumber = module_register_chrdev(
            0, "foo", &foo_fops);
    if(majorNumber < 0) {
    /* Registration failed */
        ...
    }
    /* Other initialization */
    ...
    return 0;
}
```

As you can see, the **init_module()** code performs the same function as the **init()** code in the conventional UNIX driver case, except that the code is called by **/sbin/insmod** rather than by the kernel initialization code.

The module unregisters the driver when **/sbin/rmmod** calls **cleanup_module()**, as follows.

```
void cleanup_module()
{
    int flag;
    ...
    flag = module_unregister_chrdev(majorNumber, "too");
    if(flag < 0) {
    /* Unregistration failed */
        ...
    }
    /* Other cleanup */
    ...
}
```

10

Example: A Disk Driver

The **drivers/block** directory contains various device drivers for disks. This directory contains files named **floppy.c**, **ide_floppy.c**, and **hd.c**, all device drivers for disks. The relative sizes of these three files for Version 2.0.36 are

floppy.c = 109,094 bytes, **ide_floppy.c** = 45,171 bytes, and **hd.c** = 29,009 bytes. The extra code for the two floppy disk drivers is for addressing various special cases that are unique to floppies, such as starting and stopping the drive motors. So even though you might think that the floppy disk driver should be simpler than the hard disk driver, it is not. Therefore this manual examines the code for the hard disk driver that is found in **hd.c**, given shortly. However, you are strongly encouraged to study the other device drivers on your own.

As noted previously, **blk_dev_init()** (in **drivers/block/ll_rw_bl.c**) makes a call to **hd_init()** (in **drivers/block/hd.c**), so the device driver for the **hd** device must incorporate such a function, as follows.

```
static struct file_operations hd_fops = {
   NULL, /* lseek - default */
   block_read, /* read - general block-dev read */
   block_write, /* write - general block-dev write */
   NULL, /* readdir - bad */
   NULL, /* select */
   hd_ioctl, /* ioctl */
   NULL, /* mmap */
   hd_open, /* open */
   hd_release, /* release */
   block_fsync /* fsync */
};

int hd_init(void)
{
   if (register_blkdev(MAJOR_NR,"hd",&hd_fops)) {
      printk("hd: unable to get major %d for harddisk\n",
            MAJOR_NR);
      return -1;
   }
   blk_dev[MAJOR_NR].request_fn = DEVICE_REQUEST;
   read_ahead[MAJOR_NR] = 8; /* 8 sector (4kB) read-ahead */
   hd_gendisk.next = gendisk_head;
   gendisk_head = &hd_gendisk;
   timer_table[HD_TIMER].fn = hd_times_out;
   return 0;
}
```

Notice in the **hd.c** file that the following routines are defined.

```
static int hd_ioctl(struct inode * inode, struct file * file,
        unsigned int cmd, unsigned long arg)
{
    ...
}

static int hd_open(struct inode * inode, struct file * filp)
{
    int target;
    target = DEVICE_NR(inode->i_rdev);

    if (target >= NR_HD)
        return -ENODEV;
    while (busy[target])
        sleep_on(&busy_wait);
    access_count[target]++;
    return 0;
}

static void hd_release(struct inode * inode, struct file * file)
{
    ...
}
```

The function **hd_open()** is called when a user-space program makes an **open()** system call on the kernel. This happens because **hd_open()** is registered with the kernel as the *open function* for the special file **/dev/hd*i*** (where *i* is a particular hard disk). **hd_open()** does the following:

- Gets the minor number for the device from the special file's inode.
- Checks to see whether that number is acceptable.
- Sleeps while the given target device is currently busy.
- Increases a reference count.
- Returns.

10

Notice that the **hd.c** file does not contain functions for **block_read()**, **block_write()**, and **block_fsync()**. These functions are defined in **fs/block_dev.c**, a file in the file system code. Recall that the reads and writes (and the **sync** operations) must read and write data to/from buffers rather than performing I/O on each system call. The device driver does not have enough information to know how a file is assembled—that information is kept in the file system. As a result, if blocks are going to be read and written automatically according to the amount of buffer space available, then the information needed to perform the I/O is in the file system rather than the device driver. Thus the **block_read()** and **block_write()** functions are part of the file system code, even though they ultimately will cause sector I/O in the device driver. Once the buffer management code determines which blocks to read or write—the process is complex—it calls the device driver **ll_rw_block()** function (in **drivers/block/ll_rw_blk.c**) to perform the operation.

Problem Statement

Part A

Design and implement a character device driver for a virtual FIFO device. Recall that a FIFO is equivalent to a pipe: One process can write into the FIFO, and another can read from it. The first character written to the FIFO is the first character returned by a read operation. Your driver should implement N FIFOs queues ($N = 4$) by implementing $2N$ minor device numbers. Even-numbered devices are write-only devices, and odd-numbered are read-only devices. Characters written to device i are readable from device $i + 1$.

Your driver should be a loadable device driver, that is, it should be implemented as a module. Use a major device number, K, assigned to you by your instructor. Use **mknod** to create a special file with the name **/dev/fifo***LK*, where L is a number in the range [100, 255].

Reading from an empty FIFO device should return an EOF if the other end is not currently open. Otherwise, the process calling the read operation must be blocked. Write operations (and a close on a write device) must wake up a blocked reader, if one exists.

FIFO device drivers must cope with writes that are too large by using a variant of **sleep()** and **wakeup()**. A write operation might be too large for the remaining space or for the statically allocated space. Alternatively, you may implement a FIFO device of unbounded size that dynamically obtains kernel space.

Part B

Demonstrate that your device driver operates properly. Be sure that your test program exercises the boundary conditions for the driver.

The driver in this exercise is easier to design than, for example, a disk driver, because it does not have to deal with buffers and because no actual hardware device is associated with the driver. To further simplify your driver, design it as a polling driver rather than an interrupt driver.

Design your virtual hardware—the FIFO data structure—and the interface to register with the kernel. Your module should have the following general form.

```
#include  <linux/kernel.h>
#include  <linux/module.h>
...
/* Driver entry points */
...
/* Registration information */
struct file_operations fifo_fops = {
        ...;          /* lseek */
        ...;          /* read */
        ...;          /* write */
        ...;          /* readdir */
        ...;          /* select */
        ...;          /* ioctl */
        ...;          /* mmap */
        ...;          /* open */
        ...;          /* release */
   };
...
int init_module()
{
   ...
   ... = module_register_chrdev(0, "fifo", &fifo_fops);
   /* Other initialization */
   ...
   return 0;
}

void cleanup_module()
```

10

```
{
    ...
    flag = module_inregister_chrdev(..., "fifo");
    /* Other cleanup */
    ...
```

eleven

File Systems

Exercise Goal: You will learn about how the Linux file manager is organized. Then you will design and implement a set of directory operations for a simplified file system. The Linux file manager is designed to accommodate many different kinds of disk devices, with different file system organizations and disk formats. While Linux provides its own file system organization for hard disks (**ext2**), the file manager can be extended to work with any file system format.

Introduction

Contemporary OSs provide multiple ways for a program to read or write a storage device such as a disk (see Figure 2.12(a)). An API for the device driver allows a user-space program to directly manipulate the disk hardware, thereby enabling such programs to read or write individual disk blocks. However, when a user-space program is allowed to read/write the disk directly, then the OS will have difficulty ensuring that its own data structures that are stored on the disk will not be destroyed by a rogue user program. Thus the file manager is usually the primary program that uses the device driver; other programs use only the device API under unusual circumstances. An example of an unusual circumstance is the OS's allocating the device exclusively to a process and then giving the process permission to read and write the device, for example, with a database manager. No other processes would be using the device during the time that it was allocated to the given process.

A disk device has enough capacity to store bytes for many files, but the bytes are stored in a collection of disk blocks. The file manager uses its own data structures and algorithms to implement an abstraction that enables information to be read or written from/to the disk blocks as if it were stored as a named, logical stream of bytes—that is, a *file*. File managers can usually be partitioned to include a part that manages the collection of files, referred to as the file manager's *directory operations*. For example, a process can identify a particular logical byte stream by its external name (or pathname), copy the file, remove the file, and so on. Another part of the file manager is responsible for reading and writing a specific file. Once the file has been opened, the process can read or write a variable number of bytes, independent of the block size on the underlying disk.

In UNIX systems, file systems are defined to help manage devices with removable media, such as floppy disks, and CD-ROMs.. The idea is that each removable media is organized as a hierarchical collection of files that share a single root directory, an independent *file system*. The root directory of the file system can be logically attached at a *mount point* in another file system (see the dis-

Figure 2.12
File and Device Managers

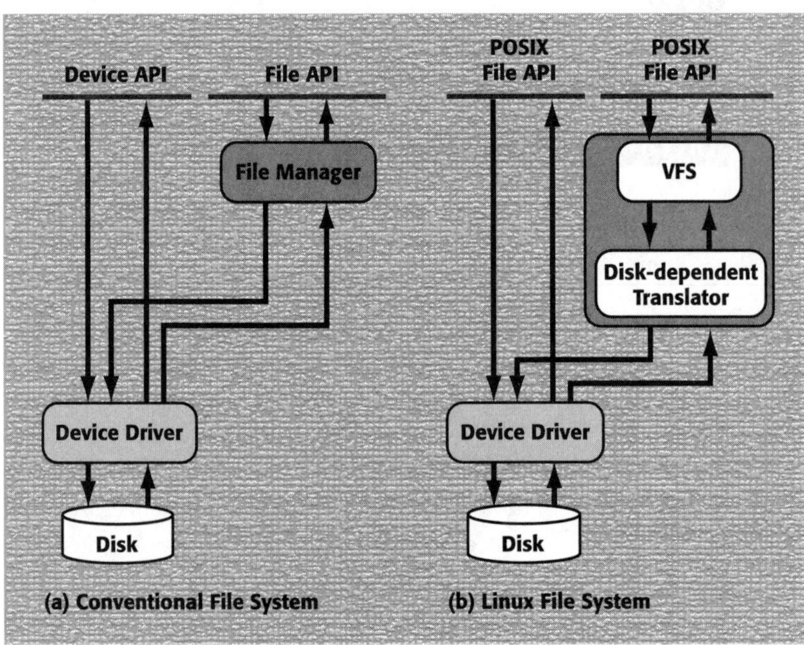

cussion in Part 1, Section 7). As a result, the mounted file system then logically appears as a subtree in a higher-level file system. UNIX systems have a boot file system that contains the system boot block and bootstrap program. It also contains the system root directory. When the system is initialized, it mounts other file systems at various mount points in the root file system according to a strategy chosen by the system's administrator.

Large disk devices can be partitioned to contain multiple file systems. Doing this has two important advantages.

1. If the file manager is limited as to the size of disk that it can manage, then it can work on an individual disk partition that has its own file system. This is common in the Windows 95/98 OSs, in which a file system is not allowed to be larger than 2GB.
2. Partitioning the disk so that it has multiple file systems enables the archiving utilities to dump or restore the disk on a file system basis. Thus dumping or restoring the entire disk at once is not necessary (instead, one file system is dumped or restored at a time).

The Linux file system organization is summarized in Figure 2.12(b). Two separate interfaces manipulate the disk device: the device driver interface and the file manager interface. However, in UNIX systems (including POSIX and Linux), the functions for the device driver API have been derived from the file manager API. Also used on the device API are the familiar **open()**, **close()**, **read()**, **write()**, **lseek()**, and **ioctl()**. You will use the device interface in this exercise, so it is discussed in more detail in the following Attacking the Problem section.

The UNIX file manager performs operations on the storage device according to which file system the relevant directory or file is located. This allows it to use the floppy disk driver when it manages files on the floppy disk and the hard disk driver when it manages files on one of the hard disk drives. Like most contemporary UNIX kernels, the Linux file manager extends this idea by incorporating the VFS (Virtual File System) switch (see Figure 2.12(b)). The VFS exports a single, logical API for manipulating files to the user-space programs. However, it is designed so that it can read and write disk drives that have radically different kinds of file systems. Specifically, a file system that has been formatted for MS-DOS, MINIX, Linux's preferred file system (**ext2**), or other formats can be mounted onto the Linux root directory. This is accomplished by designing the file manager to have certain functions that define the API and that are independent of the details of the disk or file system. However, this disk-independent component will cooperate with any disk-dependent component to translate disk-specific information into an internal VFS format. The details of how the VFS accomplishes this task are summarized in Part 1, Section 7. They are explained in more detail next.

The Virtual File System

Before a file system can be used, it must be mounted. Before an individual file can be read or written, it must be opened.

Mounting a File System

When a file system (for example, an MS-DOS file system) is mounted, the disk-dependent part of the file manager performs the following steps.

1. Read the disk geometry and FAT contents.
2. Translate the information that it needs from these records.
3. Write the information into VFS data structures (a **struct file** instance in the file structure table and **struct inode** in the inode table).

How can the VFS know how to read/write a disk (for example, to read the disk geometry and FAT contents for an MS-DOS file system) when the underlying disk could have been formatted in any of several different formats? Every file system that can be mounted first must be registered with the VFS so as to define its type. Types are usually registered when the machine is booted (by using the **register_filesystem()** system call defined in **fs/super.c**). This function's main purpose is to define a **read_super()** function for that type of file system. **read_super()**does the following.

- Reads information from a disk (actually, a file system) of the given type.
- Translates the information needed by the device-independent part of the file manager.
- Stores the information into a disk-independent *superblock* instance of the **struct super_block** data structure (see **include/linux/fs.h**).

The disk-independent part of the file manager calls **read_super()** whenever a file system of the corresponding type is mounted. This function fills in the superblock.

```
struct super_block {
   ...
   unsigned long s_blocksize;
   ...;
   struct file_system_type *s_type;
   struct super_operations *s_op;
```

```
   ...
   union {
struct minix_sb_info minix_sb;
      ...
      struct ext2_sb_info ext2_sb;
      ...;
      struct msdos_sb_info msdos_sb;
      ...;
   } u;
};
```

The superblock contains basic information about the file system type, for example the file system type (**s_type**), the block size (**s_blocksize**), and file system-specific information (**minix_sb, ext2_sb, msdos_sb**, and **generic_sbp**). The superblock also stores a set of superblock operations (**struct super_operations s_op**). The superblock operations (defined in **include/linux/fs.h**) give the device-independent part of the file manager a set of disk-dependent functions, as follows, to manipulate the on-disk superblock information—to read and write inodes, write superblock information back onto the disk surface, and so on.

```
struct super_operations {
   void (*read_inode) (struct inode *);
   void (*write_inode) (struct inode *);
   void (*put_inode) (struct inode *);
   void (*delete_inode) (struct inode *);
   int (*notify_change) (struct dentry *, struct iattr *);
   void (*put_super) (struct super_block *);
   void (*write_super) (struct super_block *);
   int (*statfs) (struct super_block *, struct statfs *, int);
   int (*remount_fs) (struct super_block *, int *, char *);
   void (*clear_inode) (struct inode *);
   void (*umount_begin) (struct super_block *);
};
```

These functions are used by the disk-independent part of the VFS to manage the specific mounted file system. The **read_inode()** function builds the Linux in-memory inode (see **struct inode in include/linux/fs.h**), and the **write_inode()** function translates Linux inode information back into the disk's form before writing it back to the on-disk file descriptor.

Opening a File

To open a file, the file manager does the following.

1. Traverses the composite file system to locate the file descriptor in its native format (for example, MS-DOS format) on the disk. The file reference is the file's external name.
2. Extracts the file description from the on-disk descriptor.
3. Translates the information needed by the VFS.
4. Stores the requisite information into VFS tables by using the disk-independent Linux format.

The design of the internal file descriptor and tables is inspired by conventional UNIX designs. That is, the VFS has a *file descriptor table* for each process, a *file structure table*, and an *inode* for each open file (see Figure 2.13). When a file is opened, entries are made into each of these data structures.

Each process's file descriptor table (the **struct files_struct files** field in the process's **struct task_struct**) has one entry for each open file for the process. The default value for descriptor 0 is **stdin**, for 1 is **stdout**, and for 2 is **stderr**. The entry defines file open and close actions and provides a pointer to a file structure table entry of type **struct file** (see **include/linux/fs.h**).

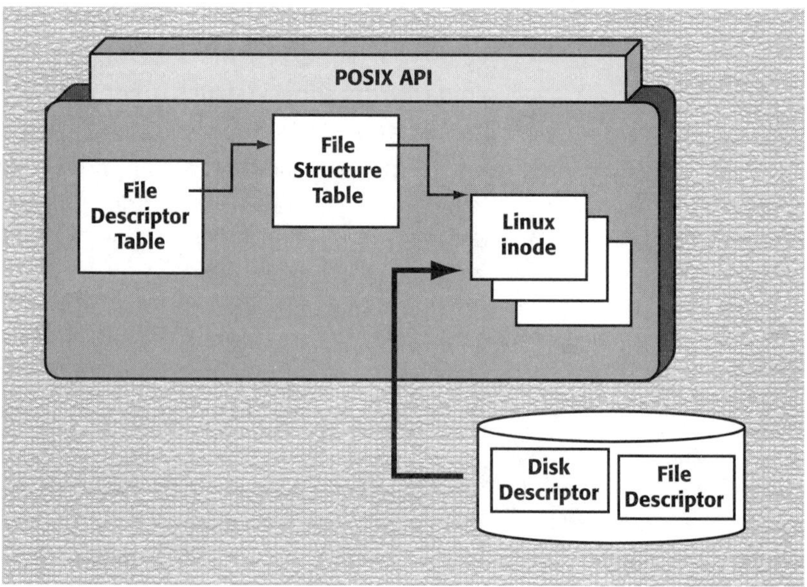

Figure 2.13
VFS-Disk Translation

The file structure table entry contains a substantial amount of the information that the disk-independent portion of the file manager uses to manipulate a disk-dependent file system. This information includes a **struct dentry * f_dentry** field (defined in **include/linux/dcache.h**) that references the **struct inode** for the file, after the inode has been loaded into primary memory. It also includes the definition of the file operations to be used to manipulate this file.

```
struct file {
    ...
    struct dentry * f_dentry;
    struct file_operations * f_op;
    ...
};
```

The internal Linux inode is derived from the file's disk-dependent file descriptor. Whenever the inode is updated, the internal version must be translated then written back to the disk. After a file has been opened, the disk-independent part of the file manager operates on the internal VFS file data structures rather than use the file data structures stored on the disk. For example, an MS-DOS-formatted disk contains the disk geometry, a boot record, a FAT, and a root directory, as well as the disk blocks as organized by the FAT contents (see the following Attacking the Problem). The **read_super()** function fills in the superblock. The **read_inode()** function defined in the superblock's **s_op** field reads inode information from the disk-dependent descriptors and fills in the VFS inode instance.

Here is an abstraction of the **struct inode** as defined in **include/linux/fs.h**.

```
struct inode {
    ...
    uid_t i_uid;
    gid_t i_gid;
    ...
    time_t i_atime;
    time_t i_mtime;
    time_t i_ctime;
    unsigned long i_blksize;
    unsigned long i_blocks;
    ...;
    struct inode_operations *i_op;
    struct super_block *i_sb;
    ...
```

```
    union {
      ...
      struct minix_inode_info minix_i;
      ...
      struct ext2_inode_info ext2_i;
      ...
      struct msdos_inode_info msdos_i;
      struct umsdos_inode_info umsdos_i;
      ...
    } u;
};
```

The inode contains many fields—all of the information that the file manager needs to manage the file. Because the disk-independent part of the file manager exports a POSIX interface, the VFS descriptors resemble classic UNIX file structure table entries and inodes. For example, the inode has fields that contain the following information:

- User and group IDs for the file
- Times at which the file was last accessed, modified, and created
- Block size and number of blocks in the file
- List of inode operations that can be used with this inode (the **struct inode_operations *i_op field**)
- A pointer to the superblock for the file system in which the file is stored
- Device-specific information about the file

Notice that just as a **read_super()** is defined for each file system type and the superblock operations are dynamically defined at mount time, the inode operation functions are defined when the VFS inode is created (when the file is opened) and are generally used for directory operations. This is described in the next subsection.

When a system call is made to the corresponding function on the system call interface, the kernel routes the call to the file manager, which ultimately uses the function as defined in the inode operations list. Finally, the **struct inode_operations** includes the **struct file_operations default_file_ops** field to define the functions that will be invoked by the system calls for manipulating the file itself (**open()**, **read()**, **write()**, and so on).

Directories

A file system may contain many files. An early study of UNIX files indicated, however, that they are likely to be typically only a few kilobytes in length

[Ousterhout, et al., 1985]. This suggests that a 1GB or larger file system might contain on the order of a million files. Such a large number of files requires a way to organize them so that people can remember which file contains what information. A hierarchical, or tree-structured, file system is a popular technique for organizing a large collection of files. In UNIX systems, the root file system has a root directory that contains entries to reference other directories and files. Each subdirectory, in turn, contains entries to reference other directories and files. This recursive definition of a directory forms the hierarchical structure for the file system. In windows-oriented interfaces to the file system, each directory is represented as a file folder that can contain other file folders or documents (files).

Hierarchical file systems are relatively easy to implement when, as is usually the case, directories are implemented by using ordinary files. Thus the nucleus of the file manager can be written with no particular knowledge of directories and a client of this nucleus can then use ordinary file operations—open, close, read, and write—to implement the directory data structures and algorithms. UNIX systems are traditionally designed in this manner, as is the Linux file manager.

A directory entry must contain enough information to allow the file manager to match a character string filename with the entry's name and, if the names match, to find the external file descriptor on the disk. For example, in a UNIX system (including Linux **ext2**), the directory entry is required to have only the filename and the inode number for the file. All specific information related to the file is kept in the on-disk inode.

Directory operations are defined by the **struct inode_operations** field in the inode (see **include/linux/fs.h**).

```
struct inode_operations {
   struct file_operations * default_file_ops;
   int (*create) (struct inode *,struct dentry *,int);
   struct dentry * (*lookup) (struct inode *,struct dentry *);
   int (*link) (struct dentry *,struct inode *,struct dentry *);
   int (*unlink) (struct inode *,struct dentry *);
   int (*symlink) (struct inode *,struct dentry *,const char *);
   int (*mkdir) (struct inode *,struct dentry *,int);
   int (*rmdir) (struct inode *,struct dentry *);
   int (*mknod) (struct inode *,struct dentry *,int,int);
   int (*rename) (struct inode *, struct dentry *,
         struct inode *, struct dentry *);
   int (*readlink) (struct dentry *, char *,int);
   struct dentry * (*follow_link) (struct dentry *,
```

```
        struct dentry *, unsigned int);
        int (*readpage) (struct file *, struct page *);
    ...
};
```

The meanings of inode operations are relatively straightforward. For example, the mkdir() function creates a new file and initializes it to be a directory (with pointers to its parent and itself). In addition, other user-space programs (library programs), for example, list the files in a directory (–ls) and traverse the directory contents (–cd). These user-space programs can be arbitrarily complex, for example ls queries the inode to retrieve information to be included in the listing.

Example: An MS-DOS File System

Linux has supported MS-DOS disks from its early releases. Over time, the code has been reorganized, modified, and extended (for example, to handle Windows 95 and NT filenames). The basic file system is implemented in the fs/fat and fs/msdos directories.

The file fs/msdos/namei.c defines the super_read() function for the file system as msdos_read_super(). This function calls fat_read_super() (defined in fs/fat/inode.c), which handles all of the details for reading the superblock. The fat_read_super() function ultimately calls ll_rw_block() in drivers/block/ll_rw_blk.c, which then reads the disk. This whole procedure includes many details that must be handled because the low-level read/write driver is designed to be called at any time that the device is to be read, and not just for super_read(). The read/write routine interacts with the virtual memory system and the file buffer caching mechanism, so it is written to be very general. Notice that msdos_read_super() is defined in the fs directory but ends up calling ll_rw_block() in the drivers directory. A careful review of this code shows that when ll_rw_block() considers the buffering strategy for the file system, it actually interacts with other code in the fs directory.

super_operations for the msdos file system are defined in fs/fat/inode.c, as follows.

```
struct super_operations fat_sops = {
    NULL,
    fat_write_inode,
    NULL,
    fat_delete_inode,
    fat_notify_change,
```

```
    fat_put_super,
    NULL, /* write_super */
    fat_statfs,
    NULL, /* remount */
    fat_clear_inode
};
```

These **file_operations** and **inode_operations** are defined in **fs/fat/file.c**.

```
static struct file_operations fat_file_operations = {
    NULL, /* lseek - default */
    fat_file_read, /* read */
    fat_file_write, /* write */
    NULL, /* readdir - bad */
    NULL, /* select v2.0.x/poll v2.1.x - default */
    NULL, /* ioctl - default */
    generic_file_mmap, /* mmap */
    NULL, /* no special open is needed */
    NULL, /* release */
    file_fsync /* fsync */
};

struct inode_operations fat_file_inode_operations = {
    &fat_file_operations, /* default file operations */
    NULL, /* create */
    NULL, /* lookup */
    NULL, /* link */
    NULL, /* unlink */
    NULL, /* symlink */
    NULL, /* mkdir */
    NULL, /* rmdir */
    NULL, /* mknod */
    NULL, /* rename */
    NULL, /* readlink */
    NULL, /* follow_link */
    generic_readpage, /* readpage */
    NULL, /* writepage */
    fat_bmap, /* bmap */
    fat_truncate, /* truncate */
    NULL, /* permission */
    NULL /* smap */
};
```

Notice that in the operations definitions, several functions are declared **NULL**, meaning that the **msdos** file system uses default functions in these cases.

Problem Statement[1]

You will implement various features of a file manager for an MS-DOS-formatted floppy disk by using the POSIX floppy disk driver API. Your solution will be user-space software. (If it were to support (and enforce) disk sharing, it would need to be kernel-space code.)

Your solution software should read a floppy disk that is written in MS-DOS format, though it will only write the on-disk file descriptor (in Part C). In Exercise 12, you will complete this simple file system by adding more software to allocate space and to write to all parts of the floppy disk.

Part A

Design and implement a function to provide a directory listing (like the **ls** UNIX shell command.) First, you need a function to make the physical disk ready for use (to call the disk driver initialization code to determine the disk geometry, as well as any other initialization that you choose):

```
int fd_load(char driveLetter);
```

Your directory listing function does not need to be as complex as a production routine–it needs to contain only the basic command, without support for options. Follow this function prototype:

```
int fd_ls();
```

After you have completed Part A, your function will be able only to list the files in the root directory.

Part B

Design and implement a function to change the current directory up one level or to a subdirectory in the current directory (you do not need to handle pathnames):

```
int fd_cd(char *directory);
```

This function assumes that you have implemented subdirectories.You will probably find it helpful to use a static variable in your file system imple-

[1] This exercise is inspired by one that Norman Ramsey created for Windows NT at Purdue University in 1996.

mentation to represent the current directory (you could implement it as an environment variable, but that is not required for this exercise). This function is to manipulate that current directory variable.

Part C

Design and implement a function to delete a file. It should take the name of a file to delete (from the current directory) as its argument:

```
int fd_rm(char *name);
```

The function needs to find the file, follow its links in the FAT, set each cluster's entry in the FAT to mark it as unused, and update the directory entry. In the case of deletion, pay attention to the hidden, read-only, and system attributes. Files with any of these set should not be deleted.

Attacking the Problem

You need to address many details to solve this problem. The exercise is broken down into parts to reduce the overall complexity of the problem:

- Part A: Construct the command to list directory contents.
- Part B: Change the current directory definition.
- Part C: Remove a file.

This section provides you with a good start on considering all of them, but you will have to discover and resolve many on your own.

The MS-DOS Disk Format

MS-DOS defines a particular format for floppy disks. The MS-DOS BIOS (Basic Input/Output System) provides a set of programs that can read and write disk sectors. It also provides an additional abstraction on the disk address called the *logical sector address*. Logical sector 0 corresponds to the sector at surface 0 (on a hard disk), track 0, sector 1 of the floppy disk. (Surfaces and tracks are numbered from zero, but sectors are numbered from 1; the reasons for this have long been forgotten.) Logical sector 1 is at surface 0, track 0, sector 2, and so on.

Before a floppy disk can be used for normal I/O operations, it must be formatted to contain essential information in prespecified locations. Specifically, logical sector 0 contains a reserved area (also called the *boot sector* or *boot record*). The MS-DOS boot sequence relies on the boot sector's being located at logical sector 0 and organized as shown in Figure 2.14; see also Part 1, Section 3.5

and Messmer [1995]. Several of the fields will not make sense until you have had a chance to read the details about the FAT and how it uses the boot record information. Hard disks also may be partitioned (see Part 1, Section 3.5), with each partition defining a file system.

Figure 2.15 shows the organization of an MS-DOS-formatted floppy disk. The FAT generally is replicated on the disk, so location **0x10** in the boot sector tells the system how many copies of the FAT are formatted onto this disk (usually two). The FAT is replicated so that if the first copy is accidentally destroyed, then the disk can be recovered by copying the second copy over the first. Each root directory entry uses 32 bytes. Location **0x11** in the boot sector indicates how many entries are in the disk (1.44MB floppy disks have space for 224 directory entries, using 14 sectors).

Each floppy disk drive has a fixed geometry that specifies the fundamental parameters for that drive. These include the number of

- bytes per disk block (a block is usually called *sector* in the disk drive literature),
- sectors in each track,
- read/write heads, and
- cylinders (tracks).

A floppy disk is formatted with the geometry in its boot sector. Logical sectors are numbered from zero, even though individual sectors on a track are typically numbered from 1. The logical sector *l* on track *T*, head *H*, sector *S* is located at

Figure 2.14
Boot Sector

0x00	0x02	<a jump instruction to 0x1e>
0x03	0x0a	Computer manufacturer's name
0x0b	0x0c	Bytes per sector
0x0d	0x0d	Sectors per cluster
0x0e	0x0f	Reserved sectors for the boot record
0x10	0x10	Number of FATs
0x11	0x12	Number of root directory entries
0x13	0x14	Number of logical sectors
0x15	0x15	Medium descriptor byte (used only on old versions of MS-DOS)
0x16	0x17	Sectors per FAT
0x18	0x19	Sectors per track
0x1a	0x1b	Number of surfaces (heads)
0x1c	0x1d	Number of hidden sectors
0x1e	...	Bootstrap program

Figure 2.15 Floppy Disk Organization

Logical Sector	Content
0	Boot sector
1	First sector in the (first) FAT
. . .	
10	First sector in the second FAT (if there is a second one; see 0x10 in the boot sector)
19	First sector in the floppy disk's root directory
xx	Last sector in the root directory (see 0x11 in the boot sector)
xx+1	Beginning of data area for the floppy disk

$l = S - 1 + T$ * (heads * sectorsPerTrack) + H * sectorsPerTrack.

The MS-DOS FAT

The floppy disk format is based on a FAT file system in which the media (floppy disk) is divided into a *reserved area* (containing the boot program), the actual *allocation tables*, a *root* directory, and file space; see Figure 2.15. The second copy of the FAT is the same as the first copy; it is used to recover the disk if the first copy of the FAT is accidentally destroyed. Space allocated for files is represented by values in the allocation table, thereby effectively providing a linked list of all of the blocks in the file. Special values designate EOF, unallocated blocks, and bad blocks. The original FAT had many limitations. It had no subdirectories and was limited to very small disks. In addition, recovering the disk if the allocation tables were damaged was very difficult.

During the time of the explosive growth of the personal computer, the size of disk drives also increased dramatically. At the same time, different variants of FAT were derived to accommodate larger disks. The basic FAT organization (see Figure 2.16) differs among disk types as follows:

- By the size of the entries (M in the figure can be 12 or 16 but can be 12, 16, or 32 in Windows 98 and Windows 2000)
- By the number of actual tables
- By the size of the logical sector addressed by a FAT entry

In the simplest variant, one FAT entry corresponds to each sector on the disk. A file is a set of disk sectors, with the FAT entry corresponding to the first entry designating the logical sector number of the second block. Similarly, the FAT entry of the second block specifies the logical sector number of the third block, and so on. The FAT entry for the last block contains an EOF designator. Thus the FAT is a linked list of disk sectors. If you know the address of the first sector, *i*—and therefore the index into the FAT—you can use the FAT to reference the next logical sector in the file (see the figure). The content, *j*, of FAT index *i* is a logical sector number, as well as an index to the second FAT entry for the file.

As disk sizes grew larger than 32MB, the FAT organization began to use the notion of a cluster of sectors. A *cluster* is a group of contiguous sectors that are treated as a virtual sector within the FAT. In contemporary implementations of the FAT file system, the FAT entry addresses a cluster rather than an individual disk sector. With the use of clusters, the FAT organization can address groups of, say, four sectors as if they were a single sector that contained four times as many bytes as a single sector. This means that disk space is allocated to a file on a cluster-by-cluster basis. However, a 12-bit FAT is still limited to 128MB. Today, floppy disks use 12-bit FATs and hard disks use 16-bit or 32-bit FATs.

Figure 2.16
FAT Organization

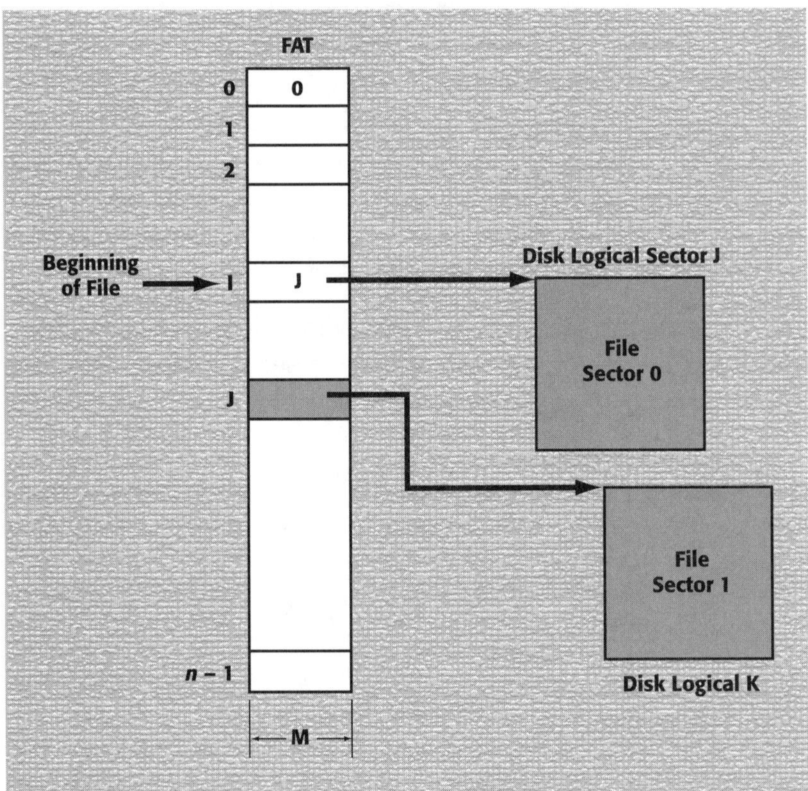

Directories and File Storage

Information about files is stored in a directory. You can look up information about a file (its size, its location on the floppy disk, the time it was created, and so on) by using the file's name. FAT-12 (the version of FAT with 12-bit FAT entries) uses a simple list of fixed-size *directory entries*. A directory entry can be found in a directory by searching linearly through the disk sectors that contain the directory list. That is, traversing the list of directory entries in a directory involves looking at multiple disk sectors and then at multiple entries within each sector.

A directory entry contains the filename and a description of the location of the file's data. The entry also contains the file's size in bytes (in case the file size is not an exact multiple of the sector size). Directory entries use the same format whether they are in the root directory or in a subdirectory. Each entry is 32 bytes long, thereby allowing 16 entries per standard 512-byte sector. The root directory has a fixed maximum number of entries (the number is stored in the boot sector) and occupies a contiguous group of logical sectors, as determined by the format. By contrast, subdirectories are stored in a set of sectors that are managed in the same manner as files. That is, logically contiguous sectors are not necessarily physically contiguous on the disk, and therefore they must be accessed by using the FAT.

Figure 2.17 shows the layout for a directory entry. All multibyte integers are in *little-endian order*, meaning that the least significant byte is stored first.

The filename and extension are stored as uppercase ASCII characters. Invalid entries have names beginning with 0x00 (the entry has not been used before) or 0xe5 (the entry was used before but has been released). The starting cluster number is slightly deceiving. Although it references the starting cluster (sector) number, it cannot reference sectors used for the boot record, FAT copies, or root directory. A starting cluster number k actually refers to logical sector number $31 + k$.

Figure 2.17
Directory Entry

Offset	Length	Description
0x00	8	Filename
0x08	3	Extension
0x0B	1	Bit field for attributes
0x0C	10	Reserved
0x16	2	Time (coded as Hour*2048+Min*32+Sec/2)
0x18	2	Date (coded as (Year-1980)*512+Month*32+Day)
0x1A	2	Starting cluster number
0x1C	4	File size (in bytes)

Figure 2.18
Directory Entry Attributes

Bit	Mask	Attribute
0	0x01	Read-only
1	0x02	Hidden
2	0x04	System
3	0x08	Volume label
4	0x10	Subdirectory
5	0x20	Archive
6	0x40	Unused
7	0x80	Unused

The attribute byte stores bits for attributes, similar to UNIX attributes. The bit fields are shown in Figure 2.18. Note that bit **0** is the least significant bit. A bit set to **1** means that the file has that attribute and **0** means that it does not. So, for example, a file with attributes **0x20** == **00100000b** has the archive bit set and all others cleared. A hidden, read-only subdirectory would be 00010011b == 0x13.

Clusters and File Storage

Files on FAT disks are divided into clusters of *N* sectors. *N* ranges from 1 to 32, depending on the format (hard disks use large clusters, so their allocation tables do not get too large). To access a file, you need to determine the list of clusters that it occupies. For example, a 2K file **FOO.TXT** might occupy clusters 34, 19, 81, and 47. Because the directory has a fixed size, there is no room to store an arbitrary list of clusters in the directory entry. Instead, the system stores only the first cluster; the FAT is used to link the rest. For example, to find out what cluster follows cluster *C*, use the Cth entry in the FAT. So for **FOO.TXT**, the system would store 34 in the directory entry for the first cluster.

FAT[34] == 19
FAT[19] == 81
FAT[81] == 47
FAT[47] == 0xff8

The special value **0xff8** marks the last cluster in the file. Any value from **0xff8** through **0xfff** may be used for this purpose. Use of this value is redundant because the file length indicates how many clusters there are, but the redundant information helps in recovering damaged disks.

More on the FAT

The first two entries of the FAT (for clusters 0 and 1) are reserved. The first one holds the media descriptor, which, for floppy disks, takes on the values shown in Figure 2.19. The FAT space, for clusters with two or more sectors, can contain the values for an entry, as shown in Figure 2.20.

FAT Packing

The data structure would be easier to manipulate if the cluster numbers in the FAT were stored in two-byte groups in the FAT sectors. But early MS-DOS machines were limited in space, so designers decided to pack *two* 12-bit FAT entries into 3 bytes. Thus bytes $3k$ through $3k + 2$ contain elements $2k$ and $2k + 1$ of the FAT array. In particular:

- Byte $3k$ contains the least significant 8 bits of FAT[$2k$].
- The least significant 4 bits of byte $3k + 1$ contain the most significant 4 bits of FAT[$2k$].
- The most significant 4 bits of byte $3k + 1$ contain the least significant 4 bits of FAT[$2k + 1$].
- Byte $3k + 2$ contains the most significant 8 bits of FAT[$2k + 1$].

As an example of how entries are packed into the FAT, suppose that a short file has been written to a new 1.44MB floppy disk. This new file begins at the first part of the file space, in cluster 2. The rest of its sectors follow contiguously (because the disk was not already fragmented when it was written). The beginning

Figure 2.19
FAT Entry Values

Descriptor	Heads	Sectors/Track	Cylinders	Capacity
0x0fe	1	8	40	160K
0x0ff	2	8	40	320K
0x0fc	1	9	40	180K
0x0fd	2	9	40	360K
0x0f9	2	9	80	720K
0x0f0	2	18	80	1.44M

Figure 2.20
FAT Space Values

Value	Meaning
0x000	Unused
0xFF0-0xFF6	Reserved cluster
0xFF7	Bad cluster
0xFF8-0xFFF	Last cluster in a file
(anything else)	Number of the next cluster in the file

of the FAT now appears as shown in the hexadecimal dump in Figure 2.21. The first 3 bytes (F0 FF FF) are the two reserved entries and can be ignored. The first entry corresponding to the example file is that for cluster 2, its beginning block. From the algorithm, the entry for cluster 2 is obtained by combining parts of bytes at offsets 3 and 4. This gives 0x003, since the first byte is less significant. This means that the FAT entry for cluster 2 is a pointer to its next cluster, number 3. To fetch number 3 then, you use the bytes at offsets 4 and 5, thereby resulting in 0x004. So the FAT entry for cluster 3 points to the next cluster in the file, number 4. Similarly, cluster 4 has 0x005 for the next cluster, and so on. Finally, at cluster 9(2 * 4 + 1), reading the entries at offsets 13 and 14 (3 * 4 + 1 and 3 * 4 + 2) gives 0xfff, a reserved value that indicates the last cluster in a file. So cluster 9 marks the end of the file that began at cluster 2. The remaining clusters, from 10 up, are still unallocated and so have the reserved value 0.

Converting Clusters to Logical Sectors

If each cluster has one logical sector, then each logical sector has an entry. However, because the FAT area stores only information about file space, and the first two entries are reserved, the first cluster in the file space is cluster number 2. To convert from a cluster number to a logical sector number, do the following.

1. Subtract 2 from the cluster number.
2. Multiply by the number of sectors in a cluster (1 for the 1.44MB floppy disks).

Thus on media that have 1 sector per cluster, with a 1-sector reserved area, 18 sectors for FAT, and 14 sectors for the root directory (exactly the description of a 1.44M floppy), the logical sector number of the first sector of file space is 0 + 1 + 18 + 14 = 33. This sector will correspond to FAT cluster 2, logical sector 34 to FAT cluster 3, and so on.

Using the Floppy Disk API

The introduction noted that the Linux device interface is the same as the file manager interface. For example, a Linux process executing in user space can open the floppy disk by executing

Figure 2.21
Example FAT

```
F0 FF FF 03 40 00 05 60  00 07 80 00 09 F0 FF 00
00 00 00 00 00 00 00 00  00 00 00 00 00 00 00 00
```

```
open("/dev/fd0", O_RDONLY);
```

The process then can use the normal kernel **read()** system call to read the entire disk device as if it were a linear sequence of bytes. The byte sequence is determined by the disk layout. That is, the first bytes in the stream are the bytes in the first logical sector on the disk, then the next block of bytes come from the second logical sector, and so on.

Depending on exactly how your laboratory machine is configured, the special file for your A: floppy disk drive could have a couple of different names, though it is probably /dev/fd0. It also might be named /dev/fd*n*H1440, where *n* is a sequence number, probably zero. You then can read the floppy disk contents as a byte stream.

To write the floppy disk, you must run your program with superuser permission. For this exercise, you are to use this device interface as though it is a simplified block device interface. That is, you are to open the file and then read or write its contents as full (512-byte) disk sectors. Use the following functions to read and write the disk.

```
int fd_fid;        /* global variable set by the open() function */
int bps;           /* Bytes per sector from disk geometry */
...
bps = ...;
fid = open(DEV_NAME, O_RDWR);        /* Must be superuser to
write */
...
int ll_fd_read(int sector_number, char *buffer) {
   int dest, len;

   dest = lseek(fid, sector_number*bps, SEEK_SET);
         if(dest != sector_number*bps) {
     /* Error handling here */
   }
   len = read(fid, buffer, bps);
   if(len != bps) {
     /* Error handling here */
   }
   return len;
}


int ll_fd_write(int sector_number, char *buffer) {
```

11

```
    int dest, len;

    dest = lseek(fid, sector_number*bps, SEEK_SET);
        if(dest != sector_number*bps) {
        /* Error handling here */
    }
    len = write(fid, buffer, bps);
    if(len != bps) {
        /* Error handling here */
    }
    return len;
}
```

The **sector_number** is a logical disk number, **sector_number** 0 is the boot record, **sector_number** 1 is the location of the first FAT table, and so on, as described in Figure 2.15.

Planning a Solution

You might find it useful to write various supporting routines that can be used to write solutions to the various parts of the exercise. Norman Ramsey, in his Windows NT solution to this problem, suggested implementing the following functions.

```
int scanFatDirectorySector(char *buf, char *name);
struct directoryEntry getEntryFromSector(
        char *buf,
        unsigned index
);
unsigned getFat12Entry(Disk d, unsigned index);
unsigned readFat12Cluster(
        Disk,
        unsigned cluster,
        char *buf
);
```

You also might find it useful to write functions to implement other routines such as

```
int getBootInfo(Disk, BootDescriptor);
```

to extract critical information stored in the boot sector and then return the information in a **BootDescriptor** structure of the following example form.

```
typedef struct BootDescriptor_t *BootDescriptor;
typedef struct BootDescriptor_t {
    unsigned     sectorsPerCluster;
    unsigned     numberOfFATs;
    unsigned     numberOfRootDirEntries;
    unsigned     numberOfLogSectors;
    unsigned     sectorsPerFAT;
    unsigned     numberOfHiddenSectors;
};
```

The scanFatDirectorySector() Function

The scanFatDirectorySector() function should search a directory in a sector, looking for an entry with a name passed as a parameter. Do not forget that MS-DOS filenames are case-insensitive, so you must match names regardless of case. (Because filenames are stored on the disk in uppercase letters, you can do this by applying **toupper()** to the name for which you are searching.)

The function should return –1 if it fails to find a matching directory entry. Otherwise, it should return the index of the matching entry, which is guaranteed to be in the range 0 to 15.

The getEntryFromSector() Function

The getEntryFromSector() function should use the index returned by scanFatDirectorySector() to retrieve the contents of the entry. Invalid directory entries have filenames that begin with 0x00 (the entry has never been used) or 0xe5 (the entry was previously used but has been released). The directory entry can be represented by the following C structure.

```
struct directoryEntry {
  char fullname[13];  /*name & extension, null-terminated */
  unsigned short year, month, day, hour, min, sec;
  unsigned short firstCluster;
  unsigned long size;
  unsigned readonly:1;
  unsigned hidden:1;
  unsigned system:1;
  unsigned vlabel:1;
  unsigned subdir:1;
  unsigned archive:1;
};
```

11

You cannot simply do bitwise copies from the directory entry into this structure. Instead, you must unmarshal it and then fill in the fields as appropriate. Integers are little-endian on the disk. Also, the 2-byte field for the time is computed as

```
2048*hours + 32*minutes + seconds/2
```

Thus you must unpack the time field by building the 2-byte value and then performing an integer divide to determine the hour value, the minute value, and the second value. Similarly, the 2-byte date field is encoded as

```
512 * (year – 1980) + 32 * month + day
```

The getFat12Entry() Function

The getFat12Entry() function should take an index (and disk descriptor) and return the unsigned index into a FAT. In the example, the FAT shown in Figure 2.21, getFat12Entry(d, 9), should return 0xfff, which is the logical sector number in the ninth entry in the FAT.

The readFat12Cluster() Function

The readFat12Cluster() function should perform the translation of a cluster to a logical sector number described in the exercise's introduction. It should return zero on success and nonzero on failure.

Following is the header file used for the solution to this exercise.

```
/* This interface is derived from one designed
 * by Norman Ramsey for CSci 413 at Purdue University, 1996
 */

#ifndef FILESYS_H
#define FILESYS_H

#include    <windows.h>
#include    "..\exercise10.h"

#define DIR_ENTRY_SIZE          32

// typedef struct open_file *Open_File;
typedef struct file_system *FileSystem;


typedef struct BootDescriptor_t *BootDescriptor;
typedef struct BootDescriptor_t {
```

```
    unsigned   sectorsPerCluster;
    unsigned   numberOfFATs;
    unsigned   numberOfRootDirEntries;
    unsigned   numberOfLogSectors;
    unsigned   sectorsPerFAT;
    unsigned   numberOfHiddenSectors;
};

typedef struct directoryEntry {
    char fullname[13];  // Filename and ext, null-terminated
    unsigned short year, month, day, hour, min, sec;
    unsigned short firstCluster;
    unsigned long size;
    unsigned readonly:1;
    unsigned hidden:1;
    unsigned system:1;
    unsigned vlabel:1;
    unsigned subdir:1;
    unsigned archive:1;
};


/* Function prototypes on the File System interface */
// File System Interface
   int fd_load(char);
   int fd_ls();
   int fd_cd(char *directory);
   int fd_rm(char *file_name);

// Function prototypes used to implement the file system
   unsigned fatOctet(Disk, unsigned);
   void findDate(
          unsigned short *year,
          unsigned short *month,
          unsigned short *day,
          unsigned char info[2]
   );
   void findTime(
          unsigned short* hour,
          unsigned short* min,
          unsigned short* sec,
```

11

```
        unsigned char info[2]
  );


  int allocSector(Disk, int);
  int getBootInfo(Disk, BootDescriptor);
  struct directoryEntry getEntryFromSector(char *buf,
        unsigned index);
  unsigned getFat12Entry(Disk d, unsigned index);
  unsigned getFATByte(Disk d, unsigned k);
  int getFreeDirectoryEntry(char *buf, char *name);
  int getRootDirSector();
  void intToExtName(char intName[], char extName[]);
  int markFATfree(Disk d, int);
  int nextRelSector(Disk d, int lastSector);
  int putEntryIntoSector(
        char *buf,
        struct directoryEntry dirEntry,
        unsigned index
  );
  unsigned putFat12Entry(Disk d, unsigned index,
          unsigned val);
  unsigned putFATByte(Disk d, unsigned k, unsigned val);
  unsigned readFat12Cluster(Disk, unsigned cluster,
          char *buf);
  int scanFatDirectorySector(char *buf, char *name);
  void toBin(unsigned char, int[8]);

#endif FILESYS_H
```

Notice that you are to read and write a single floppy disk—and with code that references the FAT. For this exercise, you should not attempt to copy the FAT into primary memory, even though not doing so will clearly impact performance negatively.

You need to derive your solution by using a floppy disk. Prepare a floppy disk under the usual Windows interface and include a dozen simple files. Your solution should be able to manipulate this floppy disk.

You need to write a simple test program to check that each of your commands works. You will likely find it natural to develop this program as you debug each command.

twelve

File I/O

Exercise Goal: You will learn how the Linux file manager reads and writes files and then modify the file manager that you created in Exercise 11. In that exercise, you learned to read, interpret, and modify the FAT and directory information on an MS-DOS floppy disk. However, you were not required to allocate new sectors to a file (or otherwise write to the disk except to change the FAT). In this exercise, you will add functions to your file manager to make directories, to copy files, and to read and write files by using buffers. You again will be using the system call interface to the floppy disk driver to read and write sectors on the disk surface.

Introduction

In Linux (and MS-DOS), a *file* is a named, linear sequence of bytes that is stored on a persistent storage device (such as a disk, a CD-ROM, or a tape). Directory operations (defined in **struct inode_operations**) are used to manipulate the file hierarchy. You implemented a few fundamental directory operations in Exercise 11. The file manager also must provide functions so that processes can manipulate the information that is stored *inside* of a file—essentially, the functions that allow the process to read and write the file. Your first goal in this exercise is to learn to read and write a file. Then you can provide additional directory operations (these require you to rewrite a directory file).

The system calls for performing file I/O operations are defined by the **struct file_operations** functions (see Exercise 11). These functions enable a user process to open/close, read/write, and move the file position pointer (**lseek**) in the file byte stream. As summarized in Figure 2.22, the file manager reacts to a **write()** function call by placing the information in one or more output buffers. If a buffer becomes full, then the file manager will enqueue a write request for the device driver. When the device driver detects that the storage device is idle, and it decides that the buffer is the next one to write, it initiates a write operation to transfer the information from the output buffer into the storage device. A read operation causes the file manager to determine the current file position and then issue a read operation to the device driver. In this way, the data will be placed in an input buffer before the user process performs a read call on the **struct file-operations** interface. The following discussion offers more details about the open/close and the read/write operations (including block buffering).

The Open and Close Operations

The open function validates the request, adjusts the file descriptor table and file structure table, and then loads the inode into the internal VFS inode table (see Figure 2.13). The **sys_open()** function in **fs/open.c** performs these functions. It allocates the file descriptor and file structure entries, validates the access, and then calls **filp_open()**, which is also defined in **fs/open.c**.

Figure 2.22
Overview of File I/O

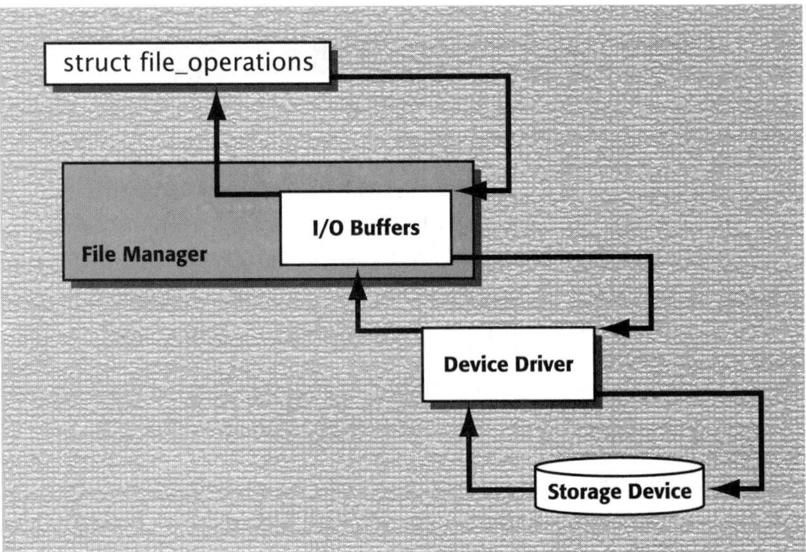

Following is an abstraction of the implementation (as usual, C++-style comments do not appear in the Linux release).

```
static int filp_open(const char * filename,int flags,int mode, int fd)
{
    struct inode * inode;
    struct dentry * dentry;
    struct file * f;
    int ...,error;

    error = -ENFILE;
    f = get_empty_filp(); // Get a file structure entry
    ...
    // Initialize the file structure
    ...
    // Get an internal inode
    inode = dentry->d_inode;
);
    ...

    f->f_dentry = dentry;
    f->f_pos = 0;
    f->f_reada = 0;
    f->f_op = NULL;
    if (inode->i_op)
     f->f_op = inode->i_op->default_file_ops;
    if (f->f_op &&  f->f_op->open) {
       error =  f->f_op->open(inode,f);
       if (error)
          goto ...;
    }
    f->f_flags &= ~(O_CREAT | O_EXCL | O_NOCTTY | O_TRUNC);

    return f;
    ...
}
```

The close operation writes all relevant information from the inode entry back to the disk, for example the size (if it changed). It also flushes any write-behind-buffer contents to the disk. Finally, it releases the entries in the file descriptor table, file structure table, and inode table.

Read and Write Operations

The essential purposes of the read and write operations is to *serialize* the byte stream on read operations (also called *unmarshaling* the data) and to *pack* (or *marshal*) the byte stream into sectors for write operations (see Figure 2.23). For example, suppose that the file pointer is addressing byte number $j + 2$ and this byte is stored in the ith sector in the file. Then the file system must determine where sector i is located on the disk. The file manager next must read the disk sector into memory so that the read routine can return byte $j + 2$ as the result of the function call. Write operations require a similar approach.

The byte stream interface allows a process to read or write an arbitrary-sized block of bytes, ranging from 1 byte to larger than a sector (or cluster). The first read operation causes the read routine to read at least one sector from the disk. If the read operation requests less information than a sector contains, then the entire sector is read and kept in an input buffer. Subsequent reads on the file will reference the remaining bytes in the buffered sector. If a read operation requests more bytes than the buffer currently holds, then the routine will read another sector (sector $i + 1$ in Figure 2.23) in order to satisfy the request. The new sector will then be buffered and the old sector (sector i) released.

A write operation behaves similarly. In many byte stream file systems, if a thread writes to some point in the file, then the new information is appended to the file at the file pointer's location. Then all old information from the original file pointer to the end of the file is released. This means that the current sector is retained but that all later sectors in the file are deallocated from the file. In some cases, the file manager might allow the thread to simply overwrite bytes in the middle of a file.

The **sys_read()** and **sys_write()** system calls are implemented in **fs/read_write.c**. Here is an annotated skeleton of **sys_read()**.

```
asmlinkage ssize_t sys_read(unsigned int fd,char * buf,size_t
count)
{
   ...
   struct inode * inode;
   ...
   file = fget(fd);          // Get the file pointer from task_structure
   // Miscellaneous error checking
   ...
   // Be sure that the kernel can write data into user's area
```

Figure 2.23
Serializing and Packing Byte Streams

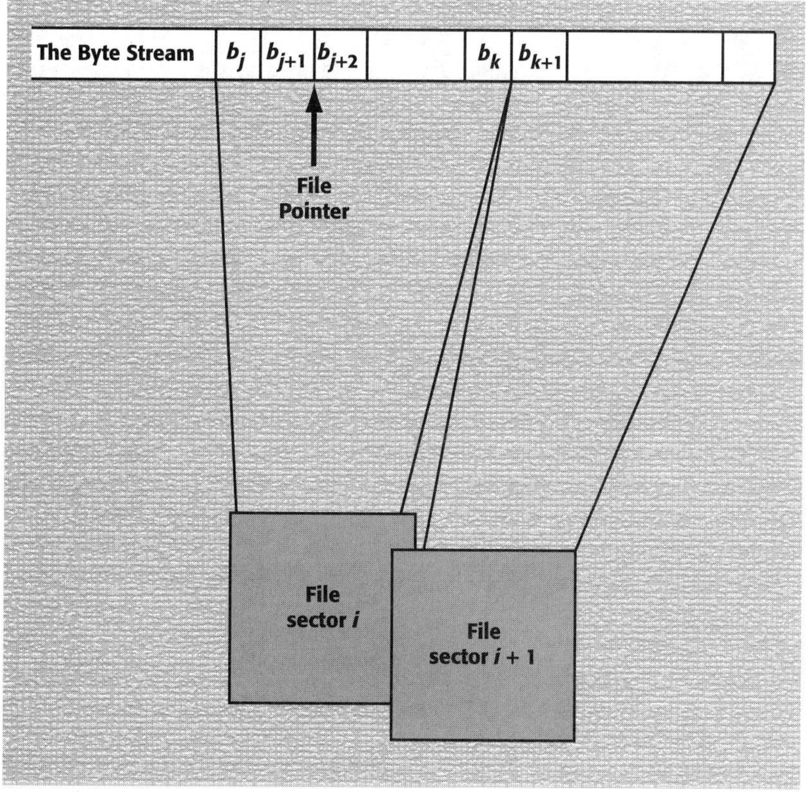


```
    ret = locks_verify_area(FLOCK_VERIFY_READ,inode,
                file,file->f_pos,count);
    ...
    ret = locks_verify_area(FLOCK_VERIFY_READ,
          file->f_dentry->d_inode,
          file, file->f_pos, count);

    if (error)
       ...
    // Here is the actual read call, using the file_operation entry
    if (!file->f_op || !(read = file->f_op->read))
       goto ...;
    ret = read(file, buf, count, &file->f_pos);
    ...
    return ret;
}
```

12

The actual read request occurs in the **file->f_op->read()** call. It is here that the disk-independent code calls the disk-dependent code. If you examine the read routine of one of the file systems (for example, **generic_file_read()** in **ext2**), then you will see where the details come into play. The read function must interact with the virtual memory so that it can be assured that primary memory space is available into which the data can be copied. It must also interact with the buffer management mechanism. This mechanism, in turn, must interact with the device driver and interrupt routines (reconsider the asynchronous activity that is implied by Figure 2.22).

Block Allocation

Every file ultimately gets stored on the block device in some collection of disk blocks (sectors). The strategy used to allocate disk blocks to a file, and to keep track of which blocks that the file is using, is determined by the individual file systems. That is, the VFS does not have a strategy for block management. It defers that strategy to the disk-dependent part of the file manager.

For example, the ext2 file system (see fs/ext2/balloc.c) uses a traditional UNIX strategy. The blocks that comprise a file are stored according to four substrategies. (See also Part 1, Section 7.)

1. **First 12 blocks**: Referenced directly from the inode.
2. **Second group of blocks**: Referenced by using a single level of indirection (via a table stored on the disk).
3. **Third group of blocks**: Referenced indirectly through two layers of indirect tables.
4. **Last group of blocks**: Referenced indirectly through three layers of indirect tables.

The ext2 file system handles free blocks by using a block bitmap. One bit corresponds to each disk block; a block allocated to some file is marked with a 1.

Buffer Management

Ordinary sector-based read and write operations implicitly cause the file manager to buffer at least one input and one output sector per open file as part of serializing and packing blocks. As summarized in Figure 2.24, you can exploit buffering by having a number of buffers used on input and output streams. The advantage of doing this is better performance. That is, the file manager can read ahead on the input stream to avoid making the application block on a sector read. Similarly, the file manager can write behind so that the thread does not have to block while waiting for a sector write operation to finish.

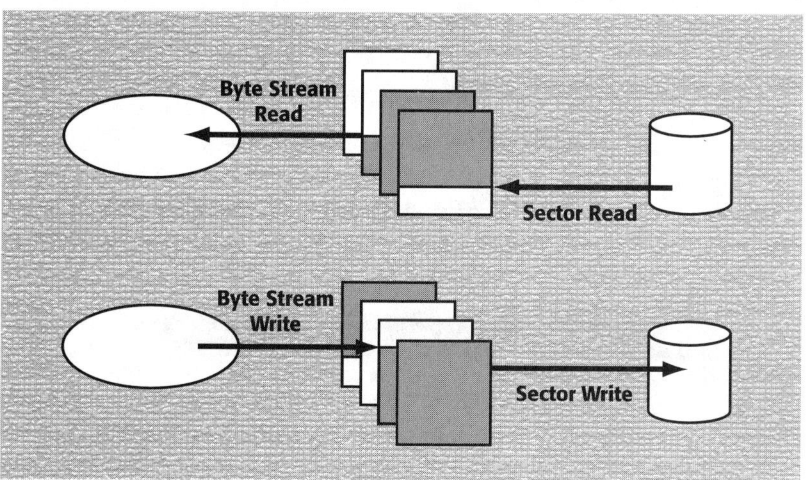

Figure 2.24
Buffering Sectors

Buffering is ordinarily implemented in kernel space, though the same mechanisms can be implemented in user space. The idea is to design the file manager so that it uses *asynchronous I/O* to start sector reads (to read ahead *N* sectors on the byte stream) and writes (that write behind the current file pointer up to *N* sectors). A read operation that requests information that has not yet been read must wait for the device read operation to complete before it can return a result to the application. As soon as it has determined that the read operation has completed on buffer *i*, it can immediately start an asynchronous read on sector *i* + 1. In a kernel-space implementation, an interrupt notifies the software when the device has completed its operation. In a user-space buffer manager, a signal (or other form of asynchronous procedure callback (APC)[1]) can be used to notify the application that the sector read operation has completed.

Figure 2.25 illustrates one way to organize a solution to the problem. The numbers refer to the following steps in a read operation.

1. The application performs a read call on the file manager.
2. The file manager interrogates the open-file table to determine if the required information resides in a buffer or needs to be read from the disk.
3. When a disk read is required, the file manager reads the FAT to determine which disk sector needs to be read next.

[1] Linux does not provide APCs except in the network RPC package. You can achieve the same effect by using signal and user-written signal handlers. See Attacking the Problem in Exercise 3.

4. The file manager reads the required disk. If other input buffers are available, then the file manager starts an asynchronous I/O operation that will call a read callback routine once the next sector has been read.
5. The kernel-level asynchronous I/O mechanism issues an APC to the file manager's read callback routine (which will perform any housekeeping to finish the read and then initiate the next read operation).
6. The block of bytes is returned to the calling program.

Problem Statement

You are to extend the file manager facilities that you created in Exercise 11. As a minimum solution, you should create functions to open/close, read/write, and seek on MS-DOS files stored on a floppy disk. You will also flesh out your directory operations by implementing a command to make new directories, to copy files, and to remove them.

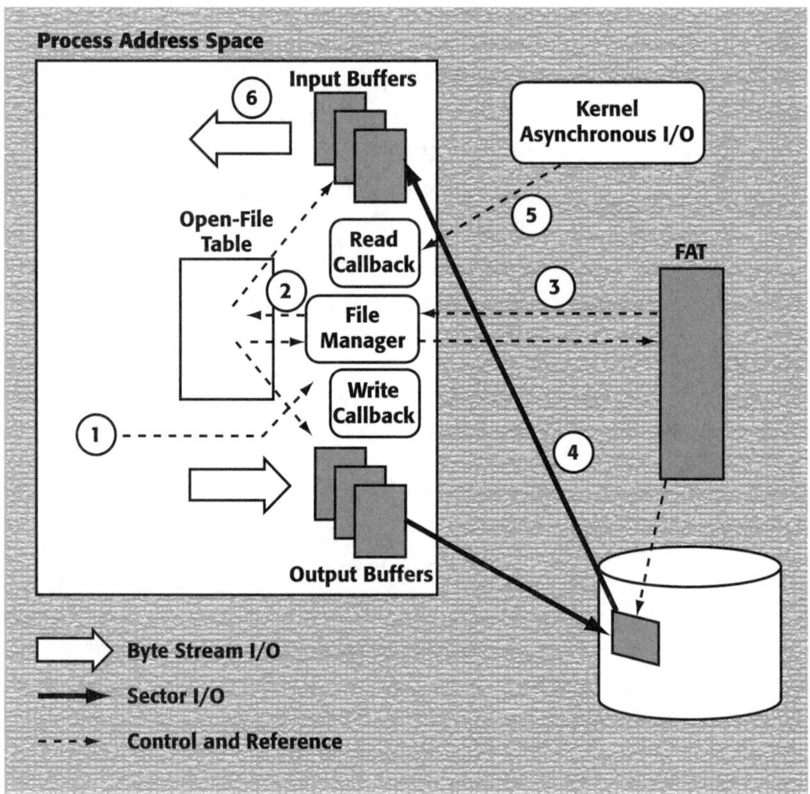

Figure 2.25 One Solution Organization

Part A

Extend the file system software from Exercise 11 so that it provides a byte stream I/O API. It should implement the following functions.

```
int fd_load(char driveLetter);
FD_Handle fd_open(char* name, int mode);
void fd_close(FD_Handle fdHandle);
int fd_read(
FD_Handle fdHandle,
char* buffer,
int length
);
int fd_write(
        FD_Handle fdHandle,
        char* buffer,
        int length
);
int fd_lseek(int offset);
```

fd_load()is an initialization routine that should perform all of the functions of **fd_load()** from Exercise 11, as well as any other initialization that you require. The **fd_open()** and **fd_close()** functions are to perform tasks that you choose when you design your read/write functions (see the discussion of the following open-file descriptor). The **fd_read()** and **fd_write()** routines are to implement byte stream writes similar to the kernel **read()** and **write()** routines. They are to be implemented on top of the FAT abstractions that you constructed in Exercise 11. Your code should work with files on an ordinary Windows NT/MS-DOS floppy disk. Thus the implementation should be able to traverse a file by using the FAT, allocating and deallocating sectors as required.

Part B

Design and implement three functions, to create a new directory, to copy an existing file to a new file, and to remove an existing file:

```
int fd_mkdir(char *name);
int fd_cp(char *source, char *destination);
int fd_rm(char *name);
```

Part C

Redesign your read routine so that it supports read-ahead buffering for up to $N = 3$. You need to use the FAT to determine which sectors to read and then perform sector reads on the floppy disk. You likely will need to add considerable new mechanism to your synchronous read routine.

Several simplifying assumptions for the buffer implementation apply, as follows.

1. You do not need to worry about shared files (so you don't have to worry about consistency).
2. A file may be opened only for reading or writing.
3. Files are accessed only sequentially.
4. Your read and write routines are synchronous.
5. Filenames are the old-style MS-DOS names (up to eight characters in the name and up to three characters in the extension).
6. You can ignore file protection.

You need to design an open-file descriptor to keep the state of the open file, for example its file pointer value and whether it is open for read or write (you need not implement files that are open for read and write at the same time). Finally, you need to design and implement a driver program to test each function.

Part D

Design your write routine to implement write-behind buffering for up to $N = 3$ buffers. You need to use the FAT to determine which sectors to write and then perform sector writes on the floppy disk handle. You likely will need to add considerable new mechanism to your synchronous read routine.

Attacking the Problem

The design of the facilities that you will add to your file manager is not difficult. However, you must consider and handle many details. The buffering exercises (Parts C and D) introduce a new level of complexity due to the need to handle asynchronous concurrency.

The open() *Function*

You need to design your own descriptor(s) that are analogous to the internal inode in VFS. Your data structure(s) should contain some information from the disk-resident file descriptor (the FAT directory entry), though other information kept in the open-file table can describe the state of the I/O session.

An open operation takes a filename and the access mode as input parameters. It finds an unused entry in the open-file table, fills in information extracted from the file system, initializes other fields, and then returns an open-file table handle (index) to the caller.

The open operation must resolve the filename, which may be a pathname, to get the directory entry for the file. Processing a pathname is laborious but straightforward. Here are the steps.

1. Start at the root directory or current directory (depending on whether the pathname is absolute or relative), and look up the subdirectory whose name appears first in the path. If the name cannot be found, then the open will fail. Otherwise, go on to the next step.
2. The found subdirectory has a directory entry, so the corresponding file is then treated as a directory as in Step 1. Continue this path traversal until the leaf name—the last name in the path—is encountered. If this name is found in the appropriate subdirectory, an open-file descriptor can be prepared.
3. Check the file access permissions.
4. Allocate space for an open-file descriptor. Then copy the information from the directory entry that you will need, including the name, attributes, start cluster address, and file size.
5. Set the file pointer to zero. Return the handle to the open-file descriptor to the calling process.

Caching the FAT

Your solution to this exercise is to perform multiple operations on the floppy disk at one time. Note that the floppy disk will become a performance bottleneck if your FAT manipulation routines read and write the FAT in place, in addition to performing the obvious read and write operations for the normal data I/O. If you have a machine with two floppy disk drives, then you should do reads on one drive and writes on the other. You might find it very challenging to support FAT I/O and data I/O on one floppy disk so that everything works correctly. If you decide to use a single floppy disk drive with two open files and to cache the FAT when you open the file, then you will need to be very careful to propagate FAT updates so that all file operations use the correct FAT values (rather than stale copies). Handing this problem will become especially difficult in Part B.

A Solution Plan

As in Exercise 11, you need to derive your solution by using a real floppy disk. Prepare a floppy disk that contains a dozen simple files by using a machine that has the usual Windows interface. Keep a copy of all of your files on the hard disk of the Windows machine. Format a floppy disk to use while you debug, but be aware that you likely will need to reformat it and restore its files as you debug your solution.

You also need a program to test all of your file system calls. Here is a code fragment that can perform some of the tests.

```
#include        <assert.h>
#include        <stdio.h>
#include        <string.h>
...

#define BLOCK_SIZE      12
#define MAX_FILE_NAME           24

void makeDOSFileName(char *, char *);


int main( int argc, char *argv[]) {
        FD_Handle inHandle, outHandle;
        char buffer[BLOCK_SIZE];
        char fileName1[MAX_FILE_NAME],
fileName2[MAX_FILE_NAME];
        int moreToRead;
        const int result = 1;

// Get parameters from the command line
        if(argc != 4) {
                fprintf(stderr,
        "Usage: test <drive_letter> <in_file> <out_file>\n");
                ExitProcess(1);
        }
        makeDOSFileName(argv[2], fileName1);
        makeDOSFileName(argv[3], fileName2);

// Initialize the file manager
        fd_load(argv[1][0]);
```

```
        fd_cd("\\");

// Open in_file for reading and out-file for writing
printf("Main: opening file %s in read mode\n", argv[2]);
inHandle = fd_open(fileName1, READ_MODE);
if(inHandle == NULL) {
                fprintf(stderr,
                "Main: fdOpenFile(\"%s\") failed ... exiting\n", argv[2]);
                ExitProcess(1);
        }
        printf("Main: opening file %s in write mode\n", argv[3]);
        outHandle = fd_open(fileName2, WRITE_MODE);
        if(outHandle == NULL) {
                fprintf(stderr,
                "Main: fdOpenFile(\"%s\") failed ... exiting\n", argv[3]);
                ExitProcess(1);
        }

        moreToRead = TRUE;
        while(moreToRead) {
                if(fd_read(inHandle, buffer, BLOCK_SIZE) == EOF) {
                        moreToRead = FALSE;
                        break;
                }
                fd_write(outHandle, buffer, BLOCK_SIZE);
        }

        fdCloseFile(inHandle);
        fdCloseFile(outHandle);

        return result;
}

void makeDOSFileName(char *rawName, char *dosName) {
        int i;

        assert(rawName);
        assert(dosName);        // This array better be big enough
        i = 0;
        while(rawName[i] != '\0') {
                if(islower(rawName[i]))
```

12

```
                        dosName[i] = toupper(rawName[i]);
                else
                        dosName[i] = rawName[i];
                i++;
        }
        dosName[i] = '\0';
}
```

Further Study

The exercises in this manual teach you how the Linux kernel is designed and organized. Each exercise focused on one or a few aspects of the kernel and then provided you with the opportunity to experiment with that aspect of the kernel. All parts of the kernel were at least touched on, but some were not discussed very deeply and might be topics for further study on your part, including the following.

- The virtual memory system is pervasive in the kernel data structures. Because the Linux virtual memory uses dynamic memory allocation, added complexity exists in understanding how and when page frames are taken away from one process (or buffer pool) and added to another. The discussion of virtual memory in this manual barely scratched the surface of the virtual memory system.
- Most of the code in a kernel is for the file system. The Linux file system is certainly one of the larger and more complex parts of the kernel. Its increased complexity results from the need to handle buffering. Many details of the file system were omitted, so a next phase of study should focus more on the existing file systems.

You can continue your study of kernels in any of several ways. This manual's goal has been to provide you with enough background and experience so that you can read and modify kernel code. By necessity, the exercises must be bounded to small problems so that they are good learning tools. After solving the exercises in this manual, you will be prepared to tackle most kernel problems (though some situations will require considerable additional study of the code). Here are a few suggestions for further study.

- Redesign and reimplement any module of the kernel.
- Extend the functionality; for example, write your own implementation of threads.

- Write a new file system that is used with VFS.
- Work on another kernel.
- Write a new kernel.
- Start a company.

References

Bach, Maurice J., *The Design of the Unix Operating System*, Prentice Hall International, London, 1986.

Beck, Michael, Harald Böhme, Mirko Dziadzka, Ulrich Kunitz, Robert Magnus, and Dirk Verworner, *LINUX Kernel Internels*, 2d ed., Addison Wesley, Reading, Mass., 1998.

Deitel, Harvey M., *An Introduction to Operating Systems*, 2d ed., Addison Wesley, Reading, Mass., 1990.

Johnson, M. K., *Linux Kernel Hacker's Guide*, Version 0.7, Linux Documentation Projectt, **http://metalab.unc.com/mdw/Linux.html**.

Linux Web page at **http://metalab.unc.com/mdw/Linux.html**.

McKusick, Marshall Kirk, Keith Bostic, Michael J. Karels, and John S. Quarterman, *The Design and Implementation of the 4.4 BSD Operating System*, Addison Wesley, Reading, Mass., 1996.

Messmer, Hans-Peter, *The Indispensable PC Hardware Book*, 2d ed., Addison Wesley, Reading, Mass., 1995.

Nutt, Gary J., *Operating System Projects for Windows NT*, Addison Wesley, Reading, Mass., 1999.

Nutt, Gary J., *Operating Systems: A Modern Perspective*, 2d ed., Addison Wesley, Reading, Mass., 2000.

Ousterhout, John K., Hervé Da Costa, David Harrison, John A. Kunze, Mike Kupfer, and James G. Thompson, "A Trace-Driven Analysis of the UNIX 4.2 BSD File System," *Proceedings of the Tenth ACM Symposium on Operating Systems Principles*, ACM (1985), 15–24.

Pomerantz, Ori, *The Linux Kernel Module Programming Guide*, Version 1.0, 1999, Linux Documentation Project, **http://metalab.unc.com/mdw/Linux.html**.

Ritchie, Dennis and Ken Thompson, "The UNIX Time-Sharing System," *Communications of the ACM*, 17, 7 (July 1974), 1897–1920.

Rusling, David A., *The Linux Kernel*, Version 0.8–3, 1996–99, Linux Documentation Project, **http://metalab.unc.com/mdw/Linux.html**.

Silberschatz, Abraham and Peter Baer Galvin, *Operating Systems Concepts*, 5th ed., Addison Wesley, Reading, Mass., 1998.

Solomon, David A., *Inside Windows NT*, 2d ed., Microsoft Press, Redmond, Wash., 1998.

Stallings, William, *Operating Systems*, 2d ed., Prentice Hall, Englewood Cliffs, N.J., 1995.

Stevens, W. Richard, *Advanced Programming in the UNIX Environment*, Addison Wesley, Reading, Mass., 1993.

Tanenbaum, Andrew S., *MINIX Version*, Prentice Hall, Englewood Cliffs, N.J., 1987.

Tanenbaum, Andrew S., *Modern Operating Systems*, Prentice Hall, Englewood Cliffs, N.J., 1992.

Tanenbaum, Andrew S., *Distributed Operating Systems*, Prentice Hall, Englewood Cliffs, N.J., 1995.

Vahalia, Uresh, *UNIX Internals: The New Frontiers*, 2d ed., Prentice Hall, Englewood Cliffs, N.J., 2000.

Welsh, Matt, "Implementing Loadable Kernel Modules for Linux," *Dr. Dobb's Journal* (May 1995).

Index

G

H

I

Linux Mandrake Quick Install Guide Version 7.0

This install guide will help you install Linux Mandrake for the first time. The install program for Linux Mandrake has been designed to eliminate some of the most common pitfalls that have plagued installation of earlier Linux distributions. Linux Mandrake has carefully designed its graphical installer, DrakX, to guide you through every step of the installation process.

With this in mind, the text will move quickly through the installation process, and notes will be made at critical intervals, so you can avoid potential problems.

Pre-installation Procedures

Before installing Linux Mandrake, you will need to make sure your system is ready. Here are a few simple tasks that you may need to perform, to ensure a clean, smooth install.

1. Make sure that your hardware is Linux compatible. If you have any doubts, check the Linux Hardware database at http://www.linux-mandrake.com/en/fhard.php3 or http://lhd.datapower.com/. The information contained on the database refers to hardware currently supported. You can also access the Linux Documentation site at http://www.linuxdoc.org/HOWTO/Hardware-HOWTO.html.
2. **Important**: Make back up copies of critical files, or perform a complete back up to save the entire disk contents. Some times things can go wrong, be prepared.
3. If your computer will support more that one operating system, such as Windows or NT, and you would like to choose which system you will use at boot time, install the Windows/NT system first. You will have to use a partition utility (such as Partition Magic or the fips program) to allocate the remaining disk space for Linux. This will allow the correct installation of the Linux boot loader, LILO, if you want LILO to handle the boot loading tasks.

4. Prepare a partitioning strategy, (how you will use the disk space efficiently) or if you are unsure how to do this, Mandrake's DrakX will handle the task for you.
5. If your computer will be used for Linux only, disregard steps 2 and 3
6. Remember, the minimum required specification for installing Linux Mandrake are as follows:
   - At least 32Mb of RAM memory if you plan to use X Windows. If the machine will be used as a server or console (text mode) use only, 16Mb is adequate.
   - Installing all the software will take up a little over 1.5Gb. A +2Gb disk would allow some growth, if required.
1. The Linux Mandrake CD that is included is bootable. If your computer BIOS supports this feature change the settings to boot the CDROM first. The computer BIOS can be accessed in many ways, depending on the manufacturer. Most computers will give you an option to access the setup menu during the "power on self-test" phase. Check your computer user guide for more details.
2. If the computer BIOS does not support CDROM boot up, you'll need to obtain a 1.44Mb floppy disk to build a boot disk. Instructions on how to build a boot disk is contained in the following section "Building a Boot Disk".

Building a Boot Disk

Creating a boot disk for Linux Mandrake is easy, follow the instructions below and you'll be on your way.

Using Windows

Insert the installation CD in the drive and change directories to the appropriate drive letter (commonly D or E, this may vary). For an example the X: drive will be our reference.

- Open winfile or the Windows Explorer, and change to X:\dosutils. Double click the ***Rawwrite*** icon, this will start the graphical rawrite utility.
- The graphical interface will allow input for Image file and Floppy. Choose the file called ***cdrom.img*** and indicate the floppy disk letter (usually a:)
- Click the Write button and ***Rawwrite*** will do the rest.
- If you are installing in a DOS environment, use the non-graphical ***rawrite*** utility. This can be done by accessing the X:\dosutils directory and issuing the following command at the DOS prompt:

```
X:\dosutils>rawrite
```

The ***rawrite*** utility will prompt you with the following

```
Enter the disk source file name:
```

You will type:

```
X:\images\cdrom.img
```

The ***rawrite*** utility will prompt you for a destination drive, indicate the correct letter for your floppy disk.

After the utility is finished you are ready to start your installation of Linux Mandrake.

Using Linux or UNIX

Insert the CDROM, using root (or super-user account) mount the CD with the following command:

```
# mount /dev/cdrom
```

Using the mount point /mnt/cdrom, type this command at the prompt:

```
# cp /mnt/cdrom/images/cdrom.img /dev/fd0
```

This will copy the boot image to the floppy (use the appropriate drive, fd0, fd1, which ever may apply). After the copying process, you ready to start your install.

Finding Installation Help

Should you encounter a problem during the installation that is not covered by this guide, please point your browser to http://www.linux-mandrake.com/ en/fdoc.php3 for more Mandrake support documentation.

Installing Linux Mandrake 7.0

To begin the installation, insert the CDROM into the computer and restart the computer.

- If the computer BIOS supports CDROM boot up, the installation program should start automatically.
- In case the BIOS does not support CDROM boot up, you can start the CDROM installation by inserting the boot disk and restarting the computer.
- Once the computer starts the installation, you should see the Linux Mandrake "splash screen". Strike the **<enter>** key to continue. The install program will begin the hardware detection phase, and start the second stage of the installation.
- The DrakX graphical installer will now take over the task of getting you through the installation process.
- One of the unique features of DrakX is the ability to move around during the install. If you input a wrong parameter, you can go back and change it. The left side of the Installation screen contains click-able buttons that will allow you to jump forward or backward.

Choose Your Language

1. The first Mandrake Install screen will allow you to change the installation language. The language selection menu is a pull down type menu. Use the mouse to scroll to the correct language.

Select Installation Class

2. **Installation Class:** The Installation class has three selections, Recommended, Customized, Expert.
   - Recommended–Suggested for the first time install of Mandrake. Contains all the packages needed for maximum performance.
   - Customized–For experienced Linux users who know exactly what they want on their systems.

- Expert—for a highly tailored installation, those who may have special application needs, i.e. kernel development or programming.
- Once you've made you choice from the three options above, DrakX will give you an opportunity to further tailor your system. You can specify, normal (everyday use), development (includes compilers and other programming tools), or server (email, webserver or DNS).

Setup SCSI Devices

1. DrakX will now prompt you to indicate any PCI SCSI devices. If you click Yes, and there are any detected devices, the drivers will be loaded automatically. If you are unsure of the type of SCSI device, click the "Hardware Info" button and the recognized components will be displayed.
2. **Note**: If there are devices that are not detected, DrakX will present a pull-down menu with SCSI drivers, choose the correct driver from the list.
3. Clicking the No button will pass you to the next screen.

Choose Install or Upgrade Method

4. DrakX will inquire whether you are installing or upgrading, click the install button for first time installations.

Configure Mouse

5. Your next pull down menu is for mouse selection. The mouse should be auto-detected by the install program. If the system choice is not correct, you can scroll up or down to find your particular mouse.
6. The install program will ask you to identify the correct port for your mouse.

Configure Keyboard

7. Next, you will be able to choose the keyboard layout for your particular use. The default is the US keyboard layout, if the US language is chosen.

Miscellaneous Questions:

The questions found in this section will allow you to configure your installation with certain goals in mind.

- Hard Drive optimization is suggested for expert users only. Leaving this unchecked is recommended
- Security level settings default to "medium". This should be sufficient for general stand-alone use. If the machine is connected to a network, then the "high" setting should be considered. You will have to configure basic network services yourself.
- Precise RAM size setting. Input your RAM amount here if it differs from what the system has found.
- Removable media auto-mounting is for first time installations
- Enable NumLock at start is based on your preference

Setup Filesystems (Partitioning Scheme)

- Correctly partitioning a hard disk will take some effort. DrakX can help you by auto allocating the space.
- Custom partitioning is detailed, and goes beyond the scope of this text. You can find more help at http://www.linuxdoc.org/HOWTO/mini/Partition.html, or if you are using more than one hard disk, this URL will help you, http://www.linuxdoc.org/HOWTO/Multi-Disk-HOWTO.html#toc21.

Format Partitions

DrakX will format all newly created filesystems (partitions)

Choose Installed Packages

If you have chosen the "recommended" install, DrakX will automatically start your package installation.

Configure Time zone

Choose you time zone from the pull down menu listing.

Configure Printer

DrakX will give you the opportunity to configure a number of printers. Choose you printer, if listed, or use one that closely resembles your model.

Set Root Password

Important: This password **should not** be easily guessed, or written down and put in a centrally accessible location. This user account has complete control over the system!

Add a User

This user account should be used to perform daily work tasks, not related to system administration.

Create a Boot Disk

Important: It is advisable to create a boot disk. This will help you boot the system in case something goes wrong. Please take precautions, have a formatted 1.44Mb available

Install Boot Loader (LILO)

DrakX will help you install the LILO boot loader. If you have special needs, (booting more than one operating system) you'll find help at http://www.linuxdoc.org/HOWTO/mini/LILO.html#toc1.

Configure X Window System

The Mandrake Installation program will auto-detect your monitor and graphics card. If you run into problems configuring X Window System, review some of the information at http://www.mandrakeuser.org/xwin/xtroub.html

Exit Installation Program

Hey, You are finished! Have a good time and "may the source be with you"!

GNU GENERAL PUBLIC LICENSE - Version 2, June 1991

Preamble

The licenses for most software are designed to take away your freedom to share and change it. By contrast, the GNU General Public License is intended to guarantee your freedom to share and change free software—to make sure the software is free for all its users. This General Public License applies to most of the Free Software Foundation's software and to any other program whose authors commit to using it. (Some other Free Software Foundation software is covered by the GNU Library General Public License instead.) You can apply it to your programs, too.

When we speak of free software, we are referring to freedom, not price. Our General Public Licenses are designed to make sure that you have the freedom to distribute copies of free software (and charge for this service if you wish), that you receive source code or can get it if you want it, that you can change the software or use pieces of it in new free programs; and that you know you can do these things.

To protect your rights, we need to make restrictions that forbid anyone to deny you these rights or to ask you to surrender the rights. These restrictions translate to certain responsibilities for you if you distribute copies of the software, or if you modify it.

For example, if you distribute copies of such a program, whether gratis or for a fee, you must give the recipients all the rights that you have. You must make sure that they, too, receive or can get the source code. And you must show them these terms so they know their rights.

We protect your rights with two steps: (1) copyright the software, and (2) offer you this license which gives you legal permission to copy, distribute and/or modify the software.

Also, for each author's protection and ours, we want to make certain that everyone understands that there is no warranty for this free software. If the software is modified by someone else and passed on, we want its recipients to know that what they have is not the original, so that any problems introduced by others will not reflect on the original authors' reputations.

Finally, any free program is threatened constantly by software patents. We wish to avoid the danger that redistributors of a free program will individually obtain patent licenses, in effect making the program proprietary. To prevent this, we have made it clear that any patent must be licensed for everyone's free use or not licensed at all.

The precise terms and conditions for copying, distribution and modification follow.

TERMS AND CONDITIONS FOR COPYING, DISTRIBUTION AND MODIFICATION

0. This License applies to any program or other work which contains a notice placed by the copyright holder saying it may be distributed under the terms of this General Public License. The "Program", below, refers to any such program or work, and a "work based on the Program" means either the Program or any derivative work under copyright law: that is to say, a work containing the Program or a portion of it, either verbatim or with modifications and/or translated into another language. (Hereinafter, translation is included without limitation in the term "modification".) Each licensee is addressed as "you".

Activities other than copying, distribution and modification are not covered by this License; they are outside its scope. The act of running the Program is not restricted, and the output from the Program is covered only if its contents constitute a work based on the Program (independent of having been made by running the Program). Whether that is true depends on what the Program does.

1. You may copy and distribute verbatim copies of the Program's source code as you receive it, in any medium, provided that you conspicuously and appropriately publish on each copy an appropriate copyright notice and disclaimer of warranty; keep intact all the notices that refer to this License and to the absence of any warranty; and give any other recipients of the Program a copy of this License along with the Program.

   You may charge a fee for the physical act of transferring a copy, and you may at your option offer warranty protection in exchange for a fee.

2. You may modify your copy or copies of the Program or any portion of it, thus forming a work based on the Program, and copy and distribute such modifications or work under the terms of Section 1 above, provided that you also meet all of these conditions:

   *a) You must cause the modified files to carry prominent notices stating that you changed the files and the date of any change.

   * b) You must cause any work that you distribute or publish, that in whole or in part contains or is derived from the Program or any part thereof, to be licensed as a whole at no charge to all third parties under the terms of this License.

   * c) If the modified program normally reads commands interactively when run, you must cause it, when started running for such interactive use in the most ordinary way, to print or display an announcement including an appropriate copyright notice and a notice that there is no warranty (or else, saying that you provide a warranty) and that users may redistribute the program under these

conditions, and telling the user how to view a copy of this License. (Exception: if the Program itself is interactive but does not normally print such an announcement, your work based on the Program is not required to print an announcement.)

These requirements apply to the modified work as a whole. If identifiable sections of that work are not derived from the Program, and can be reasonably considered independent and separate works in themselves, then this License, and its terms, do not apply to those sections when you distribute them as separate works. But when you distribute the same sections as part of a whole which is a work based on the Program, the distribution of the whole must be on the terms of this License, whose permissions for other licensees extend to the entire whole, and thus to each and every part regardless of who wrote it.

Thus, it is not the intent of this section to claim rights or contest your rights to work written entirely by you; rather, the intent is to exercise the right to control the distribution of derivative or collective works based on the Program.

In addition, mere aggregation of another work not based on the Program with the Program (or with a work based on the Program) on a volume of a storage or distribution medium does not bring the other work under the scope of this License.

3. You may copy and distribute the Program (or a work based on it, under Section 2) in object code or executable form under the terms of Sections 1 and 2 above provided that you also do one of the following:

* a) Accompany it with the complete corresponding machine-readable source code, which must be distributed under the terms of Sections 1 and 2 above on a medium customarily used for software interchange; or,

* b) Accompany it with a written offer, valid for at least three years, to give any third party, for a charge no more than your cost of physically performing source distribution, a complete machine-readable copy of the corresponding source code, to be distributed under the terms of Sections 1 and 2 above on a medium customarily used for software interchange; or,

* c) Accompany it with the information you received as to the offer to distribute corresponding source code. (This alternative is allowed only for noncommercial distribution and only if you received the program in object code or executable form with such an offer, in accord with Subsection b above.)

The source code for a work means the preferred form of the work for making modifications to it. For an executable work, complete source code means all the source code for all modules it contains, plus any associated interface definition files, plus the scripts used to control compilation and installation of the executable. However, as a special exception, the source code distributed need not include anything that is normally distributed (in either source or binary form) with the major components (compiler, kernel, and so on) of the operating system on which the executable runs, unless that component itself accompanies the executable.

If distribution of executable or object code is made by offering access to copy from a designated place, then offering equivalent access to copy the source code from the same place counts as distribution of the source code, even though third parties are not compelled to copy the source along with the object code.

4. You may not copy, modify, sublicense, or distribute the Program except as expressly provided under this License. Any attempt otherwise to copy, modify, sublicense or distribute the Program is void, and will automatically terminate your rights under this License. However, parties who have received copies, or rights, from you under this License will not have their licenses terminated so long as such parties remain in full compliance.

5. You are not required to accept this License, since you have not signed it. However, nothing else grants you permission to modify or distribute the Program or its derivative works. These actions are prohibited by law if you do not accept this License. Therefore, by modifying or distributing the Program (or any work based on the Program), you indicate your acceptance of this License to do so, and all its terms and conditions for copying, distributing or modifying the Program or works based on it.

6. Each time you redistribute the Program (or any work based on the Program), the recipient automatically receives a license from the original licensor to copy, distribute or modify the Program subject to these terms and conditions. You may not impose any further restrictions on the recipients' exercise of the rights granted herein. You are not responsible for enforcing compliance by third parties to this License.

7. If, as a consequence of a court judgment or allegation of patent infringement or for any other reason (not limited to patent issues), conditions are imposed on you (whether by court order, agreement or otherwise) that contradict the conditions of this License, they do not excuse you from the conditions of this License. If you cannot distribute so as to satisfy simultaneously your obligations under this License and any other pertinent obligations, then as a consequence you may not distribute the Program at all. For example, if a patent license would not permit royalty-free redistribution of the Program by all those who receive copies directly or indirectly through you, then the only way you could satisfy both it and this License would be to refrain entirely from distribution of the Program.

If any portion of this section is held invalid or unenforceable under any particular circumstance, the balance of the section is intended to apply and the section as a whole is intended to apply in other circumstances.

It is not the purpose of this section to induce you to infringe any patents or other property right claims or to contest validity of any such claims; this section has the sole purpose of protecting the integrity of the free software distribution system, which is implemented by public license practices. Many people have made generous contributions to the wide range of software distributed through that system in reliance on consistent application of that system; it is up to the author/donor to decide if he or she is willing to distribute software through any other system and a licensee cannot impose that choice.

This section is intended to make thoroughly clear what is believed to be a consequence of the rest of this License.

8. If the distribution and/or use of the Program is restricted in certain countries either by patents or by copyrighted interfaces, the original copyright holder who places the Program under this License may add an explicit geographical distribution limitation excluding those countries, so that distribution is permitted only in or among countries not thus excluded. In such case, this License incorporates the limitation as if written in the body of this License.

9. The Free Software Foundation may publish revised and/or new versions of the General Public License from time to time. Such new versions will be similar in spirit to the present version, but may differ in detail to address new problems or concerns.

Each version is given a distinguishing version number. If the Program specifies a version number of this License which applies to it and "any later version", you have the option of following the terms and conditions either of that version or of any later version published by the Free Software Foundation. If the Program does not specify a version number of this License, you may choose any version ever published by the Free Software Foundation.

10. If you wish to incorporate parts of the Program into other free programs whose distribution conditions are different, write to the author to ask for permission. For software which is copyrighted by the Free Software Foundation, write to the Free Software Foundation; we sometimes make exceptions for this. Our decision will be guided by the two goals of preserving the free status of all derivatives of our free software and of promoting the sharing and reuse of software generally.

NO WARRANTY

11. BECAUSE THE PROGRAM IS LICENSED FREE OF CHARGE, THERE IS NO WARRANTY FOR THE PROGRAM, TO THE EXTENT PERMITTED BY APPLICABLE LAW. EXCEPT WHEN OTHERWISE STATED IN WRITING THE COPYRIGHT HOLDERS AND/OR OTHER PARTIES PROVIDE THE PROGRAM "AS IS" WITHOUT WARRANTY OF ANY KIND, EITHER EXPRESSED OR IMPLIED, INCLUDING, BUT NOT LIMITED TO, THE IMPLIED WARRANTIES OF MERCHANTABILITY AND FITNESS FOR A PARTICULAR PURPOSE. THE ENTIRE RISK AS TO THE QUALITY AND PERFORMANCE OF THE PROGRAM IS WITH YOU. SHOULD THE PROGRAM PROVE DEFECTIVE, YOU ASSUME THE COST OF ALL NECESSARY SERVICING, REPAIR OR CORRECTION.

12. IN NO EVENT UNLESS REQUIRED BY APPLICABLE LAW OR AGREED TO IN WRITING WILL ANY COPYRIGHT HOLDER, OR ANY OTHER PARTY WHO MAY MODIFY AND/OR REDISTRIBUTE THE PROGRAM AS PERMITTED ABOVE, BE LIABLE TO YOU FOR DAMAGES, INCLUDING ANY GENERAL, SPECIAL, INCIDENTAL OR CONSEQUENTIAL DAMAGES ARISING OUT OF THE USE OR INABILITY TO USE THE PROGRAM (INCLUDING BUT NOT LIMITED TO LOSS OF DATA OR DATA BEING RENDERED INACCURATE OR LOSSES SUSTAINED BY YOU OR THIRD PARTIES OR A FAILURE OF THE PROGRAM TO OPERATE WITH ANY OTHER PROGRAMS), EVEN IF SUCH HOLDER OR OTHER PARTY HAS BEEN ADVISED OF THE POSSIBILITY OF SUCH DAMAGES.

END OF TERMS AND CONDITIONS